The United States
and Indochina,
From FDR
to Nixon

PETER A. POOLE
George Washington University
Washington, D.C.

The Dryden Press
901 North Elm Street
Hinsdale, Illinois 60521

To my parents, Caroline and William Poole

Preface

The underlying theme of this book is that each of the six Presidents who have concerned themselves with Indochina had a remarkably free hand in shaping U.S. policy toward that region. Not until the late 1960s did either the American public or Congress make any real attempt to limit what they could or could not do—and even those belated efforts were largely unsuccessful. Moreover, contrary to what some have claimed, each President was essentially free to follow, change, or discard completely the policies and "commitments" of his predecessors toward Indochina.

We are still very close to many of the events that are described in this book; I began writing it at the time of the American incursion into Cambodia and finished soon after the October 1972 agreement was made public. I have not hesitated to state my own conclusions, but, obviously, no one could expect to have the last word about events as recent as these. My aim has been to raise important questions, select themes, explore relationships of cause and effect, and generally contribute to a more fruitful discussion of what is certain to remain one of the most controversial foreign involvements in American history.

In addition to published works cited in the footnotes and discussed in the bibliographic essay, I have relied on my own observations of the foreign policy process during nine years of government service and teaching in Washington and four years in Southeast Asia. I am grateful to a large number of American officials and former officials who have taken time to discuss with me their views on our intervention in Indochina and more broadly their own experiences in the field of foreign policy. Those who were kind enough to grant me one or more substantial interviews include: the late Dean Acheson; John M. Allison; Robert W. Barnett; Winthrop G. Brown; McGeorge Bundy; William P. Bundy; W. Walton Butterworth; Marshall Green; Averell Harriman; Roger Hilsman; George F. Kennan; Edward G. Lansdale; J. Graham Parsons; Edwin O. Reischauer; the late Walter Robertson; Dean Rusk; John Service; Philip D. Sprouse; William H. Sullivan; James C. Thomson, Jr.; William C. Trimble; and the late John Carter Vincent.

I also wish to express my thanks to many officials and private citizens of South Vietnam, Cambodia, Thailand, and Laos who helped me understand the effects of U.S. policy decisions on their countries.

Professor Keith Eubank, editor of this series, provided patient and extremely helpful criticism of the manuscript which it is a pleasure to acknowledge.

I am indebted to the editors of *Asian Survey, Washington Monthly*, and the Southeast Asia monograph series of the Ohio University Center for International Studies for allowing me to include material which first appeared, in substantially different form, in their respective publications.

I wish to thank Howard University for a research grant which enabled me to revisit Phnom Penh, Bangkok, and Tokyo in the winter of 1970-71. Many long discussions with my colleagues and students at Howard over the past three years have also helped crystallize some of the ideas in these chapters. I am particularly grateful to Professor D. G. Kousoulas for his advice and support. Kenneth Wilson, Bibliographer of the Howard Library, very kindly provided access to the Bernard B. Fall collection while it was being catalogued. I knew Bernard Fall both in Washington and in Cambodia and am among the many who have missed his wise and spirited guidance.

This book is dedicated to my parents, Caroline and William Poole, in gratitude for many kinds of support which they have given me.

Once again, my thanks to Gladys Shimasaki for typing successive drafts of the manuscript with unfailing good humor.

My wife, Rosemary Poole, provided invaluable editorial support and in a thousand different ways helped and encouraged me to complete this book.

Peter A. Poole

Sugar Hill, N. H. and
Washington, D.C.
January 1973

Contents

Introduction

The question of who would rule in Indochina has engaged the interest of six American Presidents, from Franklin Roosevelt to Richard Nixon. The way in which each of them responded to the problem tells us something about their sense of proportion in the conduct of foreign relations. This is the story of how an area unknown to most Americans became a testing ground for an improvised strategy of "containing" Communist China. It is also the story of how a "limited" war mushroomed into the most divisive and demoralizing struggle in a century of American history.

Each President was necessarily influenced by the political climate at home and abroad, by decisions made and programs started by his predecessors, and by the quality of advice and information which he received.

Because of this, can we in fairness say that any President really shaped the Indochina policy of his administration? If so, what were his aims and how successful was he in achieving them? If he did not act alone, who shared his responsibilities with him—or made the key decisions on his behalf?

How can we tell whether a particular decision—such as the idea of backing Diem, neutralizing Laos, bombing North Vietnam, or sending U.S. troops into Cambodia—was justified in terms of America's world-wide interests? In spite of its obvious shortcomings, did our intervention help bring a period of relative peace and progress to other parts of Asia? Or was the killing, the terror, the destruction all in vain? Indeed, are there any yardsticks of right and wrong besides survival in a war without hope of victory for either side?

There are no final answers to any of these questions. But some light can be shed by starting at the beginning—when Japanese ambitions first turned southward in the 1930s, and Franklin Roosevelt began to lead the United States out of semiisolation into a period of unprecedented power and responsibility. We recall how our first two decades of involvement in Indochina—under Roosevelt, Truman, and Eisenhower—took place against a backdrop of awkward but sometimes splendid leadership as a world power. In the decade of the sixties, our story reaches its long, agonizing climax. At that point, precisely when the American people began to look inward at their own society and to reject the world policeman role, Presidents Kennedy, Johnson, and Nixon found themselves trapped in an escalating struggle to save the Saigon regime from impending defeat.

Compared with each of his successors, Franklin Roosevelt enjoyed certain unique advantages in dealing with the Indochina situation. In partnership with Churchill and Stalin, he held the fate of many countries in his hands during World War II. Within the U.S. government, the unprecedented emergency and the force of Roosevelt's personality allowed him to exercise greater influence over U.S. policy than any of his five successors.

At the time our story begins, in early 1939, much of the world was still at peace, but Germany, Japan, and Italy had begun to wage wars of aggression against their neighbors; these three anti-democratic powers were also moving in the direction of a formal alliance. It seemed only a matter of time before the United States would throw its weight on the opposing side. But when would the provocation be strong enough to make the American people ready to risk war? And where would the U.S. government perceive the first important threat to its interests?

CHAPTER ONE

FDR and Indochina

Franklin Roosevelt frequently expressed his belief that almost a century of French rule in Indochina had left the local inhabitants worse off than before the French arrived. Not only was he unwilling to help France retain control of its Far Eastern colony, Roosevelt even urged other Allied leaders to join him in establishing an international trusteeship to replace the French administration. However, it was power politics rather than anticolonialism that first caused Roosevelt to become involved with the subject of Indochina on the eve of World War II.

During the 1930s, Japan seized control of Manchuria and northern China and closed the "open door," which had allowed all foreigners equal rights of commercial exploitation. Prior to 1939, when Japan began to act in concert with Nazi Germany, the United States refused to take joint action with the other powers to block Japan's expansion. This was consistent with the traditional American policy of defending China's territorial integrity verbally, while avoiding a clash with Japan or Russia on the issue. Washington's policy of not "provoking" Japan failed to deter the Japanese militarists, however. It merely proved to them that they must act quickly—before Hitler's aggression in Europe polarized the United States into an alliance with England and France.

U.S.-Japanese Confrontation Over Indochina

By early 1939, the Roosevelt administration recognized the global threat posed by Japanese and German expansion; it began to meet Japanese thrusts into Southeast Asia with increasing firmness. The greatest single Japanese interest in Southeast Asia was to gain control of the oil-rich Dutch East Indies. Indochina was an important forward base for this purpose. The ports and airfields of Indochina could be useful, perhaps essential, in a Japanese invasion of Malaya, Singapore, and Indonesia; the Tonkin-Yunnan railway was of interest to both Japan and the United States, because it offered the easiest route for sending U.S. arms to Chiang Kai-shek's forces.

In February 1939, shortly after Japan proclaimed its intention of establishing a "new order" in East Asia, Japanese troops occupied Hainan, the Chinese island near Tonkin which had long been regarded as within the French sphere of influence. Undaunted by parallel "inquiries" from the French, British, and American ambassadors in Tokyo, Japan seized the Spratly Islands (near the coast of South Vietnam) the following month. Seeing this as a threat to the Philippines and the Dutch East Indies as well as to French Indochina, Roosevelt ordered the U.S. fleet, which had been conducting maneuvers in the Caribbean, to return to the Pacific. In July 1939, after further Japanese pressures against Western interests in China, the United States took the important step of canceling its commercial treaty with Japan.

In 1940, Roosevelt, seeking an unprecedented third term, was concerned about not getting too far ahead of American public opinion on the subject of involvement in the war.[1] When the Governor-General of French Indochina tried to purchase arms in the United States—to defend his territory from an imminent Japanese threat—Washington refused his request. On June 25, 1940, the pro-Axis Vichy French government signed an armistice with Hitler. Five days later, the U.S. Undersecretary of State, Sumner Welles, told the French Ambassador that the United States would not go to war with Japan over Indochina. Japan next demanded that France cede military and air bases in Indochina and allow Japanese troops to use the colony as a forward base on their way to Malaya, Singapore, and Indonesia. Again, Washington took the position that there was nothing it could do to help the French.

In September 1940, the French government accepted all of the Japanese demands and signed a treaty by which they continued to rule Indochina—though at the cost of supporting Japan's war effort in the Pacific. In the same month, a brief Japanese show of force in Indochina touched off a nationalist revolt in Vietnam, which soon attracted Vietnamese Communist support. Although they had been unable to resist the Japanese, the French suppressed this rebellion with great severity; mass executions eliminated many of the leaders of the communist and nationalist movements.

The United States took its first strong action to block Japanese aggression while these events were in progress. On July 25, 1940, President Roosevelt announced that all exports of oil and scrap metals from the United States would be subject to government licensing. This "embargo," as the press called it, actually applied only to aviation fuels and lubricants and to high grade iron and steel scrap; but the worldwide psychological impact was considerable. Two months later, after Japan signed the Tripartite Pact with Germany and Italy, Roosevelt ordered a number of additional moves to buttress the defense of the western Pacific: preliminary talks were begun between British and American staff officers; ten American submarines were sent to the Philippines; a $50 million credit was given to Chiang Kai-shek; and a large number of items were added to the list of commodities which could not be exported without government license.

In March 1941, Secretary of State Hull began his much-described series of talks with Ambassador Nomura, in which Indochina was one of the main topics. Hull had the advantage of reading the intercepted Japanese message traffic, but he had to be constantly on his guard not to reveal the extent or source of his knowledge.

In June 1941, after Hitler attacked the Soviet Union, the Japanese government faced a momentous decision; should it invade Russia from the east or concentrate on "winding up the China incident" and expanding southward? It chose the latter course, and on July 12 served the Vichy French regime with yet another ultimatum. Japan demanded the right to use air and naval bases in South Vietnam and permission to station Japanese troops there. Vichy agreed to the demands, and the United States learned of its agreement by July 21. On the same day, Undersecretary Welles told the Japanese Minister that, if Japan occupied Indochina, further discussion between the two governments would be in vain.

On July 23, 1941, Ambassador Nomura met with Welles and tried to excuse the Japanese occupation of Indochina on grounds of Japan's economic needs and the trade embargos to which his country was being subjected. When President Roosevelt received Ambassador Nomura on July 24, he warned him that "an exceedingly serious situation would immediately result" if Japan tried to seize the oil supplies in the Dutch East Indies.

At the same meeting, Roosevelt also proposed to the Ambassador that Indochina be neutralized by agreement of all interested powers (excluding France). Japan would be guaranteed the right to acquire supplies and raw materials from Indochina on a basis of equality with the other powers. Although this would have done away with the alleged "discrimination" against Japanese interests, which Tokyo used as a rationale for its expansion, it is hardly surprising that Ambassador Nomura showed little interest in Roosevelt's proposal. As the President knew, it would have only confirmed the economic concessions Japan had just wrung from Vichy, while creating obstacles to the use of Indochina for further military conquest. By this time, both Roosevelt and Nomura must have realized that there was little hope of halting the Japanese occupation of Indochina, which was already in progress.

On July 26, 1941, without waiting for a reply to his plan to "neutralize" Indochina, Roosevelt issued his famous order freezing Japanese assets in the United States. This turned out to be the pivotal event in U.S.-Japanese relations in the period leading up to Pearl Harbor. The order shook the Japanese leaders, but failed to move them off their collision course with the United States.

With the Hull-Nomura talks completely deadlocked in November 1941, Japan presented its minimum terms, designed to prevent a war while postponing settlement of the basic issues. In part, this plan called for a lifting of U.S. economic sanctions against Japan in return for Japan's abandoning her southward expansion. Indochina would be evacuated when peace was restored in China. And in the meantime (as soon as their other terms had been accepted) Japan would move its forces from South Vietnam to North Vietnam.

Some aspects of the Japanese proposal were attractive to American leaders, but a non-negotiable provision that the United States cease supporting Chiang Kai-shek's forces made the plan totally unacceptable. If the United States had agreed to this condition, it would have undermined the Chinese, British, and Dutch governments' confidence in American aims at a time when building an Allied coalition was of paramount importance.

The ten-point plan with which the United States responded merely recited for the record America's maximum conditions for peace. It called for the withdrawal of all Japanese troops from Indochina and China, recognition of Chiang's government as the only legal Chinese government, and virtual renunciation by Japan of her pact with Germany and Italy. The U.S. proposal also included the idea of an agreement by interested parties to respect the territorial integrity of Indochina. But this held no interest for the Japanese leaders, who had already forced France to place Indochina's economy at their service and to cede parts of Cambodia and Laos to Thailand.

The December 7 attack on Pearl Harbor came before a final message from Roosevelt (containing further thoughts on Indochina) could be delivered to the Japanese Emperor. While much of the American Navy was being sunk at Pearl Harbor, Japanese forces launched a rapid drive to occupy the rest of Southeast Asia.

FDR's Wartime Policy Toward France and Indochina

Roosevelt first broached his idea of a trusteeship to govern postwar Indochina when Anthony Eden, the British Foreign Secretary, visited Washington in March 1943. Hull summed up for Eden the President's general attitude toward France in the following words:

> ...no supreme political power should be set up now to exercise control over the French people. No provisional Government should be created or recognized, and any [French] political activities should be kept to the minimum dictated by necessity.[2]

Indochina was one part of the French empire in which French "political activities" would definitely be kept to a minimum. At the Teheran conference in November 1943, Churchill, Roosevelt, and Stalin discussed the future of Indochina. Roosevelt, who was doing everything in his power to gain Stalin's support on other important issues, took the line that the Allies should not help France regain control over Indochina. Stalin agreed; he said that France should be punished rather than rewarded in the peace settlement, and that the Allies should not shed their blood to restore French rule in Indochina. Churchill, coming to the defense of France, said that it could and should be quickly restored to its former status as a world power. But Roosevelt and Stalin both took the position that this could only come about after many years of "honest labor" by the French people and their government.

Nevertheless, the military decisions of the Big Three leaders at Teheran, particularly the plans to invade Normandy and southern France, had much greater influence on France's world role than any personal views that were expressed at the conference. The Allied invasion of France created opportunities for de Gaulle's Committee of National Liberation to transform itself into a Provisional Government of France, with de Gaulle as Chief of State. This in turn made it easier for him to pursue the task of rebuilding the shattered French empire. When de Gaulle visited Washington in July 1944, Roosevelt found him more reasonable and agreeable than he had expected. The visit was a success, and Roosevelt finally recognized de Gaulle's government as the "dominant political force" in France. With American support, de Gaulle then made his triumphal entry into Paris in August 1944. There remained some American opposition to the reimposition of French colonial rule abroad, but it began to seem less and less realistic.

With victory over the Axis powers in sight, the American government faced a need to clarify its position on the postwar status of European colonies in Asia. The principal statements of U.S. policy on this matter, which had been addressed to either the Vichy or Free French authorities during 1941 and 1942, generally looked toward the restoration of French territories to France after the war. This reflected a general U.S. policy of not pressing for immediate liberation of dependent peoples but of urging the colonial powers to grant all subject peoples independence as soon as they were ready for it. Hull points out in his memoirs that State Department officials held frequent talks along these lines with British, French, and Dutch representatives during the war years—although Roosevelt tried repeatedly to make a special case of Indochina and establish a trusteeship in place of the French administration.

Hull—and many State Department officials—disagreed with Roosevelt on this subject. Writing after the war, Hull recalled having thought that Indochina should fall within the "general category" of dependent peoples,

> to whom the mother countries should be pledged to grant eventual independence. I favored this method rather than placing Indo-China under a trusteeship. . . . I favored the return of Indo-China, with France's pledge of eventual independence as soon as the colony became qualified for it, along the lines of our pledge to the Philippines.

However, if France "were not prepared to do full justice" to Indochina, Hull adds, then it would have been necessary to look to an international trusteeship; "but I did not underestimate the terrific undertaking that administration by a trusteeship would represent, both in service and in money."[3]

In August 1944, Great Britain asked the United States to approve the idea of French participation in the liberation of Indochina and in the war against Japan. Roosevelt apparently failed to dissuade Churchill from this idea, for the British allowed de Gaulle to send a French military mission to the South-East Asia Command headquarters in Ceylon. But in November 1944, Roosevelt issued instructions that no American representatives in the Far East, whether civilian or military, would be allowed to make any decisions on political questions involving the French military mission.[4]

Roosevelt also opposed the idea of inviting de Gaulle to the Yalta conference, where (in February 1945) he offered one last variation of his scheme for an Indochina trusteeship. Roosevelt's proposal called for a government council which would include a French representative, one or two Asian inhabitants of Indochina, a Filipino, a Chinese and a Russian. By amending his previous plan to include a French representative, Roosevelt probably hoped to make it less objectionable to Churchill and perhaps even to de Gaulle. But Churchill still disliked the anticolonial character of the scheme, and Roosevelt needed Churchill's support elsewhere. So he did not pursue the subject of Indochina any further.

Roosevelt died less than two months after he returned from the Yalta conference; for the next four and one-half years, the U.S. government showed little interest in promoting the cause of self-determination for the peoples of Indochina. Would things have been different if Roosevelt had lived? Given his distrust of the French, it is conceivable that he might have decided to back Ho Chi Minh, who in the spring of 1945 was maneuvering his Viet Minh forces into a position where they could claim to be the chief pro-Allied group in Indochina.

Notes

1. During the 1940 election campaign, Roosevelt promised the American people that "We will not participate in foreign wars, and we will not send our army, naval, or air forces to fight in foreign lands outside of the Americas, except in case of attack."

2. Cordell Hull, *Memoirs* (New York: Macmillan, 1948), Vol. II, p. 1215.

3. Ibid., pp. 1598-99.

4. Ibid., pp. 1597-98. According to the same source, Roosevelt was told in October 1944 about an OSS proposal to aid resistance groups in Indochina. He responded with a note that said, " . . . it is my judgment on this date that we should do nothing in regard to resistance groups or in any other way in relation to Indo-China. (You might bring it up to me a little later when things are a little clearer.)"

CHAPTER TWO

China Overshadows Vietnam in U.S. Policy

Victory in Europe and Japan's unexpectedly quick defeat in the Pacific brought a host of new problems for the Allied governments. At the Potsdam conference (July and August 1945), China and Britain were given the task of accepting Japan's surrender and releasing Allied prisoners in Indochina—the Chinese to the north of the sixteenth parallel, the British south of it.

For the first few years after World War II, China's civil war caused far greater concern in Washington than any other Asian problem. In December 1945, President Truman sent General Marshall to China to try to mediate the conflict. Although it soon became obvious that the effort was hopeless, Marshall persevered throughout 1946. Right-wing congressmen had begun to attack the administration for not doing enough to help Chiang Kai-shek, but no one seriously thought of sending more U.S. troops abroad. Although American occupation units were maintained in Japan and Germany, most U.S. forces were quickly brought home and demobilized, and the defense budget was slashed.

Besides China, other Asian problems took precedence over Indochina during the early years of the Truman administration. Japan's economy was in ruins, and her people completely demoralized; the United States had no choice but to provide minimum relief funds with which to keep the Japanese people alive. The Truman administration was also drawn into mediating the bitter conflict between the Dutch and Indonesians—and this experience was not one which Washington officials cared to repeat in the case of Indochina.

Origins of the First Indochina War

In 1941, Ho Chi Minh (the founder of the Indochina Communist Party) recast the ICP as a popular front movement, which he called the *Viet Nam Doc Lap Dong Minh* (Vietnam Independence League). Since the French armistice with Germany in 1940, the French administration in Indochina had adopted a pro-Axis position; Hitler's invasion of the Soviet Union led Moscow to join the Allies. The Viet Minh (as Ho Chi Minh's front group was usually known) then sought to identify itself with the Allied cause. It received some support from the Chinese Nationalists and later cooperated with American OSS teams in Indochina.

By late 1944, while the pro-Axis French administration continued to govern Indochina under Japanese supervision, a Free French organization in the colony was preparing to expel the Japanese. In March 1945, when they could see that their defeat was inevitable, the Japanese carried out a lightning coup, killing or imprisoning most of the French forces in the colony to prevent France from reasserting its influence after the war. General Wedemeyer, the commander of U.S. forces in China, refused to aid those French who escaped this massacre, apparently on orders from President Roosevelt.[1]

The Japanese then set up puppet regimes in Vietnam, Laos, and Cambodia, but the Vietnamese regime collapsed when Japan surrendered in August 1945, leaving the Viet Minh as the only organized force in the country capable of seizing the political initiative. Their immediate aim was to disarm the Japanese before the arrival of Allied troops in Indochina and to seek recognition from Allied governments as the national government of Vietnam. On August 19, the Viet Minh marched into Hanoi and took control without firing a shot. The Emperor, Bao Dai, resigned and gave his support to the Viet Minh; he reasoned that, since they alone had been in contact with the Allies during the war, they would have the best chance of gaining Allied support now against the reimposition of French rule.

In the South, the Viet Minh's position was much weaker than in the northern and central regions of Vietnam. The first group to seize power in Saigon after the Japanese surrender was a coalition—the United National Front—composed of non-Communist nationalist parties, leaders of the powerful reformed Buddhist sects, and a group of Trotskyites (who advocated armed resistance to the French and a harsh redistribution of Vietnamese landholdings). The Viet Minh front gained a tenuous hold by killing a number of its opponents and then won the support of other groups by stressing its allegedly good relations with the Allies. Thus, the Viet Minh was able to push aside the rival United National Front and set in its place the "Executive Committee for the South."

Unlike the Viet Minh-dominated regime in Hanoi, however, the Committee for the South was never fully under Viet Minh control, and it was unable to preserve order and prevent attacks on the French community in Saigon. The first serious riots occurred on September 2, 1945, when several French citizens were killed during a large demonstration organized by the Committee for the South. A week later, the Viet Minh were forced to accept a reorganization of the committee in which they lost control of its leadership.

On September 12, a battalion of British Commonwealth troops arrived in Saigon along with a company of French soldiers. Ignoring the protests of General MacArthur and other U.S. officials in the Far East, the British commander proceeded to rearm the French and Japanese troops in Saigon and use them to expel the Viet Minh from the city. As French reinforcements arrived, they became involved in a full-scale war with Viet Minh guerrillas south of the sixteenth parallel.

In North Vietnam, meanwhile, French officials had great difficulty coming to terms with the Chinese occupation forces. But in February 1946, France agreed to pay the Chinese Nationalists' price—returning all French concessions in China—for withdrawing their troops. In March, French and Viet Minh officials reached an agreement which, if adhered to by both sides, might have led to an independent Vietnam closely associated with France.

American military personnel in North Vietnam at the end of the war tended to regard the Viet Minh as synonymous with Vietnam's movement for national liberation. Some Americans did, in fact, try to obstruct French political aims in Indochina and were on occasion extremely callous toward the suffering of the French community. This may explain the suspicion and hostility of many Frenchmen toward U.S. aims in Indochina during the 1950s and 1960s. But the fact remains that the Americans in North Vietnam at this time were politically insignificant, whatever their intentions may have been. The real obstacles to French rule were, first of all, the Chinese occupation forces and secondly, the Viet Minh.

One French official who never forgot American "obstructionism" in this period was Jean Sainteny, the head of French intelligence in China. (He became French representative in North Vietnam in 1945-46 and again in 1954-57; he was later a member of de Gaulle's government.) Sainteny saw the need to try to come to terms with the Viet Minh in the early summer of 1945, but his departure from Kunming was blocked for several weeks by General Wedemeyer. Although an American OSS officer finally flew with him to Hanoi on August 22—and arranged his first meeting with Vo Nguyen Giap, the Viet Minh military leader—Sainteny was not grateful. He sent a message to his superiors saying that he was "face to face with a deliberate Allied maneuver to evict the French from Indochina" and that "at the present time the Allied attitude is more harmful than that of the Viet Minh."[2]

However, by the fall of 1945, the Truman administration had decided that it could not afford to add Indochina to its growing list of Far Eastern problems. The hands-off policy which it adopted aided France much more than the Viet Minh. American officials in Indochina were instructed not to oppose a French return to the area. In September, President Truman disbanded the OSS, whose officers had sometimes obstructed the activities of French officials. Washington also ignored a number of appeals for aid from Ho Chi Minh during this period. The announcement, in early 1946, that the United States would supply trucks and other equipment to French forces in Indochina was taken by both France and the Viet Minh as a clear indication of where the Truman administration's sympathies lay.

While General Marshall pursued his mediation efforts in China during

1946, France and the Viet Minh drifted toward war in Indochina. At the start of the year, neither side was in a position to take the offensive; an agreement was signed in March 1946 in Hanoi which could have provided a basis for a peaceful solution to the main political problems of Vietnam. Under the agreement, France recognized Vietnam as a free state within an "Indochinese federation" and "French Union" (neither of which had yet been created or even defined).

The three segments into which France had divided Vietnam (Cochinchina, Annam, and Tonkin) were to be reunited if the people of Cochinchina voted for this in a referendum. Vietnam was to have its own government, parliament, army, and finances. In return, France would be allowed to replace the Chinese troops in the north with 15,000 French soldiers and 10,000 Vietnamese soldiers under French command; France would withdraw its troops in five annual installments. In the interim, before the agreement was implemented, the Viet Minh promised to cease their guerrilla activities in South Vietnam.[3]

From the moment it was signed, the March 1946 agreement was openly sabotaged by Admiral d'Argenlieu, the French High Commissioner in Saigon, who was determined to restore French rule throughout Indochina. Ho Chi Minh was wise enough to realize that, if possible, it would be far better to win his country's independence without fighting a long and costly war against France. At the Fontainebleau conference (July to September 1946), he tried to obtain a promise that France would implement the March agreement.

However, the French were no longer even willing to confirm all of the features of the March accord. In September 1946, Ho Chi Minh and the French Minister of Overseas Territories signed a stand-fast agreement which said nothing about French recognition of Vietnam as a "free state." Exactly why Ho signed this agreement may never be known; it is possible that he was under Soviet pressure not to embarrass the French Communists in the forthcoming national elections.[4] By delaying the outbreak of war for a few more months, the modus vivendi also gained precious time in which the Viet Minh could continue building up their forces.

October and November brought increasingly serious clashes between the two sides, culminating in the French naval bombardment of Haiphong on November 23. This created tensions that made war inevitable. The French seized Da Nang, while the Viet Minh built barricades in the streets of Hanoi and on the road connecting Hanoi with Haiphong. War began on December 19, 1946, when the Viet Minh interpreted a French order to disband their militia as a demand for surrender.

Throughout the first three years of the war, the French government was at pains to conceal from the rest of the world just how expensive and bloody the fighting in Indochina was. France was struggling to rebuild its prestige as a world power; this depended on a minimum of publicity reaching the outside world about the difficulties which the French Expeditionary Corps faced in suppressing—or even containing—the Viet Minh rebellion. American officials lacked both historical background and detailed current information with which to assess the Indochina situation. They strongly suspected, however, that the key to the problem was the French government's failure to respond to the Vietnamese people's desire for independence.

American officials repeatedly urged the French to find some political formula to accommodate the forces of Vietnamese nationalism. But by the late 1940s, owing to the rising influence of the French Communist Party, the economic recovery of France had become a major U.S. goal, and its achievement seemed to depend on reestablishing the French colonial system. The United States provided $1.9 billion in economic aid to France between July 1945 and July 1948. Thus, although no U.S. arms aid as such was given to France in those years, the United States was indirectly helping finance the French war effort.

In 1949, two major world developments compelled the U.S. government to take a more active interest in Indochina. First, the North Atlantic Treaty joined France and the United States in a formal alliance. This might have enabled Washington to press the French successfully for a liberalization of their colonial policy in Indochina, if it had not been for the second major development—the conquest of China by Mao Tse-tung's army.

The defeat of Chiang's forces brought a torrent of criticism against the Truman administration from the rightwing "China bloc" in Congress, making it extremely difficult for the U.S. government to disengage politically from Chiang's exile regime on Taiwan. During 1949, the administration decided, mainly for domestic political reasons, to adopt the policy of "containing" Communist China by encircling it with anti-Communist military forces. French leaders were not slow to see the opportunity which these events provided to gain large-scale U.S. backing for their war in Indochina, but they wanted to be sure of retaining full control over matters of policy.

When Secretary of State Dean Acheson visited Paris in September 1949, he had one of his first conversations with French Foreign Minister Robert Schuman on the subject of Indochina:

> Schuman trod warily in discussing Southeast Asia and had no welcoming response to American interest. France, he said, at great expense was fighting the battle of all democratic peoples in Indochina. The United States could help by giving economic aid to the three "infant governments"—Vietnam, Laos, and Cambodia. They could not cope by themselves. The French were sponsoring their movement toward greater independence. The French army and technical advisors were indispensable to the development of functioning and truly independent native governments. I said that I was glad to hear this. We believed that France could help more in preventing Communist domination by moving quickly to satisfy nationalist aspirations.[5]

Acheson went on to tell Schuman that he hoped the French government would ratify the Elysée accords—an agreement reached in March 1949 between France and ex-Emperor Bao Dai, making the latter chief of state and granting partial autonomy to Vietnam. France still had full control over the timing of the transfer of powers under the Elysée accords, but the agreement had reconfirmed Vietnam's independence and, for the first time, spelled out the steps which would be taken to end Cochinchina's separate status. The French also agreed, in principle, to relinquish the administration of Hanoi, Haiphong, and Da Nang.

At a meeting with Acheson and British Foreign Secretary Ernest Bevin in November 1949, Schuman pointed out the grave difficulties for France if the Communist government in Peking established relations with Ho Chi Minh's government in North Vietnam and began providing it with military aid. He expressed the wish that Britain and the United States would show support for French policy in Indochina generally, and, specifically, in regard to the new Bao Dai regime. Acheson and Bevin both stated firmly that France would have to grant real autonomy to the Indochinese states before their governments could support

French policy there. Thus, France agreed at the end of 1949 to allow the Vietnamese government in Saigon autonomy in a number of secondary matters.

This cautious move by the French raised the prestige of the Saigon regime; to redress the balance, Ho Chi Minh's government issued a general appeal for diplomatic recognition in January 1950. China was the first country to respond, and the Soviet Union soon followed suit. The other East European Communist countries recognized the Democratic Republic of Vietnam (DRV) within a few months. (During the 1950s and 1960s, the United States used its influence whenever possible to prevent diplomatic contacts between the DRV and non-Communist countries.)

The United States tried to persuade several Asian governments to take the lead in recognizing the State of Vietnam and the Kingdoms of Laos and Cambodia. But when the Asian leaders who were approached held back, the United States and Great Britain became the first nations to recognize the Associated States of Indochina (in February 1950). The U.S. government issued a statement at the time stressing its "fundamental policy of giving support to the peaceful and democratic evolution of dependent peoples toward self-government and independence."[6] Thailand recognized the Associated States later the same month; the Thai government also asked the Viet Minh to close its mission in Bangkok. Eventually, about thirty nations recognized South Vietnam, Cambodia, and Laos.

American support of French policy in Indochina did not stop at diplomatic recognition of the Associated States. In his memoirs, Acheson has described how.

During the spring of 1950, after some hesitation, we in the Department recommended aid to France and the Associated States in combating Ho's insurgency, which was backed by the Chinese and Russians. The aid was to be limited to economic and military supplies, stopping short of our own military intervention. If Chinese or Soviet forces should intervene directly, the situation would be reconsidered. The hesitation came from the belief of some of my colleagues that, even with our material and financial help, the French-Bao Dai regime would be defeated in the field by the Soviet- and Chinese-supported Viet Minh. All of us recognized the high probability of this result unless France swiftly transferred authority to the Associated States and organized, trained, and equipped, with our aid, substantial indigenous forces to take over the main burden of the fight.[7]

Thus, the U.S. aim of moving the Indochinese states toward independence began to give way to the new objective of "containing" Chinese communism. French intelligence reports of a secret military aid agreement between Communist China and Ho Chi Minh's Democratic Republic of Vietnam were made public in the *New York Times* on May 8, 1950. Reports of this type served the French interest by portraying their war in Indochina as merely one battlefield in the worldwide struggle against communism.

President Truman approved a program of economic and military aid for Indochina in May 1950, and a special technical and economic mission was set up to work directly with the Associated States on economic aid. (The French insisted on retaining full control over all U.S. military aid and most U.S. economic aid destined for Indochina until the end of 1954.) In the hope of increasing the international stature of the Associated States and of obtaining a clearer picture of the situation in Indochina, the United States sent an Ambassador, Donald R. Heath, who was accredited to all three states but resident in Saigon.

Korea and Indochina: Two Fronts in the Same War?

On July 27, 1950, two days after North Korea's surprise invasion of South Korea, President Truman announced that he had ordered U.S. air and naval units to assist South Korea; the U.S. Seventh Fleet was also being stationed in the Taiwan Strait to protect Formosa from attack (and to make certain that Chiang's forces stopped raiding the mainland). American forces in the Philippines were being strengthened, and U.S. military aid to the French in Indochina was being expedited.

In July 1950, a U.S. Military Assistance Advisory Group (MAAG) was sent to South Vietnam, and $23.5 million worth of U.S. military aid was budgeted for use in Indochina during the coming year.[8] A Mutual Defense Agreement was signed in December 1950 by representatives of the French, Vietnamese, Cambodian, Lao, and U.S. governments; U.S. support of the French war effort in Indochina rose to about $1 billion in fiscal year 1954. By that time, there were 342 U.S. officers and enlisted men assigned to the MAAG in Vietnam.

The Korean war also influenced later U.S. policy toward Indochina in certain indirect but very important ways. For example, U.S. strategy in Korea led to an outright military clash with China which made normalization of Sino-American relations impossible for a number of years. Moreover, the political constraints under which the Korean war was fought irritated the U.S. military establishment and influenced their later recommendations about intervention in Indochina.

In a communique issued in June 1952, France and the United States recognized that the war in Indochina was a part of the worldwide resistance to "Communist attempts at conquest and subversion." It was noted that France had a "primary role in Indochina," similar to the American role in Korea, and that within the authority granted by Congress, the United States would increase its aid for the purpose of building up the national armies of the Associated States.[9]

Thus, America's involvement in Korea completed the reversal of U.S. priorities in Indochina—a process which was begun in 1945 and greatly accelerated after the 1949 victory of Communist forces in China. Instead of pressing France to accommodate the nationalist movement, the United States began to emphasize the short-term aim of persuading France not to slacken its war effort. By the summer of 1952, Washington knew that the Indochina war had become extremely unpopular in France—and that many French officials no longer considered victory to be possible. American officials were instructed not to antagonize the French by continually pressing for reforms and concessions to Vietnamese nationalism. These were now regarded as being of secondary and peripheral importance compared with continuing the war to contain Chinese communism.

Notes

1. Albert C. Wedemeyer, *Wedemeyer Reports!* (New York: Henry Holt, 1958), pp. 340 and 343.

2. Jean Sainteny, *Histoire d'une paix manquée* (Paris: Amiot-Dumont, 1953), pp. 91-124.

3. The terms of this agreement are somewhat similar to those which were nego-

tiated at Geneva in 1954. (See Chapter 3.) One of the main differences is that no political relationship between Vietnam, Laos, and Cambodia is mentioned in the 1954 agreement.

4. Harold Isaacs, *No Peace in Asia* (New York: Macmillan, 1947), pp. 173-74.

5. Dean Acheson, *Present at the Creation: My Years in the State Department* (New York: Norton, 1969), pp. 671-72.

6. *U.S. State Department Bulletin*, Vol. XXII, Feb. 20, 1950, pp. 291-92.

7. Acheson, *Present at the Creation*, pp. 672-73.

8. Bernard B. Fall, *The Two Viet-Nams, A Political and Military Analysis* (New York: Praeger, 1967), pp. 219-20. However, competing demands for U.S. arms and equipment in Korea and other problems of coordination limited the actual flow of U.S. arms aid during fiscal year 1951 to less than that quite modest amount.

9. *U.S. State Department Bulletin*, Vol. XXVI, June 30, 1952, p. 1010.

CHAPTER THREE

Ending the
First Indochina War

President Eishower managed to bring about a Korean armistice early in his first year in office. This helped to set in motion the series of events which led, one year later, to the end of the first Indochina war. Realizing that the American people did not want to risk a repetition of the Korean war, Eisenhower also dampened the enthusiasm of some of his advisors for U.S. intervention in Indochina during the seige of Dien Bien Phu.

Except for these decisions, however, most aspects of U.S. policy toward Indochina during the Eisenhower administration bore the stamp of Secretary of State John Foster Dulles.[1] Although Dulles had few major differences with the Truman administration over the substance of its foreign policy, he believed, perhaps rightly, that Secretary Acheson's difficulties with Congress were based on matters of style more than substance. The solemn, implacably anti-Communist style that Dulles adopted often made him seem opposed to any settlement in Indochina that might reduce the pressure on China. Certain senators had been fond of damning Acheson for paying too much attention to our European allies; Dulles avoided such criticism by playing the condescending Yankee lawyer in his dealings with Eden and other foreign ministers. While Acheson found it hard to hide his contempt for the China bloc, Dulles came to be regarded as their ally and Chiang Kai-shek's great protector.

Korean Armistice Creates Momentum Toward Indochina Truce

Many French leaders were convinced as early as 1951 that military victory in Indochina was impossible. However, the French government held back from seeking a truce in Indochina because of their understanding with the United States (the main financier of the French war effort) that Korea and Indochina were two fronts of the same war to contain China.

On July 3, 1953 (just before the Korean armistice), the French government issued its first unqualified statement of willingness to negotiate full independence with the Associated States of Indochina. At the same time, Premier Laniel informed the newly appointed French commander in Indochina, General Henri Navarre, that his government intended to enter into negotiations with the Viet Minh for a cease-fire as soon as the conclusion of an armistice in Korea made this possible.

The Korean truce agreement was signed on July 26, 1953, after strong pressure was brought to bear on President Syngman Rhee by the Eisenhower administration. Almost immediately, there were reports (which may have been exaggerated) that the Chinese were transferring large quantities of arms to southern China and Vietnam and expediting their training and reequipment of the Viet Minh forces.[2] The Eisenhower administration took the position that it was more important than ever for France to carry on the struggle. In August 1953, in one of the first expressions of the domino theory, President Eisenhower predicted that Burma, India, and Indonesia would be in danger if the Communists overran Indochina. He added that U.S. military and economic aid to anti-Communist forces in Indochina offered the "cheapest way" to avoid a serious threat to American security. Secretary Dulles warned Peking, on September 2, that a renewal of fighting in Korea or a transfer of Communist forces to Indochina might lead to war between the United States and China.

Nevertheless, the French government persevered with its secret efforts to get truce talks started, and on November 29, 1953, Ho Chi Minh published a statement in the Swedish newspaper *Expressen* agreeing to the idea of negotiations. Only two days earlier, the Soviet Union had accepted a long-standing Western proposal for a Big Four foreign ministers' meeting, and there were rumors that the Soviets might be interested in helping mediate the Indochina war (perhaps in return for a closer understanding with France on European issues).

Meanwhile, the French and Viet Minh commanders in Indochina were each preparing one last major effort to turn the tide of battle in their favor before negotiations got under way. In November 1953, General Navarre, the French commander, began to construct a fortified camp at the town of Dien Bien Phu, in a remote valley near the border between North Vietnam and Laos. Navarre planned to station about 10,000 men there, in the hope of tempting General Giap (the Viet Minh commander) to attack with 15,000 or 20,000 of his best men. If Giap did so, Navarre was confident that the superior firepower and military skills of the French would enable them to achieve a dramatic victory over the Viet Minh on the eve of the forthcoming peace talks. As soon as General Giap discovered what Navarre planned, he began laying elaborate plans to beseige the French camp at Dien Bien Phu.

In December 1953, a Viet Minh force struck across Laos from the area of Vinh in North Vietnam and seized the Laotian town of Thakhek on the Mekong River. This move cut Indochina in half. It raised new fears in Washington of a French defeat or of Chinese intervention. Secretary Dulles tried to encourage Paris and warn Peking by announcing that, if China entered the war, the American response "would not necessarily be confined to the particular theater chosen by the Communists for their operations." He underlined the warning on January 12, 1954, when he announced the doctrine of "massive retaliation," which he called a "maximum deterrent at a bearable cost" against a "potential aggressor ... glutted with manpower." His statement was accompanied by discussion in American newspapers about the possibility of U.S. intervention in Indochina with air and sea power.

British Foreign Secretary Anthony Eden had been anxious for over a year to help the French find an honorable exit from Indochina; he considered this vital to further progress on the basic Allied problem of European defense. As long as France had a large expeditionary corps tied down in Indochina, the armed forces which it could provide for Europe's defense would be heavily outnumbered by those that West Germany could muster. Largely because of this, France had delayed ratifying the European Defense Community treaty (which would bring Germany into the Western defense system). For this reason—and because he doubted that there was much danger of direct Chinese intervention in Vietnam—Eden was greatly disturbed by Dulles' statements on the Indochina problem.

By mid-January 1954, Eden had begun to consider the idea of a negotiated settlement based on partition—as a means of helping France to extricate herself from Indochina and also to reduce the chance of a Sino-American clash which could lead to a third world war. When the British, French, Soviet, and American foreign ministers met at Berlin on January 25, 1954, Molotov advanced the idea of a five-power conference (including China) to "seek measures for reducing tension in international relations." After weeks of skillful diplomacy by Eden, this proposal was transformed into an agreement to hold a nine-power conference on Indochina, which was announced on February 18, 1954.[3]

The Question of U.S. Intervention or "United Action"

During the month of February 1954 (as the Viet Minh tightened their network of tunnels and trenches around Dien Bien Phu), the Eisenhower administration issued a series of optimistic statements about the war and disclaimers of any plans for U.S. intervention. On February 9, Defense Secretary Wilson said that the war was "going along as well as expected at this stage," and military victory was "both possible and probable." He acknowledged that a group of U.S. military mechanics and civilian pilots were aiding the French air force in Indochina, but Wilson said that no U.S. pilots or ground troops would fight in the war and that no U.S. aid was planned at "any higher level than now." The next day, President Eisenhower said that it would be a "great tragedy" for the United States to become involved in the war and that everything he did was calculated to prevent this from happening. On March 10, the

President announced that he would not involve the United States in any conflict, including Indochina, without first seeking a Congressional declaration of war.

General Paul Ely, the French Chief of Staff, arrived in Washington on March 20 on his way home from a visit to Indochina. He came to present a very pessimistic report on the military situation in Indochina and to seek additional U.S. aid (including heavy bombers and more American personnel to augment the French air force). On orders from his government, Ely stated frankly that France would not be able to continue the war effort much longer; additional aid was needed simply to keep the French expeditionary corps in the fight until a settlement could be reached at Geneva.

Ely's statement stunned the small group of top officials who heard his report. It was not the first indication they had received that the French were unwilling to carry on the fight much longer. But it appears to have been the first time the full drama of the situation struck home— the probability of a major defeat at Dien Bien Phu, followed by the complete collapse of French morale, and the replacement of the Laniel government by one prepared to make a deal with the Communists on Indochina. The fact that General Ely was known to regard the Atlantic alliance as the cornerstone of French policy made his words seem all the more impressive to his American listeners.

But it was General Ely's turn to be astonished when he called on Admiral Radford, the Chairman of the Joint Chiefs of Staff. Without even being asked, Radford suggested United States intervention in the war. His plan to save the French garrison at Dien Bien Phu called for a massive strike by American bombers on Tuan Giao, the Viet Minh supply base, about seventy miles from the French camp. Two hundred American planes would take off from aircraft carriers flying near the coast of Vietnam. These would be joined by heavier bombers from land bases in the Philippines. The planes would make one powerful attack on the Viet Minh base. If this failed to halt the Viet Minh seige, it would be followed by a second attack. While General Ely was submitting the Radford proposal to his government, the U.S. National Security Council met and debated the question of U.S. intervention. The decision reached by the NSC, and approved by President Eisenhower, was that the United States could not afford the loss of Indochina to the Communists. If there was no other way to prevent this from happening, the United States would intervene in the war—but only if two conditions were met: first, the intervention must have the support of Allied nations (preferably including Great Britain); second, the French must grant full independence to the states of Indochina to eliminate the issue of colonialism. The President had already publicly committed himself to a third condition in stating that there would be no intervention without a Congressional declaration of war.

On March 29, Secretary Dulles gave the first public hint that the administration was considering intervention in Indochina. In a speech in New York, he said that a victory by the Chinese-backed Viet Minh would lead to Communist domination of all Southeast Asia. He then indicated that the United States government felt that such a possibility should not be passively accepted but should be met by united action. While he acknowledged that this might involve serious risks, he felt the danger of not being "resolute" was far greater.

The British government had been under the impression that the United States ruled out intervention in Indochina; it was unaware of the bombing plan which Radford had just proposed to Ely. Following Dulles' speech, the British Ambassador in Washington was instructed to make clear to U.S. leaders that his own government believed a favorable solution in Indochina might no longer be possible and that the Western powers must concentrate on developing a realistic negotiating strategy to follow at Geneva. In this connection, the British government considered partition the least damaging solution.[4]

The British Ambassador learned that the U.S. government had rejected the idea of partitioning Indochina, because it was believed by leading U.S. officials that this would soon lead to Communist domination of all Southeast Asia. Dulles told the ambassador that the best hope was to compel China to cease aiding the Viet Minh by the threat of military action; if this failed, the Allies should be prepared to take military action. The first step, he said, would be a joint warning by several countries of naval and air action against the China coast. The United States would not threaten the landing of American troops.

Two days later, on April 3, Dulles and Admiral Radford briefed the leaders of Congress on Radford's intervention scheme and found that it had little support. One congressman asked Admiral Radford whether such intervention would be an act of war; Radford said it would mean the United States would be in the war. He did not give a definite answer when asked whether U.S. ground forces would be used if the air strike failed. He was also asked if his plan had the approval of the Joint Chiefs, and Admiral Radford acknowledged that it did not. In fact, he said, none of them supported it, and he explained that this was because he understood the situation in the Far East better than they did. Senator Lyndon Johnson then asked Secretary Dulles if Allied governments had been consulted about the plan; Dulles replied that they had not. The consensus of the congressional leaders was that Dulles should obtain Allied support before considering the intervention plan further.

Meanwhile, the French government had received a message from General Navarre (who was aware of Admiral Radford's intervention plan). The message said that the garrison at Dien Bien Phu would be lost without an American air strike, which Navarre believed could destroy the Viet Minh forces attacking the French camp. On April 4, with considerable hesitancy, the French government officially requested U.S. intervention. But by that time, President Eisenhower and Secretary Dulles were in agreement that the Radford plan should not be carried out. The negative response of the congressional leaders was undoubtedly one reason why the administration decided not to intervene at this stage. Secretary Dulles disapproved of Admiral Radford's action in taking it upon himself to propose intervention to the French. Dulles also felt that the limited aim of saving Dien Bien Phu and improving the French bargaining position at Geneva was not enough. He wanted to persuade the French to carry on the war in cooperation with an anti-Communist alliance, led by the United States. In short, Dulles hoped to internationalize the Indochina war and carry it through to victory.

Thus, in the first week of April 1954, Secretary Dulles sent a new proposal to the British and French governments. Before the start of the Geneva conference, an anti-Communist coalition (consisting of Britain, France, America, Australia, New Zealand, Thailand, the Philippines, Cambodia, Laos, and Vietnam) would issue a declaration of their readiness to take concerted action in Indochina against continued interference in the war by China. This declaration would contain the threat of naval and air action against the Chinese coast as well as active intervention in Indochina. Fearing that such a move would disrupt the chances for peace at Geneva, and possibly trigger a third world war, the French and British governments agreed only to examine the possibility of collective defense for Southeast Asia and the western Pacific.

In spite of this, Dulles issued invitations to the ambassadors of Great

Britain, France, Australia, New Zealand, Thailand, the Philippines, and the Associated States for a meeting on April 20. Its purpose was to set up an informal working group to study the collective defense of Southeast Asia. Eden was furious at Dulles' deliberate "misunderstanding" of his government's position. The British Amabassador in Washington was instructed not to attend the meeting (which had already been announced to the public). After Dulles agreed to turn the meeting into a briefing session on Korea, a British representative attended but took no part in the discussion.

At Dien Bien Phu meanwhile, the battle of attrition continued with mounting horror for both defending and attacking forces. The French airstrip had been knocked out of action on March 28. The wounded could no longer be evacuated, and Viet Minh antiaircraft guns made it necessary to drop supplies and reinforcements from such heights that accuracy was impossible. Both sides had totally inadequate medical facilities, and both suffered as the daily rain turned their positions into deep mud. While the Viet Minh methodically drew their ring of trenches and tunnels tighter around the French camp, training their heavy guns from newly captured hilltops, French gunners continued to make it almost suicidal for the Viet Minh infantry to attack the main French positions.

By April 21, the Viet Minh lines were only about 700 yards from the center of the French camp. General Navarre appealed to Paris for reinforcements of men and supplies "at any cost." French leaders asked Dulles to reconsider his government's earlier refusal to carry out the Radford plan for a U.S. air strike against the Viet Minh supply base at Tuan Giao. Dulles, by this time, had concluded that there was no hope of saving Dien Bien Phu. But he and Admiral Radford proposed to Foreign Secretary Eden that some form of joint U.S.-British intervention be carried out in order to show the French—and the people of Indochina—that France still had powerful allies. Neither Dulles nor Radford made clear to Eden what sort of action they had in mind, apart from suggesting that the British might send some R.A.F. units to North Vietnam.

The consensus among leading U.S. officials was that there were two minimum conditions for U.S. intervention: first, France must issue a statement approving "united action" in Indochina; and second, Great Britain must give her consent. Foreign Minister Bidault agreed on April

24 to recommend that Premier Laniel issue the required statement. But the British government held firm in its refusal to take action which might wreck the chances for peace at Geneva. At an emergency meeting of the British Cabinet on Sunday, April 25, Dulles' proposal for joint intervention was rejected. Prime Minister Churchill summed up the situation by saying:

> ... what we were being asked to do was to assist in misleading Congress into approving a military operation, which would in itself be ineffective, and might well bring the world to the verge of a major war.[5]

Nevertheless, a few senior officials in the Eisenhower administration managed to keep alive the idea of American air and naval intervention in the war until early June 1954. British approval was no longer considered necessary, but a French grant of "genuine freedom" to Vietnam, Laos, and Cambodia, and a request for American participation in the war, remained essential conditions. A new condition was evidently added in May: that American advisors in Vietnam must be allowed to take "major responsibility for training indigenous forces" and that they must "share responsibility for military planning" with the French.[6] It should have been obvious in Washington by this time that the French National Assembly was totally unwilling to prolong the war and that French officials had no interest in sharing their responsibilities with Americans.

The Fall of Dien Bien Phu

As the delegates to the Geneva conference began to assemble in late April, news of the seige of Dien Bien Phu was being carried on the front pages of major newspapers all over the world. General Giap's final onslaught began on May 1. Both sides suffered extremely heavy casualties during the last few days of fighting, but in spite of the hopelessness of their position, the defending soldiers fought on courageously until General Navarre sent the order to cease firing—at 5:30 P.M. on May 7, 1954.

During the fifty-five days of fighting, 10,000 soldiers on both sides lost their lives, including about 7,900 Viet Minh and 2,000 French

Union soldiers. More than 21,000 were wounded—including 6,400 French Union troops and 15,000 men on the Viet Minh side. Many French troops died later during the 500-mile march to Viet Minh prison camps or during the three months before a general exchange of prisoners took place.

The Geneva Conference

As General Giap probably intended, the Viet Minh victory at Dien Bien Phu set the stage for the first formal discussion of the Indochina problem at Geneva, which began on May 8. In his opening address to the conference, Foreign Minister Bidault proposed a cease-fire, as instructed by his government. But during the next few weeks he refused to meet privately with the Viet Minh delegates. In this, he was following the example of Secretary Dulles, who avoided even acknowledging the existence of the Chinese Premier, Chou En-lai, at the conference.

On May 4, Secretary Dulles left his deputy, Undersecretary Bedell Smith, in charge of the U.S. delegation and departed for Washington, announcing that the conference was "going just as expected." Dulles faced strong criticism among conservative forces in Congress for his failure to organize a Southeast Asian defense pact—although he had done everything he could to promote the project, even at the risk of wrecking the Geneva conference. Once back in Washington, however, Dulles counseled the Congress and American public to be patient; he said he was at a loss to see how anyone could call what had happened thus far at Geneva a defeat for the West. Eisenhower supported him, saying that it was never expected that a defense organization for Southeast Asia would spring into existence overnight. On May 11, Dulles and Eisenhower both made public statements indicating that the administration had become reconciled to a compromise settlement in Indochina.

The task of trying to develop a coherent Western position at Geneva, as well as much of the negotiating with Molotov and Chou En-lai, fell to Foreign Minister Eden. The British government was not obsessed with the fear of Chinese aggression as was the United States; nor was it faced with a major loss of prestige and territory, like the French. Eden had a smooth, friendly relationship with Bedell Smith, who led the American delegation during the major part of the conference. However, he regarded Dulles' sudden and unpredictable changes of direction as dangerous and infuriating.

Foreign Minister Molotov took the lead among the Communist dele-gates for much the same reason that Eden did on his side: the Soviet Union had nothing to lose from a settlement based on the partition of Indochina. The fact that France failed to ratify the European Defense Community treaty after the Geneva conference has led some observers to conclude that this was the price demanded for Soviet "influence" in restraining the Viet Minh negotiators. Molotov's manner was so un-characteristically mild throughout the long and hectic conference that Eden suspected him of trying to drive a wedge between the United States and Britain.

On the other hand, the Chinese Premier and Foreign Minister, Chou En-lai, apparently felt the need to be cold and dogmatic during the first few weeks of the conference; but it gradually became apparent that he, too, was prepared to work toward a settlement that did not bring all of Indochina under Communist rule. It was he who made the important announcement, in June, that Viet Minh forces would be withdrawn from Laos and Cambodia after a cease-fire was signed.

The Viet Minh delegation was led by Pham Van Dong, Premier of the Democratic Republic of Vietnam. Dong and his delegation pro-duced conflicting impressions on different observers at the conference. It is generally thought that they settled for less than they believed they deserved because of Soviet and Chinese pressure. However, in judging their effectiveness as negotiators, three points should be remembered. First, although they had just won an enormous psychological victory at Dien Bien Phu, they had by no means driven the French expeditionary corps out of Indochina. Second, their own forces were desperately weakened by the battle of Dien Bien Phu; they were dependent on Chinese aid to continue the struggle at anything like the level they had been waging since 1952. Third, the terms of the Geneva agreements were widely regarded at the time as putting them in sight of their goal of reunifying Vietnam under Communist rule.

Of the three delegations from the Associated States, the one from Saigon was in the most difficult position. Its leader, Foreign Minister Tran Van Do, was excluded from the negotiations between the French and the Viet Minh. Since the Saigon regime lacked both the will and the means to continue the war alone, its interests were largely ignored at Geneva.

From June 24 to 29, an important meeting took place in Washington between Churchill, Eden, Eisenhower, and Dulles. By then, relations between Eden and Dulles had become so strained over the latter's efforts to promote "united action" at the expense of a peace settlement that it was apparently necessary for Churchill and Eisenhower to repair the damage to Anglo-American relations. As a result of this meeting, the United States and Great Britain sent a secret message to the French government saying that they would each respect a truce in Indochina which would: assure the withdrawal of the Viet Minh from Laos and Cambodia; preserve at least the southern half of Vietnam (and if possible an enclave in the Red River delta); not impose any restrictions on Laos, Cambodia, or South Vietnam that would prevent them from maintaining stable, non-Communist regimes; not contain any political provisions which would risk loss of South Vietnam to Communist control; not exclude the possibility of reunifying Vietnam by peaceful means; allow for the peaceful and humane transfer, under international supervision, of people desiring to move from one zone of Vietnam to another; and provide effective machinery for international supervision of the agreement.

Mendès-France and Eden both tried to persuade Dulles to return to Geneva for the final days of the conference to show solidarity with France and Britain. Dulles argued that even if the settlement conformed to the Anglo-American principles which had been agreed to in Washington, the United States still could not sign it. However, after Eden worked out a procedure with the Communist delegations by which the conference participants would not actually sign the Final Declaration, Dulles agreed to let Bedell Smith represent the United States at the closing session.

Premier Mendès-France managed to get two major concessions from the Communists just before the July 20 deadline which he had set himself. First, the dividing line between North and South Vietnam would be the seventeenth parallel of latitude, rather than the thirteenth, as the Communists had first proposed. Second, the nationwide elections which were supposed to be held as a step toward unifying the two halves of Vietnam would be held in 1956; this would allow the non-Communist South Vietnamese politicians time to prepare for an electoral campaign against the much better organized Communists in North Vietnam. In a dramatic, last-minute move, the Cambodians succeeded in forcing the other delegations to recognize their country's right to do whatever might be necessary to defend itself.

Separate truce agreements were signed for Cambodia, Laos, and South Vietnam in the early morning hours of July 21. Under the agreement for Vietnam, the country was divided in half along the seventeenth parallel; the Viet Minh were given control of the northern zone and the State of Vietnam the southern zone. Within 300 days, Viet Minh forces were to move into North Vietnam, and in the same period, all forces under French command were to leave North Vietnam. Civilians were also allowed to move between North and South Vietnam during the first 300 days of the truce. Neither side was supposed to strengthen the military forces in its half of Vietnam or to allow foreign military bases to be set up on their territory. The agreements were to be carried out under the supervision of an International Control Commission, which would be made up of equal numbers of Indian, Canadian, and Polish representatives, with an Indian serving as chairman.

The Geneva conference ended on July 21, 1954 with a Final Declaration, which stated that the division of Vietnam was temporary. The two halves of the country were to be joined together after a government had been chosen in a general election (to be supervised by the International Control Commission). Preparations for the election would begin a year after the Geneva conference. The actual elections would be held in July 1956.

The Final Declaration of the conference was not signed by any country. The names of all nine participating nations were listed in the heading of the document, and it was agreed to by voice vote of the representatives at the conference. Because they were unwilling to recognize the legitimacy of the Communist regime in North Vietnam, the United States and the State of Vietnam both announced that they were not prepared to join in the Final Declaration of the conference. But both governments also promised not to use force to upset the agreements. Bedell Smith added that the United States was in favor of the principle of free elections under United Nations supervision and that all three Indochinese countries should be permitted to determine their own future.

With the exception of the State of Vietnam and possibly the Democratic Republic of Vietnam, most of the governments thought the agreements reached at Geneva were the best possible under the circumstances. President Eisenhower expressed this view on July 21, although members of his administration privately recorded their opinion at the time that the Geneva settlement was a "disaster" that might lead to the "loss of Southeast Asia."[7] Historians have been inclined to take the view that the agreements were highly favorable to the non-Communist forces, given their military position at the time.

Half of Vietnam, two provinces of Laos, and no provinces of Cambodia were placed under Communist control. The war was over; the killing had been stopped. But the conference had not even attempted to solve the major political problems dividing the peoples of Indochina. And there was no automatic guarantee that the terms of the agreement would be respected by the governments with interests in the area.

Notes

1. Dulles had long been involved in the formulation of American foreign policy before he took charge of the State Department in 1953. As Republican advisor to U.S. delegations to the United Nations and to Big Four meetings of the foreign ministers and as chief negotiator of the Japanese Peace Treaty, Dulles was committed to the broad lines of U.S. foreign policy that evolved in the postwar period. The Truman administration found him a valuable advocate who could, and often did, persuade senior members of his party to support certain policies on a bipartisan basis.

2. See Fall, *The Two Viet-Nams*, pp. 122-24.

3. Dulles' main objective at the Berlin conference was to avoid conferring the status of a major power on Communist China—as the original Soviet proposal for a five-power conference with a worldwide agenda would have done. The idea of a conference with broader participation and a strictly limited agenda removed this obstacle. After the Berlin meeting, Dulles returned to Washington and persuaded the China bloc that it had been a "victory" for the West.

4. Anthony Eden, *Full Circle* (Boston: Houghton Mifflin, 1960), p. 102.

5. Ibid., p. 117.

6. Neil Sheehan et al., *The Pentagon Papers* (New York: Bantam, 1971), pp. 12-13 and 44-46.

7. Ibid., p. 14.

CHAPTER FOUR

"Sink or Swim with Ngo Dinh Diem"

Once Dulles had decided that the days of French rule in Indochina were numbered, he was impatient to take up the faltering ally's burdens. By July 1954, his plans for postwar Indochina were well advanced. The Southeast Asia Treaty Organization, a deliberately vague concept useful for bluffing potential enemies, was to be the cornerstone of his strategy. Although SEATO remained the most skeletal of military alliances, Dulles believed that it would have enough potential military forces at its disposal to deter any Communist power from attacking South Vietnam, Laos, or Cambodia. Ngo Dinh Diem, the anti-French Premier of South Vietnam, would receive direct American economic backing, and the Vietnamese national army (with American aid and advisors) would be in charge of South Vietnam's internal security. This would leave the French armed forces in Indochina with nothing to do except protect the local French community.

Formation of SEATO and Its Aims

Once the danger of disrupting the Geneva conference was over, Dulles had little difficulty in persuading a number of governments that were already closely associated with the United States to join SEATO. America was expected to play by far the major role in the alliance. In the unlikely event that Communist forces risked an attack on a country in the treaty area, an American response would be promptly sanctioned by the other SEATO members. On September 8, 1954, representatives of Australia, Britain, France, New Zealand, Pakistan, the Philippines, Thailand, and the United States met in Manila and signed the SEATO treaty. This pledged each member to "act to meet the common danger in accordance with its constitutional processes" in the event of armed aggression against any one of them.

The member states also agreed to develop their individual and collective capacity to resist armed attack and "subversive activities directed from without" and to seek solutions to common economic and social problems. The word "Communist" did not appear in the treaty, but the U.S. government filed a separate statement indicating that its commitment applied only in the case of Communist aggression—although the United States would also consult SEATO members in the event of "other aggression or armed attack."

The treaty area covered by the Manila pact was defined as the "general area of Southeast Asia," including the entire territories of the Asian parties to the treaty and the "general area of the Southwest Pacific" below a line running to the south of Formosa. A protocol to the treaty extended its protection to Cambodia, Laos, and South Vietnam, though the treaty did not specify that the SEATO "umbrella" had to be accepted by the Indochinese states to be valid. When Cambodia renounced SEATO's protection a short while later, the SEATO military planning staff probably continued to make plans for Cambodia's defense. However, when Laos formally renounced SEATO protection under the 1962 Geneva settlement, this ended any possibility of SEATO intervention in Laos.

The United States Backs Diem

In June 1954, Ngo Dinh Diem was named premier of the State of Vietnam by Bao Dai. He was fifty-three years old and had been in voluntary retirement for twenty years. His name meant nothing to the younger generation of Vietnamese, but as a member of one of Vietnam's most illustrious Catholic families, Diem was known to the older Vietnamese elite as a man of rigid integrity; he had resigned his post as Minister of Interior in 1933, when he realized he was only expected to be a French puppet. Over the years, Diem had often declined the Emperor Bao Dai's offers of high government posts for the same reason. In 1946, he also refused to serve as Minister of Interior of the DRV, when Ho Chi Minh held him prisoner, because the Viet Minh had killed his brother and his nephew.

Diem was released by the Viet Minh when the March 1946 agreement was signed, and he traveled abroad extensively during the next few years. He met Dulles and other American political figures while living in the United States in the early 1950s, but there is no reason to believe that any American influenced Bao Dai's choice of Diem in June 1954. He was simply the only person of stature who was willing to serve as Premier of South Vietnam at that unpropitious moment. The reason Diem accepted, after so many refusals, was that Bao Dai agreed to give him full civil and military powers. During the nine and a half years that he ruled South Vietnam, Diem remained the unbending autocrat, who trusted no one completely except his closest relatives.

The Ngo family's political base was in central Vietnam, where Diem's younger brother, Ngo Dinh Can, acted as unofficial proconsul of the national government. Diem's older brother, Archbishop Ngo Dinh Thuc of Hue, was the senior Roman Catholic prelate of Vietnam. He helped to make the Catholic Church one of the regime's main sources of political strength.

During his nine and half year reign, Diem came increasingly under the influence of another younger brother, Ngo Dinh Nhu, whose control of the secret police and intelligence networks reflected his fascination with totalitarian methods. Nhu provided Diem with daily reports on the hatred and disloyalty which, according to his spy network, certain key officials felt toward him. Although Diem was no coward—as he proved a number of times when his life was in danger—Nhu's reports gradually unnerved him and drove him to paranoia. Eventually, the circle of people whom Diem trusted included almost no one except his three brothers and Nhu's wife, Tran Le Xuan ("Beautiful Spring"), who was official hostess for the bachelor President.[1]

As a Roman Catholic from central Vietnam, Diem had no political base in Saigon or in the southern provinces of the country. He could count on the loyalty of only two battalions of the 270,000-man national army. A gangster group known as the *Binh Xuyen* had purchased from the French for 40 million piasters the right to organize the police force of Saigon. The *Cao Dai*, an eclectic religious sect, controlled much of the territory west of Saigon; and the *Hoa Hao*, a reformed Buddhist sect, was strong in the southern tip of the country. Many other provinces were effectively controlled by the Viet Minh. Although Viet Minh military units moved north of the seventeenth parallel in accordance with the Geneva agreements, they left their political cadres, who immediately began preparing for the 1956 elections.

Most Americans who dealt with Diem during his first months in office had doubts about his being able to cope with the massive problems he faced. He refused to accept the advice of Americans or other foreigners and seemed incapable of decisive action. But not all American officials considered Diem incompetent. One of his earliest American backers was Edward G. Lansdale, a U.S. Air Force colonel on loan to the CIA, who had been sent to Saigon by the Eisenhower administration in June 1954 to organize covert warfare activities against the Vietnamese Communists.[2] Within a few weeks after Diem's appointment—and before either he or Lansdale knew much about the situation—Lansdale had gained Diem's confidence and was urging Washington to give him maximum support.

The idea that Diem was the best available anti-Communist leader was viewed with initial skepticism in Washington, but it seems to have been accepted by the Eisenhower administration in September 1954, the same month in which the administration privately informed the French government that the United States intended to play the leading role in Indochina. Senator Mike Mansfield, the influential Democrat, visited South Vietnam in September. His October 15 report to the Senate Committee on Foreign Relations acknowledged that Diem's position was weak, and concluded that the United States "should consider an immediate suspension of all aid to Vietnam and the French Union forces there" if Diem's government fell.

On October 1, President Eisenhower wrote Diem a letter (which was made public on October 25, 1954) pledging full American support. This letter was of great importance to Diem, because it told potential or actual rivals in South Vietnam that he was the chosen instrument of U.S. policy. Eisenhower's letter formed the basis of the United States' commitment to support an anti-Communist government in South Vietnam, but it made U.S.backing conditional on Diem's "assurances as to the standards of performance" by his administration. Specifically, Eisenhower noted that the U.S. government

> . . . expects that this aid will be met by performance on the part of the Government of Vietnam in undertaking needed reforms. It hopes that such aid, combined with your own continuing efforts, will contribute effectively toward an independent Vietnam endowed with a strong government. Such a government would, I hope, be so responsive to the nationalist aspirations of its people, so enlightened in purpose and effective in performance, that it will be respected both at home and abroad and discourage any who might wish to impose a foreign ideology on your free people.[3]

With American policy hardening at this time around the idea of supporting Diem, excluding French influence, and making South Vietnam an anti-Communist bastion, it was logical for the French to support the man who could most easily topple Diem and preserve the French presence in Indochina. This man, General Nguyen Van Hinh, chief of staff of the Vietnamese army, was known to be pro-French and anti-Diem. General Paul Ely, the French civil and military chief in Indochina, was opposed to an anti-Diem coup because he attached great importance to preserving close relations with the United States. But with the Vietnamese army, a large part of the French community, and the Binh Xuyen police on his side, Hinh would have had little difficulty deposing Diem.

The French and British governments, eager to see the Geneva accords implemented, favored the overthrow of Diem. Their strategy was to assert that the growing danger of a North Vietnamese attack made it necessary to put the country in the hands of the South Vietnamese army. A number of prominent French people in Vietnam called for Franco-American military cooperation (with France playing the leading role) to meet the North Vietnamese "threat." News reports from "French sources" described how North Vietnam was rearming with Chinese aid. An article in the French newspaper *L'Express* by Buu Hoi, a prominent anti-Diem Vietnamese scientist, produced speculation that he might be the French and British governments' candidate to replace Diem.

In Washington, Secretary Dulles responded coolly to this campaign to block his aims in Vietnam. He told a congressional committee that any "external" threat to South Vietnam had been warded off by the SEATO alliance. He also sent a message to the French government (on the eve of an important visit to Washington by Premier Mendès-France) saying that the United States was opposed to anyone with views like those of Buu Hoi being given responsibility in Saigon. At that point, war began in Algeria, and much of Mendès-France's visit was taken up with the question of U.S. aid to French forces in North Africa. The French Premier had no choice but to reaffirm publicly what his government had already agreed to secretly two months earlier—that the United States would play the "leading role" in Indochina.

Meanwhile, President Eisenhower had sent General Lawton Collins to Saigon as his special ambassador, with broad powers to coordinate the activities of American agencies in South Vietnam. Shortly after his arrival, Collins met with High Commissioner Ely, who was an old friend, and presented him with the draft of an agreement which would transfer most of the remaining military responsibilities in Indochina to the United States. Although Ely knew the United States intended to make such a move, he was shocked at the speed with which Washington hoped to liquidate the remaining French military presence. From the point of view of the French, the one good thing about the Americans' attitude was that they showed no signs of wanting to replace French commercial interests in Indochina.

General Collins next took firm steps to discourage General Hinh and his supporters from overthrowing Diem. He announced that the United States would give every possible aid to Diem's government—and to his alone—and that it would not consider training or otherwise aiding a Vietnamese army that did not give implicit obedience to its premier. Hinh refused to obey Diem's orders to leave the country, but after

American representatives met with Bao Dai in France, the Vietnamese chief of state summoned Hinh and relieved him of his command. Both Hinh and Bao Dai claimed they had acted out of patriotic motives—to spare South Vietnam a disastrous loss of American aid. With Hinh out of the way, Premier Diem's position was a little more secure, although other challenges awaited him.

On December 13, 1954, Ely and Collins signed a highly important agreement which provided for the substitution of American military influence for that of France in South Vietnam. Full responsibility for assisting the Saigon government in the organization and training of its armed forces would pass to the chief of the U.S. Military Assistance Advisory Group, although he would operate under "supreme authority" of the French commander in chief, General Ely. While both American and French personnel would be used as advisors and instructors, all would be under the direction of the chief of MAAG.

The United States had decided to reduce the size of the Vietnamese national army from 270,000 to 90,000 men. With American instructors and modern training techniques, it was hoped that the smaller national army could keep order within the country and perform a civic action role which would contribute to economic development and help create popular support for the government. (Vietnam's defense from external aggression would be the responsibility of SEATO rather than the Vietnamese national army.) By reducing the size of the army and substituting American for French instructors, there would be no further need for French military personnel in Vietnam, except for a small force to protect French nationals in the Saigon area. The United States government therefore informed the French that it planned to cut its financial support for these troops by almost seventy-five percent in 1955. This would virtually force France to reduce its expeditionary corps in Indochina from 150,000 to 30,000 men by the end of the year.

The Vietnamese army, although slated to be cut by two thirds from its 1954 strength, would receive $200 million in aid from the United States in 1955; this was more than half the amount it had received during the last year of the Indochina war. Finally, U.S. economic aid would be increased from $25 million in 1954 to $100 million in 1955. France would be pressed to transfer all remaining administrative functions to the State of Vietnam by January 1, 1955. Once that was done, U.S. aid could be given to Vietnam directly rather than through the

French government. Eliminating French "intermediaries" had become one of the major aims of U.S. officials, who often found French procedures no less baffling than those of the Vietnamese.

The following table shows the amount of U.S. aid provided to the government of South Vietnam from mid-1952 to mid-1966. (The cost of direct U.S. intervention in Indochina is not included.)

U.S. Economic and Military Aid to South Vietnam,
Fiscal Years 1953 to 1966* (in millions of U.S. $)

Fiscal Year	U.S. Economic Aid	U.S. Military Aid	Total U.S. Economic and Military Aid
1953-57	$ 823.3	$ 277.8	$1,101.1
1958	188.7	53.2	241.9
1959	207.1	41.9	249.0
1960	180.3	70.9	251.2
1961	144.1	65.0	209.1
1962	142.9	144.0	286.9
1963	186.0	190.0	376.0
1964	216.1	186.9	403.0
1965	268.2	274.7	542.9
1966	729.2	170.8	900.0
Total, 1953-1966	$3,085.9	$1,475.2	$4,561.1

*Note: Military assistance under the Foreign Assistance Act was transferred to regular Department of Defense funding after 1966.

Source: U.S. Agency for International Development, *U.S. Overseas Loans and Grants and Assistance from International Organizations* (Special Report prepared for the House Foreign Affairs Committee), Washington, D.C.: Agency for International Development, March 29, 1968, p. 59.

Much of the aid classified as "economic" in Table 1 was "supporting assistance." Under this program, commodities were made available to the Saigon government for sale in South Vietnam to offset the inflationary effect of the government's heavy expenditures on its army and police. About four fifths of all U.S. aid to South Vietnam in the 1950s and early 1960s was directly or indirectly used to keep the Diem regime in power by supporting the "internal security" forces. Only a small percentage of U.S. aid was devoted to education, health, agricultural and industrial development, and related areas that would have improved the people's living conditions.

Diem's Struggle with the Sects

In early 1955, France touched off a new crisis by announcing that it would discontinue its subsidies to the Hoa Hao and Cao Dai sects. Their leaders then joined with the head of the Binh Xuyen in demanding that Diem form an anti-Communist government of national union. France and Britain supported this approach, but Diem refused, taking the position that he must either dominate the sects or be ruled by them. His brother, Ngo Dinh Nhu, organized a "revolutionary committee" of assorted politicians (including two former Viet Minh) to support Diem during the crisis.

In the midst of this turmoil, the chief of state, Bao Dai, ordered Diem to come to France for consultations. Premier Faure of France supported Bao Dai's order by announcing that Diem was no longer fit to lead Vietnam. But the American Embassy in Saigon stood firmly behind Diem. In so doing, it reflected the consensus of political leaders in Washington, both Democrat and Republican.

Diem was able to divide the leadership of the sects by giving large bribes to some and by promising others that he would integrate their private bands of soldiers into the national army. The United States gave Diem some $12 million which he dispensed to various opposition leaders during March and April 1955. In late April, the national army finally engaged the Binh Xuyen in a major battle and drove them out of Saigon. Just before this successful move, General Collins (who had returned to Washington) persuaded Secretary Dulles to instruct the embassy in Saigon to look for alternatives to Diem's leadership. As soon as news of Diem's victory over the Binh Xuyen reached Washington, Dulles cancelled these instructions. For the next eight years, the U.S.

government gave Diem its full support, although it also tried (with very mixed results) to influence the Saigon regime's programs and policies by manipulating its massive aid program.

The Geneva Accords and Elections

According to the Geneva agreements, North and South Vietnam were supposed to begin preparatory talks about unifying national elections in July 1955. Soon after the cease-fire went into effect (in July 1954), Hanoi began broadcasting instructions to its followers in South Vietnam to avoid violence and work toward the goal of gaining power through the electoral process. On June 6, 1955, Premier Pham Van Dong announced that the DRV was ready to hold preparatory talks with "competent representative authorities" from the South.

U.S. officials advised Diem to take the position that the election should be by secret ballot and carried out under strict international supervision. They hoped that North Vietnam would reject these conditions—or make it obvious that it was not complying with them—and that it would thus be possible to place the onus on Hanoi for not carrying out this crucial aspect of the Geneva accords. But Diem was not prepared to take this risk. On July 16, 1955, he told his people in a radio speech:

> We are not bound in any way by those agreements signed against the will of the Vietnamese people. . . . We shall not miss any opportunity which would permit the unification of our homeland in freedom, but it is out of the question for us to consider any proposal from the Viet Minh if proof is not given us that they put the superior interests of the national community above those of communism.

Six days later, France, Great Britain, and the United States decided during a summit conference at Geneva to recommend that South Vietnam reconsider its position and enter into talks with North Vietnam on the subject of unifying elections. France was still technically responsible for implementing the Geneva agreements; Britain and the United States were worried about the resumption of war in Indochina if Diem failed at least to go through the motions of implementing the 1954 accord.

However, it was not in Diem's nature to yield, whether to foreign advisors, to the DRV, or to his rivals in South Vietnam. He ignored all suggestions that he enter into talks with Hanoi and devoted himself to shoring up his own position in the South. On October 23, 1955, he held a referendum in which the South Vietnamese people were asked to choose between Bao Dai and himself. Although Diem might have won a fair election in the South at this stage (because of his unexpected success in consolidating his regime), he ignored the warnings of American officials and conducted a grossly unfair election in which he received a spectacular but unconvincing 98.2 percent of the vote.

Colonel Lansdale, who was in Washington at the time of the election, urged the Eisenhower administration to put more pressure on Diem to carry out democratic reforms, such as granting political freedom to opposition parties. Lansdale argued that only a popular and democratic government (such as Magsaysay's in the Philippines) could stop the growth of Communist support among the South Vietnamese people. But the consensus among leading U.S. officials at the time was that it was more important for the Saigon regime to be strong and anti-Communist than democratic.

In May 1956, the United States took an important step in defiance of the Geneva accords, although Washington still tried to give the appearance of upholding the agreement. After learning that the Indian member of the International Control Commission in Vietnam would not make an issue of the matter, the United States doubled the size of its military mission in Saigon—from 342 to 685 men—by sending in a "temporary" weapons recovery team; this became an integral part of the U.S. military advisory group.

Meanwhile, Hanoi continued to press for nationwide elections, confident that it would win if they were held and that Diem's government would be severely discredited if they were not. Saigon allowed the July 1956 deadline to pass without even responding to an invitation from Britain and Russia (the Geneva co-chairmen) to submit an estimate of the time required to organize elections. North Vietnamese leaders continued to seek diplomatic support for holding the elections, but they received little backing from any of the countries that took part in the 1954 Geneva conference.[4]

Because of this, and because Diem's position seemed to be growing stronger all the time, the U.S. government came out publicly in support of his stand on the elections; together, Saigon and Washington took the position that Hanoi must prove that it would take part in a nationwide election without intimidating the voters. Since neither North or South Vietnam had ever held a free election, this demand gave some of the Geneva powers a convenient excuse for inaction. By being unwilling to challenge the United States on this matter, these powers helped deprive Hanoi of what it had been promised at Geneva. Most of the Geneva powers gave the impression, at this time, of implicitly recognizing the division of Vietnam as one of the facts of international life.

In 1956, many people believed that Diem's American-backed regime had accomplished a minor miracle by providing South Vietnam with a reasonably stable anti-Communist government. This was the high water-mark of the United States' China containment policy—when the governments of South Vietnam, Laos, and Cambodia seemed to be progressing rapidly behind a SEATO "shield" which cost the United States only a small fraction of its peacetime defense budget. Vice-President Nixon visited South Vietnam and Taiwan in July 1956 and confidently assured both Diem and Chiang Kai-shek of the American government's steadfast support. President Eisenhower began the 1956 election campaign by telling newsmen that the Geneva settlement had given the free world a "firm foothold" in Indochina and placed the non-Communist countries there under "stronger leadership."

Notes

1. Madame Nhu was an outspoken member of the National Assembly, where her specialty was social action. Her crowning achievement, which undoubtedly helped hasten the end of the regime, was the Law for the Protection of Morality. This law tried to enforce a puritanical code of behavior on the South Vietnamese people and deny them most of the worldly pleasures to which they were accustomed. Among other things, it outlawed divorce, prostitution, dancing, fortune-telling, beauty contests, gambling, cockfighting, the use of contraceptives, and marital infidelity (which could be defined as merely being seen in public with a member of the opposite sex). In 1963, shortly before the overthrow of the regime, Madame Nhu succeeded in banning the singing of "sentimental songs."

2. Lansdale had made his reputation in the Philippines, where he supported Magsaysay, the man who demonstrated to his people that a dynamic, liberal administration could defeat the communist Huk movement.

3. For the text of President Eisenhower's October 1, 1954 letter to President

Diem, see George McT. Kahin and John W. Lewis, *The United States in Vietnam* (New York: Delta, 1967), pp. 382-83.

4. Communist China was in the midst of an intensive "peace offensive," which included overtures for improved relations with the United States. The Eisenhower administration made it clear that it had no intention of relaxing its tough policy toward China, including trade and travel controls, until Peking offered unmistakable signs that it would abide by accepted norms of international behavior.

CHAPTER FIVE

Origins of the
Second Indochina War

The determination of the Vietnamese Communists to reunify their country under Communist rule made war inevitable—once Diem, with American support, decided to block the national elections which were agreed upon at Geneva. Through the creation of SEATO and separate military aid agreements with countries close to North Vietnam, Secretary Dulles had fostered polarization rather than reconciliation in the region. He seemed to believe that the Diem regime was "democratic" and that its interests were the same as those of the United States simply because Diem was anti-Communist. He regarded North Vietnam as a puppet of the "Sino-Soviet bloc" and an enemy of the United States because its government was Communist.

American aid during the 1950s freed Diem from the

necessity of seeking the support of the South Vietnamese people. Although North Vietnam was much less well endowed with foreign aid and natural resources than the South, its leaders more than made up for this fact by the zeal and ruthlessness with which they pursued their chosen aims. The Hanoi regime had a detailed blueprint for the future, and the *Lao Dong* ("Workers") party of the North was a far more effective political instrument than Diem's family oligarchy.

Until his death in 1959, Secretary Dulles kept a tight rein on all U.S. agencies operating abroad which might influence U.S. policy through their activities. Without John Foster Dulles' control at the top, many U.S. agencies (including the CIA and various units of the Defense Department) began to play a semi-independent role in Indochina. This led to unprecedented confusion in U.S. policy and a constant series of "crises" which exhausted the leading U.S. officials in Washington. Unhappy with the existing situation, but unable to find a better approach, President Eisenhower chose to do nothing during his last year in office which would bind the hands of his successor. However, he also failed to crack down on freewheeling U.S. agencies in the field. Thus, by the end of 1960, it was almost impossible for Washington officials to raise their sights above day-to-day crisis management and view the Indochina problem in any sort of rational perspective.

North Vietnam's Agricultural Crisis

In September 1956, while President Eisenhower was voicing cautious optimism about the situation in South Vietnam, North Vietnam was in the throes of a major upheaval. To gain the support of the poor farmers, the DRV had issued decrees, during 1953, reducing rents and absolving debts. The rural population was then classified into five categories: landless agricultural laborers, poor peasants, middle peasants, rich peasants, and landlords. During the year 1954-56, each of North Vietnam's 15,000 villages was assigned a quota of "feudalists" among their local residents to be singled out and punished, often by death.[1] This campaign, instead of aligning the mass of Tonkinese peasants with the regime, succeeded in provoking bitterness against the DRV's excesses on the part of those who survived the purge. Thousands of members of the ruling Communist party were also jailed for criticizing the agricultural program.

The reign of terror was finally halted by Ho Chi Minh's personal intervention in the fall of 1956. For a few months, intellectuals were permitted to criticize the government, but the fervor with which people took part in this "mistakes rectification campaign"—and in the peasant rebellions which followed—caused the regime to reestablish strict controls over all forms of political expression.

The economic effects of this upheaval were far-reaching; food shortages became even more acute and the government had to rely on imports financed by other Communist states to avoid famine. By the end of the 1950s, the first painful steps toward collectivization and a Socialist society had been taken, and the North had begun to progress beyond 1939 levels. But the lack of economic incentives in the socialized system of agriculture, coupled with treacherous weather conditions, still hampered North Vietnam's progress. The DRV's need for economic reunification raises the tantalizing question of whether Hanoi would have been satisfied if Saigon had agreed to economic ties. Diem refused to consider such ties, and this was undoubtedly one of the main reasons for Hanoi's gradually increasing pressure against his regime during the late 1950s and early 1960s.

Slow Pace of Land Reform in the South

In South Vietnam, as in the North, the problem of reorganizing and reforming the rural sector of the economy offered a major test of the government's ability to lead. Land was more unequally distributed in the South than in the North, but the South had a much more favorable ratio of people to arable land. An effective agricultural program might have made South Vietnam less dependent on foreign aid; it might also have provided Diem with the solid political base he lacked. Thus, American officials repeatedly tried to persuade Diem to move ahead boldly in this crucial area.

The problem was Diem's unwillingness to change the country's class structure. His approach to the subject of land reform was at the opposite extreme from that of the North Vietnamese leaders. While they used the most ruthless means to get rid of the few remaining landlords and many prosperous peasants in the North, Diem shrank from taking steps that would reduce the incomes of South Vietnam's major landowners. His government moved so slowly and reluctantly in redistribut-

ing land that it even alienated many of the tenant farmers who were
turned into small-holders by the program. Above all, it did nothing for
Diem's political stature among the South Vietnamese people to have it
become widely known that even the limited reforms he achieved were
the result of American prodding.

The Ngo Family and Democracy

Not only did Diem fail to develop support among the poorer people by
means of his land-reform program, his authoritarian style of leadership
also antagonized most of the country's educated, non-Communist
nationalists. Vietnam has no tradition of loyal, purposeful opposition
forming part of the political system. Before the French arrived, all
major decisions were made bureaucratically by the mandarins and approved by the Emperor. Under French rule, political parties appeared;
but they were almost invariably illegal resistance movements (sometimes linked to foreign governments, as in the case of the Communist
and Chinese Nationalist backed parties). During World War II, the
Japanese and pro-Axis French taught the Vietnamese that political
parties could be used for totalitarian control—a point which impressed
Diem's brother, Ngo Dinh Nhu, among others.

After the first Indochina war, some of the non-Communist parties
began to surface and play a slightly more open role in the political life
of the country. Nhu chose this moment to organize his "personalist
Revolutionary Labor Party" (*Can Lao*), a semisecret network of leading
officials whose main task was to report to Nhu on any signs of disloyalty within the bureaucracy. The nature of the Can Lao's activities
persuaded the other non-Communist parties that Diem and Nhu were
not interested in promoting representative government.[2]

War Returns to South Vietnam

In 1956, after defying the Geneva agreement on national elections,
Diem launched an extensive manhunt against the Viet Minh leaders who
had remained behind when the 1954 truce was signed. In the course of
this roundup, a great many innocent people were killed or imprisoned,
while others had their homes destroyed by vicious army "sweep" operations. Officially, between 20,000 and 30,000 "Communists" were

placed in concentration camps, although foreign observers who visited the camps reported that most of those who were confined were not Communists.[3] Over the next few years, Diem's paranoia led to whole-sale arrests of people vaguely suspected of disloyalty to the regime.

Beginning in 1957, the Viet Minh responded with a campaign of terrorism, often involving the murder of policemen, school teachers, and other village-level officials appointed by the central government. The Viet Minh campaign, which was designed to make the people afraid to support the central authorities, quickly grew into a nationwide up-rising that was supported by a large portion of the rural population, either voluntarily or involuntarily. Some became part-time guerrillas, some were unpaid intelligence agents, and others supplied food or shelter to the insurgents. Following tactics which they had used success-fully against the French during the first Indochina war, the Communists formed a new coalition of anti-Diem elements that was soon administer-ing those areas of South Vietnam which they had wrested from Saigon's control.

In spite of temporary disagreements over tactical matters, there is no reason to doubt that Vietnamese Communist leaders in the North and South shared the goal of reunifying Vietnam under a Communist gov-ernment. Neither the northern or southern Communist leaders ever ruled out the use of violence to defeat the Saigon regime and "liberate" the South. However, Hanoi was preoccupied with major political prob-lems in the North during the latter half of the 1950s and tended to regard the use of force to overthrow Diem's regime as premature.[4] North Vietnamese leaders were also extremely sensitive to the growing Sino-Soviet dispute, which had begun to polarize the world Communist movement.[5] Hanoi had everything to lose and nothing to gain by of-fending either of the Communist giants—as was likely if it were forced to adopt a position toward an overt southern rebellion.

In 1958, Le Duan (one of the most prominent southerners in the Hanoi regime) visited the South and made a detailed study of the situation. A year later, in July 1959, Ho Chi Minh published an article in a Belgian Communist journal which stated cautiously that his govern-ment still had to "direct and bring to a close the middle-class demo-cratic and anti-imperialistic revolution" in the South.[6] Six months later, General Vo Nguyen Giap issued a more militant pronouncement. He said that the North had become a "large rear echelon of our army . . . the revolutionary base of the whole country." But Giap's strong words were not yet matched by deeds. They may have been aimed at impressing the Chinese or those southerners who felt Hanoi had abandoned them.

Later in 1960, Le Duan directed Hanoi's campaign to place the southern insurgency under a unified military command. He also carried directives to the southern leaders for a political program broad enough to gain the support of all anti-Diem elements; at the third congress of the Lao Dong party in September 1960, Hanoi finally endorsed the goal of overthrowing Diem and "liberating" the South by force. Three months later, at a meeting of a dozen parties and religious groups "somewhere in the South," the southern insurgent movement was formally launched as the "National Front for the Liberation of the South."[7]

The NLF was the old Viet Minh Front reincarnated. In both organizations, the Communists emphasized the fact that they were a minority, although in both cases they were the guiding force. To avoid frightening the non-communist members of the NLF, the southern Communists did not demand immediate reunification of the country, but there is no reason to suppose that they ever abandoned this aim.

It is hardly surprising that there is almost nothing in common between the way Hanoi and its allies on the one hand and Saigon and its supporters on the other have described the outbreak of the second Indochina war. Communist writers claim the 1957-60 uprising in South Vietnam was a spontaneous movement of the people which Communists joined but did not control. Although the movement did achieve broad popular support, there is little doubt that it was organized by the Communists exactly as they organized the effort to expel the French. Although Hanoi did not immediately support the southern insurrection, it would not hold back indefinitely because its own vital interests were at stake.

The United States and South Vietnamese governments have claimed that the second Indochina war began because of North Vietnamese aggression. They have generally ignored the repressive character of Diem's regime that drove many southerners into militant opposition. The theory of northern aggression propounded by the U.S. and South Vietnamese governments also disregarded those governments' own statistics; these showed that infiltration of men and weapons into the

South was insignificant prior to 1960 (when Hanoi finally endorsed the "liberation" strategy) and that it was on a small scale until 1964.[8] Until that time, virtually all of the antigovernment guerrilla forces (though not all of their leaders) were recruited in the South, and they were armed mainly with American weapons captured from Diem's army.

In an effort to discredit the uprising, both at home and abroad, the Saigon regime dubbed the insurgents *Viet Cong* (meaning "Vietnamese Communists") and asserted that all antigovernment forces were Communists, which was far from true. However, the term Viet Cong later came into general usage to describe insurgents recruited in the South; its use ceased to imply agreement with the proposition that all anti-Saigon forces are Communist.

Gathering Storm Over Laos

As the struggle for control of South Vietnam became more intense, both sides viewed the kingdom of Laos as an important testing ground for their programs and policies. After full-scale war broke out in Vietnam, it became essential to Hanoi's logistical operations that eastern Laos be under Communist control. For the United States, control of the western half of Laos was vital to the defense of Thailand, the strongest U.S. ally on the Southeast Asian mainland.

Of the four Indochinese states that emerged in 1954, Laos faced the greatest problems in trying to become a nation. Ethnically, just under half of its 3 million people are Lao, while the rest belong to various hill tribes, who are closely related to the people in the adjoining areas of northern Thailand. The national borders of the region have little meaning for them. The kingdom of Laos is much too poor to support an army or police force capable of defending its thousands of miles of frontiers. The ease with which China, Vietnam, and Thailand can invade this fragile kingdom seems to consign it to the role of a perpetual buffer zone between its neighbors.

The problems of Laos were compounded by the rivalry of two royal brothers, Prince Souvanna Phouma and Prince Souphanouvong. When the Geneva accords were signed in 1954, Souvanna Phouma was Premier of the royal government, which had sought independence from France through negotiation. Souvanna's half brother, Souphanouvong, was prominent in the *Pathet Lao*, a liberation movement which had close ties with the Viet Minh. Souphanouvong's wife was Vietnamese and a member of the Lao Dong party. Souvanna Phouma claimed to speak for the moderate members of the Lao elite; Souphanouvong said he represented the radical nationalists. No one could say just how much authority either of them actually wielded over their respective factions—or how much support either of them had among the population generally.

The 1954 Geneva accords had called for the withdrawal of Viet Minh forces from Laos and the integration of the Pathet Lao troops into the Royal Lao Army. Souvanna Phouma declared that his regime would seek to "integrate all citizens, without discrimination, into the national community." Under the Geneva agreements, the Lao government renounced military alliances and foreign military aid except for defensive purposes, but France was permitted to retain two military bases in Laos. The United States was allowed to provide economic aid and military equipment, but not military advisors or instructors.

Secretary of State Dulles favored the creation of a 25,000 man Royal Lao Army as one of the "trip-wire" forces with which he sought to surround China and Russia. (If the Communist powers attacked, these local forces were supposed to be able to put up enough resistance to justify U.S. intervention.) Dulles also intended the Royal Lao Army to be a unifying institution around which the new Laotian nation could be formed. This scheme was opposed by Pentagon officials, who were against the idea of arming forces which could not also be trained by U.S. military personnel, but Dulles' view prevailed. The Royal Lao Army was brought into existence at a cost to U.S. taxpayers of over $90 million during the second half of the 1950s. Under the Kennedy administration, military aid to Laos rose well above this level.

Neither its French training nor its American equipment prepared the Royal Lao Army to combat Communist guerrilla-warfare tactics. The corruption of its officers (who pocketed U.S. aid funds and used the army as a power base from which to topple civilian governments), coupled with the arrogant behavior of its troops, failed to inspire the population. Moderate members of the Lao elite were antagonized by the support which Lao generals received from U.S. Defense Department and CIA officials.

Throughout the 1950s, Souvanna Phouma's constant aim was to put together a government of national union which would include all major factions within the country. Fearing that this would lead to a Communist take-over, the U.S. government tried to dissuade Souvanna from forming a coalition government. In May 1968, left-wing Lao politicians scored major gains in supplementary elections for the National Assembly—in spite of a crash aid program designed by the U.S. Mission to win support for anti-communist candidates. After the election, Souvanna resigned and claimed that U.S. pressure made it impossible for him to form a new government. For the next two years, Laos was run by a moderately right-wing government; its American-supported army clashed periodically with the North Vietnamese-backed Pathet Lao.

In August 1960, a coup led by Captain Kong Le restored Souvanna Phouma to power. The ousted government was accused of allowing American domination of Laos and waging a fractricidal war. General Phoumi Nosavan, the head of an American-backed, right-wing faction, served briefly in Souvanna's government and then withdrew to form a "revolutionary committee" in southern Laos.

American policy toward Laos became thoroughly muddled in the latter half of 1960; the U.S. Ambassador's authority was openly flouted by CIA and Pentagon officials because of the lack of firm leadership in Washington. Although the United States recognized Souvanna Phouma's government in Vientiane and continued to provide it with economic aid, American officials also announced that they would give military aid directly to Lao military units wherever they were located. Thus, the United States provided arms and money both to government troops and to the right-wing forces which were in open rebellion against them. Thailand, which supported General Phoumi Nosavan, added to the pressure on Souvanna's regime by refusing to allow any goods to be shipped from Bangkok to Vientiane, thus depriving the Lao administrative capital of its main surface supply route.

In September 1960, Souvanna announced that he would establish diplomatic relations with Moscow. He also reopened negotiations aimed at bringing the Pathot Lao into his government. The United States promptly suspended economic aid to Souvanna Phouma's regime while continuing to send military aid to the right-wing troops led by Phoumi Nosavan. Assistant Secretary of State Graham Parsons (former Ambassador to Laos) was dispatched to Vientiane to warn Souvanna that economic aid would be withheld permanently unless he allied himself with the right-wing forces and moved his capital to Luang Prabang (away from Kong Le's influence). Souvanna denounced these demands, which were hardly strengthened by the current state of U.S. policy. He told Parsons that he would get aid elsewhere if he had to. U.S. economic aid was resumed shortly thereafter.

During November, agreement was reached between Souvanna and the Pathet Lao on the formation of a neutral coalition government which would receive aid from the Soviet Union. The United States continued to support the build-up of Phoumi Nosavan's troops until the end of the month, when Phoumi began to march toward Vientiane. With Thailand continuing to blockade Vientiane's normal supply routes, Souvanna requested Soviet aid, and a Soviet airlift of food and fuel from Hanoi began in early December.

On December 9, 1960 just before the right-wing troops attacked Vientiane, Souvanna Phouma fled to Phnom Penh. His capital fell one week later, and Kong Le's neutralist troops retreated to the Plain of Jars, where they linked up with the Pathet Lao.

In Washington, meanwhile, the Eisenhower administration was preparing to hand over the burdens of office to the newly elected President and his advisors. Although more than a generation separated Dwight Eisenhower and John F. Kennedy, and their backgrounds were almost as different as those of two American leaders could be, they both subscribed to the domino theory and viewed the Laos crisis as a major challenge to U.S. policy. Both felt that people and governments all over the world would judge the United States by its ability to prevent a remote mountain kingdom on China's southern border from being overrun by Communists.

Notes

1. It is generally believed that the number of people killed after these trials was at least 10,000. Between 50,000 and 100,000 were sent to prison or labor camps or starved to death because people were afraid to help them. See Joseph Buttinger, *Vietnam: A Political History* (New York: Praeger, 1968), pp. 426-28.

2. In April 1960, a group of non-Communist politicians issued a series of demands for reform, which became known as the "Caravelle manifesto" after the name of the Saigon hotel where they met. This document offers one of the few indications of what South Vietnam's political elite really thought about Diem. The manifesto, which was signed by eighteen of South Vietnam's most distin-

guished political personalities, called for a liberalization of Diem's government and an end to the domination of the civil and military services by Diem's family. Most members of the Caravelle group were imprisoned until after Diem's assassination in 1963.

3. See P. J. Honey, "The Problem of Democracy in Vietnam," *The World Today*, February 16, 1960, p. 73.

4. For evidence of differences between Hanoi and the southern insurgents between 1957 and 1960, see Kahin and Lewis, *The United States in Vietnam*, pp. 110-114.

5. Khrushchev's regime ordered its followers to adopt a policy of peaceful coexistence toward the West, while Peking called for militant struggle against imperialism. In the hope of preserving the monolithic strength of the world Communist movement (on which North Vietnam's future seemed to depend), Ho Chi Minh even tried to mediate the quarrel between Khrushchev and Mao.

6. The emphasis on passing through a democratic revolution before a Socialist one reflected Moscow's approach rather than militant Maoism.

7. It was usually referred to as the National Liberation Front or NLF. On the same principle—that they could achieve their goal of a unified, Communist Vietnam only by concealing the degree of unity between northern and southern Communists—the latter established a new party, the People's Revolutionary Party, in January 1962. The PRP was supposed to appear independent of the Lao Dong Party in the North, although it is universally regarded as the southern branch of the Lao Dong.

8. According to testimony of U.S. Defense Department officials before Congress, the number of men infiltrated from North Vietnam in 1961 was 6200; in 1962 it was 12,800; in 1963 it was 7900; in 1964 it was 12,400; while in 1965 it rose to 46,000. For commentary, See Bernard B. Fall, *Viet-Nam Witness*, 1953-66 (New York: Praeger, 1966), pp. 307-312.

CHAPTER SIX

The Neutralization of Laos

The internal Laotian crisis of the early 1960s was of world importance because the United States and the Soviet Union chose to become involved. It was part of the highly dangerous world setting in which President Kennedy and Chairman Khrushchev began to take each other's measure. Peking claimed to see in this process a budding conspiracy between the two superpowers against China and the Third World. And indeed, the Laotian settlement, that resulted mainly from Averell Harriman's tough but patient diplomacy, reduced Soviet-American tensions while deepening the Sino-Soviet split.

Kennedy's Perception of the Problem

The year 1961 began with the Lao neutralist and left-wing forces allied and in control of the eastern half of the country. A right-wing prince, Boun Oum, was named Premier with General Phoumi Nosavan as his deputy. Phoumi's forces held the administrative capital, Vientiane, which they had seized in December 1960. Souvanna Phouma, the leading neutralist politician, was in exile in Cambodia.

By the time President Kennedy was inaugurated, Phoumi had begun a very cautious advance north from Vientiane. A month later, his troops reached an important junction where roads fork off to the west toward the royal capital of Luang Prabang and to the east toward the Plain of Jars. In early March, the neutralist and Pathet Lao forces attacked, and Phoumi's troops broke and ran. Within a few days, nothing was left to prevent the combined Pathet Lao and neutralist forces from seizing Luang Prabang or Vientiane. If they did so, they would threaten Thailand, an American ally, whose stability and economic development benefited the whole region.

Like his predecessor, President Kennedy believed in the domino theory. He felt that the world situation required the United States to protect non-Communist countries and prevent them from being overrun by the Communist powers. If even so remote and indefensible a country as Laos were overrun, President Kennedy and his advisors feared that American military prestige would suffer a major blow. Many countries that had looked to the United States for protection might decide that nonalignment or membership in the Communist block was safer.

In terms of domestic American politics, both Eisenhower and Kennedy feared the loss of any "free world" territory to Communist control might lead to a revival of McCarthyism in the United States. This could paralyze the government, as happened in the early 1950s, and prevent the passage of important liberal legislation. It could even set the country on a collision course with Russia. In the early 1960s, President Kennedy and moderate leaders of both major parties still felt the need to endorse the China containment policy to gain the cooperation of conservative congressmen on other foreign and domestic issues.

Laos was always one of the more surrealistic elements of the China containment policy. The Royal Lao Army, created at huge expense to U.S. taxpayers, had a disconcerting tendency to melt away when they came in contact with the Hanoi-supported Pathet Lao. (A Royal Lao Army colonel once explained to the author that when his soldiers fired at the enemy their bullets turned into flowers.) Moreover, serious-minded American diplomats found it almost impossible to persuade Lao politicians to act along ideological lines. Foreign Communist advisors probably had the same problem with the Pathet Lao.

As one of the first major decisions of his administration, President Kennedy decided to gamble on the possibility that a de facto partition of Laos was more acceptable to all parties concerned than a major war. Thus, the U.S. government's minimum aim in Laos was defined as preventing Communist and pro-Communist forces from overrunning the heavily populated lowlands of western Laos. The administration believed that this would prevent the Laotian war from spreading into Thailand. If this could be achieved, the "dominoes" of Southeast Asia would not fall. An answer would have been found to the subversive "war of liberation" tactics which were being tested in Laos and South Vietnam—and which seemed potentially capable of engulfing the entire Third World. Moreover, when Soviet leaders realized that the U.S. government could be both firm and reasonable, they might agree to take further steps to reduce cold war tensions.

On March 23, 1961, President Kennedy told a televised news conference that the United States was prepared to take part in a Geneva conference aimed at guaranteeing the neutrality of Laos. What the United States wanted in Laos, he said, was "peace, not war; a truly neutral government, not a cold war pawn; a settlement concluded at the conference table and not on the battlefield." But the President also pointed out that local Communist forces in Laos had received "increasing direction and support from outside" the country, and this seemed to be aimed at destroying Laotian neutrality. He warned that the United States was prepared to take stronger action if the Communist side tried to seize the western half of Laos.

To underline the seriousness of his warning, President Kennedy felt it necessary to demonstrate that the United States was prepared to intervene in Laos. U.S. forces in Japan and Okinawa were put on alert, and the Seventh Fleet was sent into the Gulf of Thailand. About 500 U.S. troops were flown to northeast Thailand to set up a helicopter repair base, and supplies for U.S. ground forces were also stockpiled in northeast Thailand.

It was assumed that all of these moves would soon become known to the Pathet Lao through their North Vietnamese, Chinese, and Russian contacts, and it was hoped that further American intervention would be unnecessary. The President's basic policy statement on March 23 was intended to make all parties understand that the American aim was limited to preserving an independent and neutral Laos—that it did not include seizing Laotian territory, expelling the Pathet Lao forces, or launching an attack on China or North Vietnam.

Both Sides Prepare for the Peace Conference

After making clear his position that a truce in Laos was a necessary condition for U.S. participation in a Geneva conference, President Kennedy did everything in his power to bring about a cease-fire. First, he met with the British Prime Minister, Harold Macmillan, who reaffirmed his country's support for a Geneva conference and cease-fire. (Macmillan privately urged the President not to consider U.S. intervention in Laos unless it should prove absolutely necessary.) At a SEATO conference in Bangkok, Secretary Rusk tried to rally support for the idea of neutralizing Laos. But the Thai government was bitterly opposed to any withdrawal of U.S. military support from their Lao neighbors.

President Kennedy next met with Soviet Foreign Minister Gromyko and warned him of the danger of misjudging America's aims in Laos. In early April, Moscow took an important step toward meeting the U.S. position that a cease-fire must be in effect before the start of negotiations. The Soviets indicated that they would agree to holding the Geneva conference after a truce went into effect—provided the United States would agree in principle to attend the conference before the cease-fire began.

However, Russia's ability to restrain the North Vietnamese and Pathet Lao seemed questionable, because these forces continued to advance slowly into western Laos, creating deep concern in Thailand. The State Department proposed sending American combat troops to Thailand. It was argued that this would demonstrate American determination to repel the Communists and help reassure the government and people in Thailand that the United States was not on the verge of cutting its losses in Laos.

This idea of *limited* intervention in Indochina was opposed by Pentagon officials, who remembered the frustrations of fighting a war in Korea under political constraints, such as the prohibition against bombing Chinese bases. The Joint Chiefs of Staff wanted an advance commitment from the President that technical military considerations would play the decisive role in the conduct of any war in Indochina before they would agree to any form of U.S. intervention. Some of the Joint Chiefs wanted the President to approve, in advance of any U.S. intervention, the use of nuclear weapons, if this should prove necessary in the Joint Chiefs' judgment. Such a condition would have usurped the President's prerogatives and was completely unacceptable to Kennedy.[1]

In April 1961, an event occurred which had the effect of reducing the influence of senior Pentagon and CIA officials who had been retained from the previous administration. This was the invasion of Cuba at the Bay of Pigs. On April 17, a force of about 1200 CIA-trained Cuban refugees began their amphibious attack on the island. Encountering much heavier resistance from the Cuban militia than Washington had foreseen, the refugees were overwhelmed within two days. When he realized how ill-conceived the operation had been and how much it had hurt his own reputation and that of the United States, President Kennedy was deeply disturbed. It was only proper that he should assume full responsibility for the invasion which he had approved. But the experience made him less willing to take the advice of either the CIA or the Pentagon, which had planned and recommended the invasion.

Since he had not been willing to commit American forces to the Cuban invasion, the President felt it would be wrong to send combat troops to Thailand or Laos. It seemed necessary, however, to show the world that the U.S. government had not lost its resolve in the face of universal condemnation of the Bay of Pigs fiasco. So President Kennedy ordered a group of U.S. Army advisors, who had been in Laos since the start of the year, to wear uniforms rather than less conspicuous civilian dress.

The Geneva Conference on Laos, 1961-62

Great Britain and the Soviet Union, which had been co-chairmen of the first Geneva conference in 1954, announced on April 24, 1961 that a cease-fire had been arranged for May 3. After some delays and tense moments, the International Control Commission declared that the truce was in effect, and the conference opened on May 12.

Fourteen countries had agreed to attend. These included the nine which had taken part in the 1954 conference: Cambodia, China, the Democratic Republic of (North) Vietnam, France, Great Britain, Laos, the Republic of (South) Vietnam, the Soviet Union, the United States, as well as the three members of the International Control Commission— India, Canada, and Poland. Also taking part were the two other neighbors of Laos, Thailand, and Burma. After a heated dispute between the Soviet and American delegations over whether the Pathet Lao delegates should be seated as well as the neutralist and right-wing Lao groups, an agreement was reached to seat all three Lao groups as "spokesmen" for forces operating in Laos.

Averell Harriman, the permanent American representative, dominated the conference on Laos, much as Anthony Eden had dominated the 1954 Geneva conference. Harriman's long experience at the top levels of diplomacy and government gave him great prestige, even though he held the rather nebulous rank of Ambassador-at-large at the start of the conference.[2] Deputy Foreign Minister, Georgi M. Pushkin, took charge of the Soviet delegation. Most governments sent their foreign ministers or other high officials to the opening sessions.

When President Kennedy and Chairman Khrushchev met for the first time in Vienna in June, they disagreed ominously on almost every subject they covered. The important exception was Laos. Both leaders endorsed the concept of a neutral and independent Laos and recognized the importance of making the cease-fire effective. Harriman drummed the latter point home by presenting his fellow delegates at Geneva with a list of thirty Pathet Lao violations of the truce. He announced that the United States would withdraw from the conference unless the truce were honored.

During most of the rest of the summer of 1961, the major power delegates marked time in Geneva, while the leaders of the three Lao factions met elsewhere to debate the internal politics of their country. On June 22, 1961, the three princes (Souvanna Phouma, Boun Oum, and Souphanouvong) approved in principle the idea of a national union government in which all three factions would be represented. But they failed to agree on the most difficult question—the composition of the government.

In September 1961, a meeting of the three princes was held in Rangoon at Harriman's invitation. Souvanna Phouma was persuaded by Harriman to try to put together a government of sixteen ministers;

eight neutralists, four members of the right-wing faction and four members of the left wing. It seemed essential, for the coalition to have any chance of succeeding, to assign the Defense and Interior ministries to neutralists. But General Phoumi Nosavan balked at relinquishing these posts (which he held in the interim government).

Phoumi's efforts to block the formation of a coalition government were all the more frustrating because the work of the others attending the conference had been largely completed by December 1961. Agreement was reached not to use Laotian territory for intervention in other countries. Foreign troops and paramilitary personnel were to be withdrawn from Laos within seventy-five days of the signing of new accords. On the other hand, China still opposed disbanding the Pathet Lao and integrating its troops into the Royal Lao Army. Also, the International Control Commission was unlikely to work very effectively under the terms of the December 1961 agreement, which gave each of its members a veto over the ICC's investigatory activities.

At this point, Harriman decided that the time had come to deal firmly with the obstructive General Phoumi and his American supporters. He recommended to President Kennedy that cash payments to Phoumi for the support of his army be stopped, and that every American official in Laos who was a personal friend of Phoumi be reassigned. This produced an outcry from the CIA and the Defense Department, but the President supported the recommendation. The United States did however continue to provide Phoumi's forces with arms and equipment.

Battle of Nam Tha Brings U.S. Warning Signals

The event which finally broke Phoumi Nosavan's resistance to forming a coalition government was the battle of Nam Tha, in northeast Laos. The town was besieged by Pathet Lao and North Vietnamese forces from January to May 1962. Disregarding the obvious parallel with the battle of Dien Bien Phu, Phoumi sent in reinforcements by air, bringing the garrison's strength to 5000 men. In the climactic battle, Pathet Lao and North Vietnamese troops took the town on May 6, almost exactly eight years after the fall of Dien Bien Phu. The twelve American advisors present were evacuated by helicopter, and the Royal Lao Army survivors fled in disorganized panic.

As in 1961, President Kennedy's advisors disagreed on what the United States should do. Harriman and other State Department and White House staff members wanted to move U.S. troops into Thailand and send the Seventh Fleet to the Gulf of Thailand as a political "signal" to warn the Communists. Pentagon officials opposed the idea of a limited intervention designed to achieve mainly political aims. Their position was the same as it had been a year earlier. They wanted no U.S. intervention at all or intervention without any political constraints. However, they agreed to send the Seventh Fleet to the Gulf of Thailand and also proposed a crash effort to rebuild Phoumi's demoralized forces.

President Kennedy was in favor of sending troops to Thailand. But he deferred making a final decision until Secretary McNamara and General Lemnitzer (Chairman of the Joint Chiefs of Staff) returned from a visit to Bangkok. Meanwhile, the President tried to muster more support before overriding the advice of the Pentagon. He sent two representatives to Gettysburg to ask General Eisenhower for his views. Eisenhower said that he favored a very strong U.S. response, even going as far as sending U.S. troops into Laos. When McNamara and Lemnitzer returned from Thailand, they agreed with the idea of limited intervention. At a meeting of the National Security Council on May 12, the decision was made to send U.S. forces into Thailand. However, the President only made public his decision to move the fleet to the Gulf of Thailand. On the same day, the last Lao government stronghold in northwestern Laos fell to Pathet Lao and North Vietnamese forces.

On May 15, President Kennedy announced that 1000 U.S. troops, who had been retained in Thailand after a recent SEATO exercise, would be augmented immediately by 4000 more. He said the move was "considered desirable because of recent attacks in Laos by Communist forces, and the subsequent movement of Communist military units toward the border of Thailand." The emphasis in his statement was on defending Thailand; the President called the move "a defensive act." Two days later a task force of 1800 U.S. Marines arrived in Thailand.

Meanwhile, no further breaches of the cease-fire in Laos were reported, and the left-wing Lao faction agreed to resume negotiations for a coalition government. On May 18, Chairman Khrushchev called the American move imprudent and predicted that Laos and South Vietnam would go Communist even if Americans fought there for fifteen years. Radio Peking said that China "can absolutely not permit the establishment of a new military bridgehead aimed against her in an area near the Chinese border.

Coalition Government Formed

On May 25, 1961, Souvanna Phouma agreed to return to Laos for negotiations; he also set a three-week deadline for success or failure in forming a coalition government. On the same day, Khrushchev said that the Soviet Union continued to support the aim of a neutral Laos, even though the American moves in Thailand had "hindered" a settlement. On June 11, four days before his self-imposed deadline, Souvanna Phouma announced his formation of a government of national union. The neutralists received eleven cabinet portfolios and four each were assigned to the right-wing and Pathet Lao factions.

Premier Khrushchev and President Kennedy promptly exchanged messages which called the development "good news" and "encouraging" and said that it offered hope that other international problems could be solved. Although the Chinese did not refuse to sign the new Geneva accords, their attacks on Khrushchev's "revisionism" became more and more bitter. (The Cuban missile crisis, just three months later, strengthened Khrushchev's critics in China and the Soviet Union.)

Souvanna Phouma's government was formally installed on June 24. A month later, the Geneva conference approved the Lao declaration of neutrality. Laos agreed to join no military alliance that might violate this neutrality. It disassociated itself from SEATO's protection, and undertook to allow no foreign military bases on its territory and to refrain from using its forces in ways that might hinder world peace. The other Geneva powers signed a separate declaration guaranteeing the neutrality of Laos; a limit of seventy-five days was set for the withdrawal of all foreign troops from Laos.

U.S. Policy Toward Laos After the 1962 Agreement

On October 5, 1962, one day before the deadline, all U.S. military advisers were out of Laos, in spite of strong indications that North Vietnam planned to leave several thousand troops there indefinitely. On October 9, it was announced that the U.S. forces which had been sent to Thailand during the previous spring would be withdrawn as well.

Many leading Pentagon officials had argued in favor of leaving

American military advisers in Laos until the North Vietnamese withdrew their forces. Harriman had no illusions about North Vietnamese intentions in Laos, but he felt that the United States must let the Communist side incur the blame for breaking the Geneva agreements, and this view became the administration's policy. He also insisted on giving the strongest possible backing to Souvanna Phouma, the neutralist Premier. If the coalition split apart, Harriman argued, the U.S. must be certain that the break came between the neutralists and the Pathet Lao—so that these two factions would not team up together again.

By the summer of 1963, Souvanna Phouma had aligned his neutralist group closely with the right wing. The left-wing faction held the eastern half of the kingdom, including the main infiltration routes to South Vietnam. But they appeared to be too isolated, politically and militarily, to pose an immediate threat to the areas lying next to Thailand.

In the years that followed, the United States continued to supply military aid to forces loyal to Souvanna Phouma's government, in accordance with his wishes. But the United States government tried to keep its military activities in Laos as secret as possible, even after many of the details of these activities had been described in the world press. The reason offered by each succeeding administration was that the United States did not want to give Hanoi or Peking an open invitation to violate the Geneva agreements. It was also hoped that Moscow would exercise a restraining influence on Hanoi. The United States had therefore to adopt a "low posture," which in practice meant not admitting publicly its own violations of the 1962 agreements. Another (unstated) reason for Washington's secrecy about U.S. activities in Laos was that Congress and the American public might not approve of the whole range of these activities if they knew about them. This was probably the Johnson administration's main concern from 1966 on, when a vocal opposition to the Indochina war developed in the United States.

During the rest of President Kennedy's administration, however, the Geneva accords on Laos were attacked more by hawks than by doves. The administration was accused, by foreign as well as domestic critics, of "selling out" Laos. Yet given the inherent factionalism of Laos and the lack of any direct U.S. security interest, it is hard to see what more the United States could or should have done. Laos was, in effect, divided in half with left-wing forces controlling the east and neutralist right-wing forces holding the much more heavily populated west. The danger of the Laotian war spreading into Thailand was temporarily averted, as was the much more serious risk of major power involvement leading to general war.

Although the charge of having sold out Laos was unfair, it had far-reaching consequences for U.S. policy during the remaining year and a half of the Kennedy administration. President Kennedy and his closest advisors became concerned that the Laotian accords might be used to undermine the President's weak position at home or cause foreign powers to suspect his administration of softness. This explains why they adopted an unusually tough position during the Cuban missile crisis (September 1962). Moreover, it explains why they decided to reinforce a losing hand in Saigon—even though it was obvious by late 1962 that massive U.S. military and economic aid would not suffice to save Diem. Thus, ironically, the end result of Harriman's statesmanlike effort to avoid a major war by reconciling the main political forces in the area was to draw the United States deeper into the Vietnam war.

Notes

1. See Roger Hilsman, *To Move a Nation* (New York: Dell, 1967), pp. 133-134.

2. Harriman had been Ambassador to Great Britain and the Soviet Union, Secretary of Commerce, and governor of New York. President Kennedy promoted him to the rank of Assistant Secretary of State for Far Eastern Affairs in November 1961 and Undersecretary for Political Affairs in April 1963.

CHAPTER SEVEN

Kennedy Backs
a Losing Horse

Roger Hilsman, a former member of the Kennedy administration, has argued that the President could not refuse to give South Vietnam more of the same kind of aid it had received in the past "so long as the recipients could use it effectively." To cut off aid might have meant "disrupting the whole balance of power and fabric of the security structure of the region, where so many countries had based their policy on continued American involvement."[1]

President Kennedy himself complained to close associates that the United States was "overcommitted" in South Vietnam; yet he was undoubtedly aware that his predecessor had promised to support Ngo Dinh Diem only if he lived up to certain standards in his conduct of South Vietnam's affairs. By the time President Kennedy was inaugurated, the American Embassy in Saigon and the main intelligence agencies in Washington were convinced that Diem's increasingly autocratic regime was headed for disaster.[2]

Yet instead of reexamining U.S. aims in South Vietnam, the Kennedy administration concentrated on learning the art of walking a political tightrope between direct involvement in the war and disengagement. For two years prior to the 1963 Buddhist crisis, the administration not only continued but steadily enlarged the U.S. commitment to Diem personally and to South Vietnam as a nation. In the fiscal year beginning July 1961, U.S. aid rose to $287 million, compared with $209 million the year before. In fiscal 1963, $376 million was provided. That the Kennedy administration backed Diem reluctantly is indicated by the speed with which it cut its ties with him once the Buddhist crisis revealed his true character to the American public and Congress.

The steady expansion of American support for Diem and his regime during 1961-62 was not based on any formal alliance or on any apparent threat to the United States' security. The "commitment" to defend South Vietnam was primarily an understanding between the White House and two other great power centers in Washington: the Pentagon and Congress. Many important figures in both of these institutions were critical of Kennedy's policy toward Laos, and the decision to take a tougher line in South Vietnam was designed to show them, and the Russians, that the administration would not invariably retreat when faced with the challenge of subversive warfare.

McNamara Given Leading Role in Vietnam

When the Joint Chiefs of Staff began to criticize the Kennedy administration's policy on Laos, Secretary of Defense Robert McNamara was given the responsibility of producing a policy for Vietnam that would command the support of the whole U.S. defense establishment. McNamara was supposed to keep the Joint Chiefs of Staff sufficiently satisfied so that they would not air their objections publicly or in private committee hearings before Congress. (The Chairman of the JCS has the right to advise the President and Congress directly on military matters, without going through the Secretary of Defense.)

McNamara became fascinated with the challenge of communist subversive warfare generally and the problem of Vietnam in particular; he was attracted by the assignment of shaping the U.S. response because the new administration regarded Vietnam as one of the most difficult foreign affairs problems it faced. Although he lacked Dean Rusk's depth of governmental experience, McNamara's extraordinary energy and competence as an administrator—and the colossal size of the Defense establishment—made it seem only natural to define Vietnam as an essentially "military" problem and to include it within the scope of his responsibilities.

At first, Secretary of State Dean Rusk was satisfied with the decision that McNamara would play the leading role in Vietnam policy. Rusk had been raised in the Stimson-Marshall-Acheson school, which holds that military strength is the key to effective foreign policy. During World War II, Rusk had served in Asia, and he was obviously impressed by China's latent power; his public statements on Far Eastern policy during the 1950s and 1960s often dwelt on the theme that the United States' main task in Asia was to hold the line militarily against Chinese expansionism. Thus, when he first took charge of the State Department, Rusk was prepared to accept the view that Vietnam was a military problem. To the annoyance of some State Department officials, Rusk made less effort than many cabinet officers to protect his department's interests in the bureaucratic wars of Washington. He considered it to be his main duty to advise the President on foreign policy.

In April 1961, the President appointed an interagency task force on Vietnam, with McNamara's deputy, Roswell Gilpatric, in charge.[3] A few weeks later, on the basis of a report submitted by this task force and a series of parallel recommendations by Walt Rostow of the White House staff, Kennedy approved the following statement of U.S. objectives and operating principles:

> . . . to prevent Communist domination of South Vietnam; to create in that country a viable and increasingly democratic society, and to initiate, on an accelerated basis, a series of mutually supporting actions of a military, political, economic, psychological and covert character designed to achieve this objective.[4]

In addition, 400 members of the Special Forces—a group trained in counterinsurgency—and 100 other U.S. military advisors were ordered to Vietnam. This increase of the U.S. military presence in Vietnam was not announced publicly, although it clearly violated the 1954 Geneva accords and was the largest increase since 1954. The assignment of the Special Forces advisors pointed the way toward active U.S. involvement in the war. One of the Vietnam task force recommendations which President Kennedy did not approve (until about a year later) was a proposal to send over 3000 more advisors to train the South Vietnamese army.

Lyndon Johnson's Far Eastern Tour

In May 1961, President Kennedy sent Vice-President Johnson on a tour of some of the major U.S. aid recipient nations in Asia, including South Vietnam, to assure the leaders of those countries that the new administration would continue to support them. Johnson's report offers glimpses of the approach which he himself would adopt a few years later.[5]

The Vice-President described Vietnam and Thailand as the most important trouble spots in Asia and said they were "critical" to the United States. He argued that the United States had only two policy alternatives: "to help these countries to the best of our ability or throw in the towel in the area and pull back our defenses to San Francisco and a 'Fortress America' concept." In the latter case, he added "we would say to the world . . . that we don't live up to treaties and don't stand by our friends. This is not my concept. . . ."

Although Johnson hailed Diem publicly as the "Winston Churchill of Asia," his report described him somewhat more accurately as a "complex figure beset by many problems." He had "admirable qualities" but he was remote from the people and "surrounded by persons less admirable and capable than he." Johnson's report also indicated that the American Embassy in Saigon, the U.S. Information Service, the Military Assistance Advisory Group, "and related operations" left much to be desired. "They should be brought up to maximum efficiency. The most important thing is imaginative, creative, American management of our military aid program."

Johnson's role in the planning of Kennedy administration programs for Indochina was, however, peripheral. Indeed, he was seldom consulted on any foreign policy matters by senior members of the administration. His report suggested that "$50 million of U.S. military and economic assistance will be needed if we decide to support Vietnam." In fact, and apparently without his knowledge, the administration had already asked Congress to approve nearly six times this amount of aid for South Vietnam during the year beginning July 1961. Probably the main value of the Vice-President's tour, in the eyes of the administration, was in helping reassure such Asian leaders as Diem, Chiang Kai-shek, and Ayub Khan. And since those leaders all had their admirers on Capitol Hill, Johnson's trip may have gained a few votes for the foreign aid bill, which had an unusually difficult time in Congress that year.

During the summer, the news from South Vietnam continued to get worse instead of better. In September 1961, there were 450 separate instances of Viet Cong violence reported throughout the country.[6] On September 18, the Viet Cong seized a provincial capital fifty-five miles from Saigon, beheaded the province chief, and escaped with large amounts of arms and ammunition before the South Vietnamese army arrived.

The Taylor-Rostow Mission

On October 5, 1961, a paper, known as a National Intelligence Estimate, was produced by the main U.S. intelligence services. It indicated that 80 to 90 percent of the 17,000 Viet Cong believed to be in South Vietnam had been recruited locally—not infiltrated from outside the country. It also indicated that the Viet Cong obtained most of their arms and supplies by buying, stealing, or capturing them in South Vietnam. The paper had been prepared to help adminstration leaders evaluate new proposals for sending U.S. combat forces to South Vietnam. It tended to invalidate two of these proposals—submitted by the Joint Chiefs of Staff and by Walt Rostow of the White House staff—to cut off the infiltration of Viet Cong troops and supplies from North to South Vietnam.

Nevertheless, a high State Department official attempted to combine the Joint Chiefs' plan and the Rostow plan into a single proposal, perhaps altering the original purpose of those plans in the process. The State Department paper recommended for the first time that the United States adopt "as our real and ultimate objective the defeat of the Viet Cong." The State Department paper estimated that about three divisions of U.S. troops would be needed to accomplish this. The next day, the Pentagon provided a more specific (although, as it turned out, equally unrealistic) estimate that 40,000 U.S. troops would be needed to defeat the Viet Cong, while 128,000 would be needed to cope with possible Chinese or North Vietnamese intervention in the war.[7]

Faced with these conflicting estimates and recommendations, President Kennedy sent General Maxwell Taylor, his personal military advisor, to Saigon. Walt Rostow was the senior civilian in General Taylor's party. The purpose of the mission, President Kennedy told a press conference on October 11, was to discuss with Diem and with U.S. officials in Saigon "ways in which we can perhaps better assist the government of Vietnam in meeting this threat to its independence." When asked whether General Taylor was going to consider the need for U.S. combat forces, President Kennedy was noncommittal; he said that the administration would reserve its position on new measures to aid South Vietnam until after General Taylor and his party returned. But he also indicated that there had been a large increase in the number of enemy troops involved in South Vietnam and that there was evidence that some of them came from beyond that country's borders. This statement, which did not reflect the overall estimate of the intelligence community, was obviously designed to keep open a wide range of policy choices.

On the same day, a State Department spokesman denied that the U.S. was considering sending troops to Vietnam. He told reporters that the South Vietnamese government had assured the United States that, with the help of U.S. military supplies and training, it could manage. Two days later, however, the South Vietnamese minister of defense privately requested U.S. combat units, or "combat trainer units," to be placed near the North Vietnamese border. The purpose, he said, was to free the South Vietnamese army from the task of guarding the border, allowing them to concentrate on fighting the Viet Cong within South Vietnam.

At the first meeting between President Diem and General Taylor, Diem asked for a bilateral defense treaty, American funds to expand the Vietnamese army, and a long list of expensive military equipment. But he did not ask for American combat forces. At his second and last meeting with Diem during this visit to Saigon, General Taylor presented a long list of recommendations, which fell into three main categories: 1) reforms and new administrative procedures to be adopted by the Diem regime to broaden its base and make it more receptive to American advice; 2) U.S. aid for counterinsurgency advisors, funds, and equipment; and 3) the dispatch of a so-called flood relief task force to South Vietnam.

The latter unit was to be composed of about 8000 U.S. combat troops, who would help the Saigon government cope with extensive flood damage in the Mekong delta area—and then remain in South Vietnam after completing their nominal flood relief duties. The idea was to enlarge the U.S. military presence in Vietnam as inconspicuously as possible.

After this second meeting, General Taylor cabled Washington that Diem's reaction to all of his recommendations had been favorable. However, Diem and Taylor may not have understood each other so well as Taylor thought. After all, Diem had not requested U.S. combat forces at their first meeting, and he may not have understood the full implications of the "flood relief task force" proposal. This was only one of a large number of complex recommendations made by General Taylor. Diem was by now in a very bad mental state because of overwork, the crumbling military situation, and his brother Nhu's constant reports of treachery within the Saigon government. It was hard for anyone to know whether Diem or Nhu was in command and what their real thoughts were. Finally, General Taylor did not seek Diem's views but only his concurrence in an American military operation which he (Taylor) considered necessary.

Reaction of Leading U.S. Officials

Secretary Rusk, in Tokyo at the time, was sent a copy of Taylor's recommendations. Rusk immediately cabled the President opposing the idea of sending combat troops to Vietnam. He said that if Diem remained unwilling to trust his military commanders and to broaden the base of his government, he (Rusk) found it difficult to see how a "handful of American troops can have decisive influence." He did not like to see the United States become too deeply committed to a "losing horse."

Ranged on the same side as Secretary Rusk were the main intelligence agencies in Washington. On November 5, they issued a National Intelligence Estimate warning that any increase in American forces would probably be matched by infiltration of troops from North Vietnam, that U.S. threats of bombing North Vietnam would not deter Hanoi from supporting the Viet Cong, and that Moscow and Peking would react strongly to an actual U.S. attack on the North.

Secretary McNamara, speaking for the Deputy Secretary and for the Joint Chiefs of Staff, supported General Taylor's recommendations— but on condition that the President commit the government to the aim of preventing the fall of South Vietnam to Communism. Secretary McNamara warned the President that the 8000-man task force which General Taylor had recommended probably would not be enough to accomplish this aim; he indicated that 6 divisions or 205,000 men would probably be the maximum number of U.S. troops required.

On the basis of available evidence, it is quite certain that President Kennedy did not want to send U.S. combat forces to South Vietnam. But having sent the Taylor-Rostow mission to Saigon, and having received their recommendations for a task force (with Secretary McNamara's cautious endorsement of the idea), the President needed to have the case for more moderate action made as strongly as possible before he could announce his decision. Thus, President Kennedy apparently asked Rusk and McNamara to produce a joint recommendation by their two departments. And the President probably directed Rusk and McNamara not to propose the immediate deployment of combat forces.

With two exceptions, President Kennedy accepted all of the major recommendations in the memorandum which Rusk and McNamara sent to him on November 11, 1961. He did not approve the proposal that the U.S. government commit itself to preventing the fall of South Vietnam to the Communists. Nor did he accept the idea of admitting openly, in a public letter to President Diem, that the expanded U.S. involvement in South Vietnam violated the 1954 Geneva accords. By failing to clarify his objectives in Vietnam—or to announce publicly the type of force he was prepared to use at this stage—President Kennedy opened the door to massive confusion about U.S. aims (and indeed the honesty of his statements) both at home and abroad.

With a minimum of public fanfare, the President approved the immediate deployment of a number of small, specialized American military units for the purpose of aiding the South Vietnamese armed forces with specific tasks (e.g., communications, intelligence, airlift, air reconnaissance, and naval patrols). He also approved a large increase in the number of U.S. military advisors and authorized changes in the rules of engagement for U.S. military personnel in South Vietnam. Henceforth, the United States would assume a much more active role in directing and controlling South Vietnamese military operations. U.S. military prestige would be much more directly involved in the success or failure of the Saigon forces. American aircraft flown by American crews would be allowed to take part in offensive operations against the Viet Cong— and resulting U.S. casualties would make it harder for the United States to withdraw without some form of victory. Finally, the President agreed to a large increase in the number of American civilian advisors working with Vietnamese officials in the Saigon government.

The reasons cited in the Rusk-McNamara memorandum for not sending U.S. ground combat units to South Vietnam undoubtedly coincided closely with the President's own thinking on this matter. The two Secretaries pointed out that sending such forces might raise a number of serious domestic and international political problems including the possibility of "Communist bloc escalation" in Vietnam. The memorandum also pointed to the basic dilemma of U.S. intervention: if South Vietnam were making a strong effort, no U.S. combat forces would be needed; if South Vietnam were not making a strong effort to defend itself, U.S. forces could not operate successfully in the midst of an apathetic or hostile population. This was why the two Secretaries advised a policy of sending small, specialized U.S. units, which would serve primarily to bolster South Vietnamese morale. Nevertheless, President Kennedy and his associates almost certainly realized that the decision to send such a large number of U.S. advisors and support troops to Vietnam was likely to lead, sooner or later, to their direct participation in the war.

Diem's Reaction to Increased U.S. Involvement

On November 14, 1961, the President's decisions were cabled to Ambassador Frederick Nolting in Saigon. Nolting, a career Foreign Service Officer, had developed a close relationship with Diem (and a personal commitment to Saigon's cause) during his first eight months in Vietnam. Ambassador Nolting was instructed to tell Diem that he must provide "concrete demonstrations" that he was prepared to work in an "orderly way" with his subordinates and "broaden the political base" of his government. Moreover, Diem was to be told that the U.S. government expected to share in the decision-making process in the political, economic, and military fields as they affected the security of his country.

This amounted almost to a demand for a joint U.S.-South Vietnamese administration. It would be interesting to know what response Washington officials expected from a man as proud and independent as Ngo Dinh Diem. According to available information, they and Ambassador Nolting expected Diem to be disappointed over the decision to send no U.S. combat troops. But in fact, he had not asked for them and was apparently of two minds about the desirability of having foreign troops on his territory. After seeing Diem, Ambassador Nolting cabled Washington that he took the news about combat troops "rather better than I expected."[8]

Within a few days, however, the embassy began to get reports that Diem was upset and brooding. These reports were relayed to Washington. On December 7, the embassy in Saigon received new instructions, softening the United States' demand for "reforms" and requesting "close partnership" and frequent consultation instead of an outright U.S. role in decision-making. After more than six years of dealing with U.S. advisors, Diem knew how to make them feel they needed him more than he needed them. His astonishing success resulted from his own sincere conviction that he alone had the wisdom, integrity, and patriotism to prevent South Vietnam from being overrun by Communists.

Results of Growing U.S. Involvement

During 1962, the number of U.S. forces in South Vietnam rose from 2600 to 11,000. In addition to military advisors, the U.S. supplied pilots and mechanics to assist the South Vietnamese air force. American personnel began to take part in bombing of suspected concentrations of Viet Cong, as well as providing close support and airlift for South Vietnamese forces. The Viet Cong were also temporarily thrown off balance by the U.S. bombing attacks and by the increased mobility and firepower of the ARVN (Army of the Republic of Vietnam). According to an Australian journalist, the National Liberation Front almost decided, during 1962, to evacuate the Mekong delta and pull their forces back into the mountains of South Vietnam.[9]

On February 5, 1962, newspapers carried the first report of an American helicopter being shot down by the Viet Cong. At his press conference two days later, President Kennedy responded cautiously to a general question about the basis of U.S. involvement in South Vietnam. He said that the United States had been "assisting Vietnam economically to maintain its independence" and had also sent training groups "which have been expanded in recent weeks, as the attacks on the government and the people of South Vietnam have increased." He added that the United States was helping the South Vietnamese people "in every way we can" to maintain their freedom.

This deliberately vague formulation of U.S. policy was obviously intended to serve the dual purpose of reassuring the American public, warning potential enemies of America's resolution, and encouraging the Saigon government. However, as dangers of open-ended U.S. involvement in Indochina became more obvious to the American people and Congress, this type of vague formulation of policy would lead to serious doubts about the credibility of the U.S. government.

On February 8, the *New York Times* reported that there were 5000 U.S. personnel in South Vietnam, mostly "advisors"—and pointed out that the 1954 Geneva accords had set a much lower limit.[10] When questioned about this the following day, a Defense Department spokesman told reporters that "this is a war we cannot afford to lose" and "we're drawing a line" against Communist aggression in South Vietnam. At his February 14 press conference, President Kennedy said that the United States was attempting to prevent a Communist take-over in South Vietnam. (This, of course, was precisely the formulation of U.S. aims which he had rejected three months earlier when it was proposed to him by Rusk and McNamara.)

At the same February news conference, President Kennedy was also asked if his administration was being "less than candid" about American involvement in Vietnam. He replied that, although U.S. troops were "firing back" to protect themselves, these were not combat troops in the generally understood sense of the word. He also said that the U.S. government was attempting to make available all the information on its actions in Vietnam that was consistent with security needs, and that it was keeping bipartisan groups in Congress informed.

In March 1962, administration officials acknowledged publicly that the training of South Vietnamese military personnel by Americans "occasionally takes place under combat conditions." On April 11, 1962, after two American soldiers were killed in a Viet Cong ambush, the President was asked by reporters what he planned to do about this type of situation. He answered that the United States could not "desist" in Vietnam, which it was trying to keep from falling under Communist domination. [11]

One of the major programs begun in early 1962, and which for a time gave rise to great optimism within the U.S. government, was the strategic hamlet program based on the British experience in Malaya during the 1950s. The program was intended to deny the Viet Cong recruits or supplies by fortifying rural hamlets and instituting strict controls over the movement of people and food in and out of the fortified areas.

Ideally, the program would not only make it possible for the people to defend themselves but would also provide the people with better health and education services than those to which they had previously had access. But if the emphasis were simply on controlling the population and preventing them from aiding the Viet Cong, it could produce enough resentment to make the government's position hopeless.

Diem put his brother Nhu in charge of the strategic hamlet program in March 1962. This gave Nhu access to an enormous amount of U.S. aid funds and a mandate to place hundreds of thousands of people behind barbed wire and control them. Under Nhu's direction, an impressive number of strategic hamlets were completed—but often only on paper; a great deal of the aid money was pocketed by Nhu's circle of friends, and very little was used to provide social services for the people inside the hamlets. Moreover, hamlets were dotted around the country in a helter-skelter pattern wherever Nhu chose to locate them and with whatever fortifications he chose to give them, while the plan called for building them only in areas which had been cleared of the Viet Cong.

By the end of 1962, U.S. intelligence analysts had begun to see signs that all was far from well. The Viet Cong were still managing to recruit thousands of young men in South Vietnam, and they were still capturing weapons from the South Vietnamese army, though in smaller numbers. There was no centrally controlled civil, police, and military program aimed at protecting the mass of people and winning their support.

The Diem regime and the U.S. civilian and military officials in South Vietnam were all pursuing separate ends. The strategic hamlet program was being run by Nhu for the purpose of tightening the regime's control over the people. South Vietnamese military commanders had become so afraid of incurring the displeasure of Diem and Nhu they had lost almost all initiative. The American military command in South Vietnam (which had grown large enough to have twenty-two generals) was preoccupied with the "shooting war." And the American Embassy was trying desperately to coordinate the enormous range of American civilian and military programs in South Vietnam and to influence the policies of the Diem regime.

But as the U.S. military presence grew, the Embassy was more and more relegated to the role of a service organization. Ambassador Nolting and General Harkins, the senior U.S. military commander, had established an excellent personal relationship by agreeing tacitly to recognise an artificial boundary between "political problems" and "military problems'. Military considerations were increasingly given overriding importance by U.S. officials in Saigon and Washington. Diem and Nhu showed themselves adept at playing off one American organization against another within the large and growing U.S. Mission.

By the end of 1962, the temporary improvement in the Saigon regime's military situation, produced by the massive increase in U.S. aid, had been nullified by the Diem family's baneful influence on the South Vietnamese bureaucracy and army. President Kennedy realized this, although neither he nor his advisors had a solution. When asked for his assessment of the Vietnam situation at his December 12, 1961 press conference, Kennedy's reply seemed more somber than the optimistic statements which Secretary McNamara, General Taylor, and other high administration officials had made throughout the year. The President pointed out that fighting a guerrilla war was extremely difficult; a ratio of ten or eleven government troops to one guerrilla was needed, and the terrain of South Vietnam presented special problems. Thus, he concluded, "We don't see the end of the tunnel, but I must say I don't think it is darker than it was a year ago, and in some ways [it's] lighter."

Notes

1. Hilsman, *To Move a Nation*, p. 420.

2. *Pentagon Papers*, pp. 86 and 87.

3. Rusk finally saw the importance of having the State Department head this interagency task force, and with typical soft-spoken humor he told McNamara, "If you want Vietnam, give me the marines."

4. See *Pentagon Papers*, pp. 126-27 for the text of National Security Action Memorandum 52, May 11, 1961.

5. Excerpts from Vice-President Johnson's report on his 1961 trip to Asia are contained in *The Pentagon Papers*, pp. 127-30. See also Lyndon Johnson's memoirs, *The Vantage Point* (New York: Holt, Rinehart and Winston, 1971), pp. 53-55.

6. Such figures are meaningful only insofar as the quality and objectivity of the reporting system are known. Some incidents may have been fabricated, some may have been omitted, and some may have been provoked by the local authorities.

7. *Pentagon Papers*, pp. 79-157.

8. *Pentagon Papers*, pp. 107-09.

9. See Wilfred G. Burchett, *Vietnam: Inside Story of the Guerrilla War* (New York: International Publishers, 1965), p. 193.

10. *Pentagon Papers*, p. 110, indicates that U.S. *military* personnel in South Vietnam rose from 948 in November 1961 to 2646 on January 9, 1962. On the latter date, the Pentagon anticipated that the number would reach 5576 by June 30, 1962.

11. It was not until December 12, 1962 that the President told a press conference the approximate number of American troops in Vietnam and acknowledged publicly that there had been "a number of casualties." (During 1962, 109 Americans were killed or wounded in South Vietnam, compared with fourteen the previous year.)

CHAPTER EIGHT

The Buddhist Crisis
and Its Aftermath

On May 8, 1963, South Vietnamese army troops attacked a group of unarmed Buddhist demonstrators in Hue (the Ngo family's main political stronghold). The Buddhists were protesting a government ban on the flying of religious flags, which had been applied in their case but not for a Catholic celebration a few weeks earlier. Nine demonstrators were killed and many more were wounded. Instead of admitting its mistake and adopting a more reasonable attitude to keep the crisis from spreading, the government took the position that its prestige was involved. Its tactics, aimed at intimidating the Buddhists and their growing ranks of supporters, became more and more ruthless.

Until late July 1963, the United States avoided a

public break with the Saigon government, while making an intensive behind-the-scenes effort to persuade Diem and his family to moderate their position. The regime's August 21 attack on the main Buddhist pagodas marked the point of no return in Diem's relations with his own people and with the U.S. government. By September, many of the educated people in South Vietnam's cities were said to regard Diem's overthrow as more urgent than defeating the Viet Cong. Although Washington was not entirely aware of the fact, its policy in South Vietnam had reached a dead end.

Buddhism as a Vehicle for Vietnamese Nationalism

The great majority of South Vietnam's 15 million people probably regard themselves as Buddhists, but only a minority (perhaps 3 to 5 million) take part regularly in organized meetings or in other Buddhist functions. Roughly 2 million people belong to the Hoa Hao, Cao Dai, and other sects; and there are believed to be one and a half million practicing Catholics. (Over half of the Catholic families in South Vietnam came from the North as refugees in 1954.) Many Vietnamese who regard themselves as members of one or another of these religions or sects also follow the ethical precepts of Confucianism and practice its cult of ancestor worship.

The complex attitude of the Vietnamese people toward Buddhism lies at the heart of their sense of nationality and nationalism. Chinese missionaries brought the Mahayana form of Buddhism to Vietnam about 2000 years ago. By 939 A.D., when the Vietnamese people expelled their Chinese overlords, Buddhism had become part of their lives, along with the ancestor cult of Confucianism and the animist beliefs of the aboriginal people of Tonkin. Some of the greatest rulers of Vietnam's history, revered for their determined resistance to the Chinese, were patrons of Buddhism.

During the French colonial period, when political activity was outlawed, Buddhist associations provided one of the few outlets for Vietnamese nationalism. Many Vietnamese people today feel that Vietnamese rulers have a responsibility to preserve this traditional element of the national culture. They believe that Buddhism is more "Vietnamese" than Confucianism (with its Chinese roots) or Catholicism, which they associate with French influence.[1]

Buddhists Challenge Diem's Leadership

After the May 8 massacre, a government spokesman claimed that army troops had not fired on the demonstrators. He said that the crowd had panicked when a Viet Cong agent threw a grenade and that the people who were killed or wounded had been trampled underfoot. The next day, several thousand Buddhists gathered quietly outside the province chief's house to protest this statement of the government's position. The Diem regime's response was to ban all further demonstrations.

In the eyes of the United States Mission in Saigon, each day that President Diem delayed making some gesture of conciliation toward the Buddhists, the chances of his government's survival grew more uncertain. On May 13, a group of militant Buddhist leaders publicly demanded that the government: 1) lift the ban on flying religious flags; 2) accord Buddhism and Buddhists the same status as Catholicism and Catholics; 3) allow Buddhists to preach their religion freely; 4) compensate the May 8 riot victims and their relatives; and 5) punish the officials responsible for the May 8 incident.

In charging the Diem regime with religious discrimination, the Buddhists were voicing a sense of injustice felt by many Vietnamese over the preferential treatment given Catholics since the days of French colonial rule. Under the French, most of the opportunities provided to Vietnamese for a western-style education were in Catholic schools. As a result, Catholics were often the best qualified applicants for jobs in the colonial administration or in private French firms. Catholics were also exempted from performing unpaid labor on the roads. And the Catholic Church was given the right to acquire land, while Buddhism was denied this right because it was classified as an "association," rather than a "religion."

The Ngo family, which was one of the oldest Catholic families in Vietnam, continued many of the discriminatory practices of the French colonial regime and added a few new ones of their own. For example, Catholics were not required to help build the strategic hamlets, and Catholic refugees from North Vietnam (who were among the few positive supporters of Diem's anti-Communist policy) received preferential treatment from the regime.

Thus, the charge that Diem had discriminated against Buddhists by favoring the Catholic minority could be easily substantiated. But before

Buddhism emerged as a political protest movement, the Saigon government did not limit the freedom of Vietnamese Buddhists to practice their religion. As described earlier, the government persecuted many individuals whom it considered "Communist" or "disloyal." But it was only in the summer of 1963 that the regime began to regard Buddhists in this light.

As the Buddhist protest movement grew, thousands of students in universities, high schools, and even elementary schools—representing the best families in South Vietnam—courted persecution at the hands of the Diem regime by joining in a massive campaign of civil disobedience and antigovernment demonstrations. Their rallying cry was "Buddhism in danger!" However, the basic aim of the movement was not simply to protect Buddhism but to undermine the Diem regime by revealing its political incompetence and repressive character.

Seven Buddhists committed suicide by burning during the summer and fall of 1963. This convinced most observers that Diem had lost the support of the people. An elderly monk, Venerable Quang Duc, committed the first act of self-immolation on June 10. Because Buddhist leaders had passed the word that "something important" would happen, an American reporter attended the demonstration and photographed the fiery sacrifice. The pictures of the Venerable Quang Duc sitting upright in the lotus position while flames engulfed his robes and body were published on the front page of newspapers all over the world.

Quang Duc's extraordinarily painful death—to the accompaniment of hypnotic chants and moans by the surrounding circle of monks and nuns—was no less horrifying than the reaction of Ngo Dinh Nhu and his wife. Madame Nhu gave the world press grisly quotes about "monk barbeques" and told how she had "gaily clapped her hands" when she heard of the suicide. Her husband boasted publicly of the strong-arm tactics his police used to harass the Buddhist demonstrators and American journalists who reported on them. The Nhus probably started the rumor that the Buddhist movement had been infiltrated by Communists. (No one ever proved this charge; indeed the Communists seem to have been just as unprepared as the government for the Buddhists' sudden emergence as a major political force.)

During this period and in the absence on leave of the American Ambassador, the American Embassy in Saigon worked frantically to persuade President Diem to change his policies toward the Buddhists. Both Embassy and administration leaders in Washington believed that Diem could prevent the Buddhist movement from undermining his regime if he silenced the Nhus, abolished official discriminiation in favor of Catholics, and indemnified the victims of the May 8 incident. Under instructions from Washington, Chargé d'Affaires William Truehart repeatedly urged Diem to adopt some or all of these measures. But Diem turned a deaf ear.

In July, when Ambassador Nolting returned to Saigon for the last few weeks of his tour, he also tried to make Diem listen to reason. Nolting managed to obtain Diem's promise that there would be no crackdown on the Buddhists, whatever the Nhus were openly advocating, and U.S. pressure was temporarily relaxed. Diem also agreed, on the eve of Nolting's departure from Saigon to issue a public statement calling for reconciliation with the Buddhists. But the statement was far from reassuring; it even sounded somewhat deranged. Diem announced that he had "always" followed a conciliatory policy but added, ominously, that it was "irreversible."

In Washington, meanwhile, these events were being followed with the deepest concern. Henry Cabot Lodge, who had been chosen to succeed Nolting, was being briefed for his assignment. Lodge had lost his Senate seat to John F. Kennedy in 1952; he served as Ambassador to the United Nations in the 1950s, and was Republican Vice-Presidential candidate in 1960. By appointing a Republican of Lodge's stature to head the U.S. Mission in Saigon, President Kennedy hoped to prevent the question of U.S. policy toward Vietnam from becoming a partisan issue.

The August 21 Attack on the Pagodas

Six days after Diem's "conciliatory" statement, during the predawn hours of August 21, police and military units attacked the main Buddhist pagodas throughout South Vietnam. Hundreds of monks, including most of the leading figures in the protest movement, were arrested. Many were injured, and some may have been killed. Many religious statues and sacred relics inside the pagodas were desecrated. In Saigon, three monks, including Venerable Tri Quang, a leader of the militants, took refuge in U.S. Mission building. In the city of Hue, thousands of local residents fought in the streets against government troops who destroyed the main pagoda. A state of martial law and a curfew were proclaimed by President Diem. He announced that "a number of political speculators who had taken advantage of religion" had abused the government's "extremely conciliatory goodwill."

The attack on the pagodas was the Ngo brothers' way of showing that neither the Buddhists nor the U.S. Mission could dictate to them. On the day of the attack, the State Department issued the first public criticism by any U.S. agency of the Diem regime's handling of the Buddhist crisis. The statement called the attack on the pagodas a "direct violation by the Vietnamese government of assurances that it was pursuing a policy of conciliation with the Buddhists." Here was an implied warning that the U.S. government might reconsider its support for Diem if he did not change his course.

Initial reports from the American Embassy and from American correspondents in Saigon indicated that South Vietnamese army troops had taken part in the raids on the pagodas. When these reports were rebroadcast to Vietnam by the Voice of America, two senior Vietnamese generals protested privately to the U.S. Mission that no regular army troops had been involved. They said the forces used in the raids were South Vietnamese Special Forces, who were under Nhu's personal control.

The generals asked the U.S. Mission to investigate the situation and satisfy itself that these statements were true. When this had been done, they wanted the Voice of America to broadcast a retraction of its earlier report, which had been harmful to the morale of the Vietnamese army and to its relations with Buddhist civilians. Finally, and most important, the generals asked for a definitive statement of what U.S. policy would be in case they decided to overthrow the regime.

The August 21 attack on the pagodas had been timed for the interval between Ambassador Nolting's departure from Vietnam and the arrival of Ambassador Henry Cabot Lodge. Lodge arrived in Saigon just thirty-six hours after the pagoda attacks; thus, he was barely on the scene when this new element—a possible Vietnamese army coup—was injected into the situation.

The Decision to Withdraw U.S. Support from Diem

On the morning of August 24 (a Saturday), the State Department received word from Saigon of the generals' request. American officials in Washington had by this time obtained evidence, which they regarded as conclusive, that regular Vietnamese army units had nothing to do with the assault on the pagodas. The attack, it was believed, had been planned by Nhu and carried out by his secret police and Special Forces.[2]

On the basis of this evidence, a cable was sent to Ambassador Lodge on August 24 instructing him to tell "appropriate levels" of the Saigon government that the United States would not accept the actions of Nhu and his collaborators against the Buddhists, and that "prompt dramatic actions" must be taken by the Saigon regime to redress the wrongs committed against the Buddhists. At the same time, Lodge was told to inform "key military leaders" that U.S. military and economic aid would cease if these steps were not taken immediately. Lodge was to say that the United States wanted to give Diem a "reasonable opportunity" to remove the Nhus; otherwise "we can no longer support Diem." Lodge was also authorized to tell the generals that Washington would give them "direct support in any interim period of breakdown" of the "central government mechanism."[3]

This decision, to support an anti-Diem coup, was one of the most controversial actions of the Kennedy administration. When it became known that the United States had secretly provided encouragement to those who were planning to assassinate Diem and Nhu, some people concluded that no political figure who obstructed U.S. policy was safe from assassination.

The August 24 cable was drafted by Undersecretary Ball, Deputy Undersecretary Harriman, Michael Forrestal of the White House staff, and Assistant Secretary of State Hilsman. President Kennedy and Secretary Rusk were both within easy reach by secure communication channels, and they participated in several revisions of the cable. Because Secretary McNamara and CIA Director McCone were on vacation, the cable was cleared for them by their deputies. General Maxwell Taylor cleared it for the Joint Chiefs of Staff.

Lodge replied the following day (Sunday) saying that the chances of Diem meeting the U.S. government's demands were virtually nil; going to Diem with the demands would only give Nhu a chance to forestall a coup by the military. Lodge asked that he be instructed to go directly to the generals (without informing Diem) to demand that action be taken to right the wrongs against the Buddhists. Lodge also wanted to tell the generals that the United States was "prepared to have Diem without [the] Nhus but it is in effect up to them" whether to keep Diem or not. After a quick check of the responsible top officials in Washington that Sunday, Hilsman and Ball at the State Department sent Lodge a telegram authorizing these changes in his August 24 instructions.[4]

Meanwhile, as the Vietnamese generals had requested, arrangements were made on August 25 for the Voice of America to broadcast a statement to Vietnam saying that the U.S. government had proof that Nhu's secret police and Special Forces (not the Vietnamese army) were to blame for the attacks on the pagodas. Following its usual procedure, the Voice of America quoted a wire service report as its source for this information. This report ended by speculating that "the U.S. may sharply reduce its aid to Vietnam unless President Diem gets rid of secret police officials responsible for the attacks." Voice of America officials included this statement in their summary of the wire-service report broadcast to Vietnam: this gave the erroneous impression that the United States was officially and publicly threatening to cut off aid to the Diem regime.[5]

The Voice of America broadcast, which was heard in South Vietnam on the morning of August 26, warned Diem's brother Nhu that the United States might be considering ways of getting rid of him. This exposed the Vietnamese generals and members of the official American community in Saigon to the danger that Nhu or Diem might act against them to prevent a coup. Ambassador Lodge, who was due to present his credentials at Gia Long Palace only three hours after the broadcast, told General Harkins (head of the U.S. military mission) not to accompany him—just in case Diem or Nhu tried some "funny business."[6]

The Voice of America broadcast probably made the Vietnamese generals wary of confiding further details of their plans to the U.S. Mission. Besides, the anti-Diem generals also had to contend with the wavering attitude of the senior Vietnamese troop commander in the Saigon area, an extremely ambitious and erratic individual. Until the generals were certain that he would not oppose them, they did not dare attempt a coup. Thus, on August 31, the U.S. Embassy in Saigon reported to Washington its impression that the antigovernment generals had decided to stop preparing for a coup "at this time".

Notes

1. Buddhism spread out from India in two great arcs. The Mahayana form of Buddhism reached Vietnam via Tibet and China, while the Theravada form came via Ceylon and Cambodia. In South Vietnam, Mahayana Buddhism has its largest following around Hue; the Theravada form is more common in the southern provinces. Mahayana Buddhists from Hue have played the leading role in the nationwide protest movement which began in 1963.

2. Hilsman, *To Move a Nation*, p. 485. The South Vietnamese Special Forces had been established, with CIA funding and assistance, as an elite counterinsurgency unit, but Nhu had kept them close to Saigon to use as his own private army.

3. The August 24, 1963 telegram containing these instructions to Ambassador Lodge in Saigon is cited on pp. 194-95 of *Pentagon Papers*.

4. Hilsman, *To Move a Nation*, page 489 and *Pentagon Papers*, page 169.

5. Hilsman, pages 489-90.

6. John Mecklin, *Mission in Torment* (Garden City, New York: Doubleday, 1965), page 194.

CHAPTER NINE

Downfall of Diem and the End of a Policy

Back in Washington, the National Security Council met on August 31. In the absence of the President, who was in Hyannisport, Secretary Rusk presided. The discussion centered mainly on the question of how the events of the past few weeks had affected the war effort—and what U.S. policy should be, now that there seemed to be little immediate prospect of a coup.[1]

The view that the war effort had been adversely affected was expressed by the State Department representatives (Rusk, Harriman, Hilsman, and Paul Kattenberg, head of the Interdepartmental Working Group on Vietnam). Kattenberg took a more pessimistic view of the situation than did anyone else present. He made what was perhaps the first suggestion of its kind at an NSC meeting: that the United States should withdraw from Vietnam before the politico-military situation deteriorated to the point that it was forced to leave.

Secretary McNamara and General Taylor, who had so often claimed that the situation was improving, may have felt that Kattenberg's statement challenged their judgment. Secretary Rusk called Kattenberg's assessment "speculative" and proposed that the United States "not pull out of Vietnam until the war was won," and that it should not "run a coup." The Pentagon representatives promptly agreed.

For the first time at an NSC meeting, Vice President Johnson was asked to present his views. He supported Secretary Rusk's position completely. Johnson had great reservations about a coup because he saw no alternative to Diem. At the same time, he thought it would be disastrous for the United States to withdraw. The Vice-President also endorsed Secretary McNamara's statement that Lodge and Harkins should reestablish "communication" with Diem. After this had been done, he said, perhaps General Taylor or someone should "talk rough" to the Vietnamese. But the main order of business was to get on with "winning the war."[2]

Secretary Rusk's formula—that the United States should not withdraw from Vietnam until the war was "won" and that it should not "run a coup"—summarized the main points on which administration leaders seemed to agree. But the shades of meaning given by the President and some of his top advisors to these points were so different as to be almost irreconcilable.

President Kennedy's Views on Vietnam

The President himself probably devoted more attention to Vietnam during the last three months of his life than during any other time in his administration. He was under considerable domestic political pressure to redefine the basis for U.S. policy, since Diem's attack on the pagodas had finally driven home to the American people the repressive character of the Saigon government.

In a September 2 television interview, President Kennedy issued a blunt invitation to Diem to remove the Nhus from power. He said the Saigon government had "gotten out of touch with the people" during the past two months, although "with changes of policy and perhaps . . . personnel" he thought they could regain the South Vietnamese people's support. Without those changes, however, he did not think its chances of winning the war would be very good.

On September 9, in another television interview, President Kennedy said that he had no plans for reducing aid to South Vietnam. He also reaffirmed the domino theory, saying that if South Vietnam were overrun by the Communists, the world would consider communism the wave of the future. But he did not quite commit himself to Rusk's formula—that the United States should stay in Vietnam until the war was won.

On September 12, Senator Frank Church proposed withdrawing U.S. aid and personnel from South Vietnam if the government continued its "cruel repressions" of the Buddhists. At a news conference the same day, President Kennedy indicated that he did not favor withdrawing American aid. But he added that he and Senator Church were in agreement in wanting to see U.S. aid used as effectively as possible. By this time, the President had reduced his policy to a simple formula: "What helps to win the war we support; what interferes with the war effort we oppose."

In President Kennedy's private messages to Ambassador Lodge during September and October, he urged the adoption of a position of "surveillance and readiness," which included making contact with alternate leadership. However, Lodge was *not* to actively promote a coup. Moreover, he should do everything in his power to insure that the U.S. government would be able to deny involvement in either a successful or an unsuccessful coup. The White House wanted to be kept closely informed of developments so that it would be able to withdraw U.S. support from any plan that seemed likely to fail.

Lodge in Saigon

Ambassador Lodge was much more certain than the administration leaders in Washington that a coup was inevitable, and his messages show that he was impatient to have the action begin.[3] He probably believed that any type of regime which emerged after Diem's overthrow would be more receptive to U.S. advice than the existing government and would stand a better chance of achieving the results desired by the United States. Lodge strongly urged the administration not to discourage the generals from carrying out their coup plans. In fact, he doubted that the coup could be stopped. And while he promised to keep the President fully informed of developments, he warned that it might prove impossible to control such a delicate situation from Washington.

Lodge said that there was no point in going to Diem and repeating the U.S. government's position when Diem understood it perfectly well and had thus far chosen to ignore it. On October 5, President Kennedy gave Lodge the power to make selective cuts in the U.S. aid program, and these pressures began shortly afterward. But Diem showed no sign of yielding. As a consequence, Diem and Lodge did not see each other between October 2 and October 27.

At the latter meeting, Diem asked Lodge about the suspension of American aid. Lodge replied by asking about the release of arrested Buddhist and student demonstrators. When Diem offered only excuses and complaints, Lodge pointed out that he had rejected every specific suggestion for a more conciliatory policy made by the United States. When Lodge asked Diem for one conciliatory gesture to impress American public opinion, Diem gave him a blank look—as if to say "mind your own business."

Having been thrust into the breach with no previous background in Asia, Lodge could not provide what administration leaders in Washington needed most (whether they knew it or not)—a clear, dispassionate analysis of the various alternatives the United States faced—including deeper involvement with or without Diem or gradual or rapid disengagement. Lodge had been sent out to "get results." Both he and administration leaders interpreted this to mean making Diem agree with their viewpoint or finding a successor to Diem. Thus, Lodge and senior officials in Washington focused on the immediate question of Diem's fate so completely that they failed to come to grips with the fact that U.S. policy—for nine years based on keeping him in office—had reached a dead end.

There were constant press reports of friction between Lodge and the U.S. generals and CIA leaders in Saigon. General Harkins, chief of the U.S. military mission, was repelled by the thought of abandoning Diem to his enemies after working closely with him for so many years. Harkins also feared that a coup would be harmful to the war effort. But the reports of inter-agency conflict were often inaccurate and greatly exaggerated. Everyone in Saigon knew that Lodge was in charge of the

U.S. Mission. And whether they liked the fact or not, American officials there obeyed orders.

The "Great Debate" in Washington

In Washington, however, a far more significant split occurred between top Presidential advisors. Instead of reducing its objectives to fit its means, the administration was struggling to find the right combination of military, economic, and psychological programs to counter the Communist challenge. State Department and White House officials agreed that political considerations should play the leading role in an effective "counterinsurgency" strategy. The Joint Chiefs of Staff viewed counterinsurgency as essentially a military problem.

Fact-finding missions were an important tactical device used by all of the contestants in Washington's tense bureaucratic struggle over Vietnam policy. Saigon was a grueling, fifty-two hour round-trip jet journey from Washington, and it was rarely possible for an exhausted traveler to learn much from a quick visit there. But he was usually assured a top-level hearing when he returned to Washington. Thus, a never-ending procession of fact-finders came and went, placing an enormous burden on the U.S. Mission in Saigon. Their reports were written on the return journey from Saigon (or, in some cases, *before* the journey to Saigon, in anticipation of what they would discover).

Following a particularly stormy NSC meeting in September 1963, Secretary McNamara ordered Marine General Krulak to be on a plane for Saigon in one hour. The State Department decided to send Joseph Mendenhall, a foreign service officer who had served in Vietnam. They were ordered to get the latest "assessment" of the situation and report back to Washington in four days—including travel time!

General Krulak talked with a large number of American military advisors, sometimes in the presence of their commanding officer, General Harkins. To a man, they supported the Pentagon view that the war was going well in spite of the Saigon regime's preoccupation with the Buddhist crisis.

Mendenhall talked with Vietnamese acquaintances in the major cities of Vietnam, who generally agreed with him that educated urban Vietnamese were more anxious to be rid of Diem than to fight the Viet Cong.

Krulak and Mendenhall returned to Washington in the same plane, speaking to each other only when absolutely necessary, and spending every waking moment polishing their reports for the NSC. Mendenhall brought with him the American advisor to the strategic hamlet program and John Mecklin, chief of the U.S. Information Service in South Vietnam. Mecklin was appalled by the fact that everyone in Washington seemed to be lobbying hard for his own Vietnam policy and that no one was paying any attention to what anyone else said. Indeed after listening to Krulak and Mendenhall's totally contradictory impressions, President Kennedy asked, "Were you two gentlemen in the same country?"[4]

McNamara's October 1963 Visit

To help resolve the conflict, Secretary McNamara proposed that he and General Taylor make yet another high-level fact-finding trip to Saigon. President Kennedy agreed, and after an intensive survey of the situation, including several field trips to combat areas, they delivered a report to the President which tried to reconcile the contradictory impressions brought back by the Krulak-Mendenhall mission.

The McNamara-Taylor report indicated that the "military campaign had made great progress and continues to progress." It also acknowledged that there were "serious political tensions in Saigon (and perhaps elsewhere in South Vietnam) where the Diem-Nhu government is becoming increasingly unpopular."[5] The report recommended that the United States "work with the Diem government but not support it." The rationale offered for this puzzling recommendation was that "effective performance in the conduct of the war" was the main U.S. interest in Vietnam.

President Kennedy approved the main military recommendation of the report. General Harkins was instructed to take up with Diem a list of internal changes aimed at winding up the military campaign in the northern and central areas of South Vietnam by the end of 1964 and in the Mekong delta by the end of 1965. The main political recommendations, also approved, were to withhold economic aid funds and stop payment for the Vietnamese Special Forces until these troops were used to fight the Viet Cong. Meanwhile, Ambassador Lodge was instructed to maintain "correct" relations with Diem; the rest of the

U.S. Mission was told to maintain necessary contacts with their South Vietnamese counterparts to keep them supplied with advice on the conduct of the war.

On Secretary McNamara's strong recommendation, President Kennedy also released a statement on October 2—one of many that were issued during the decade of the 1960s in order to reassure the American people about the Pentagon's conduct of the war. (Such statements were usually designed to counteract news of some new disaster that had befallen our Saigon allies.) On this occasion, the President declared that the military program had made progress and that Secretary McNamara and General Taylor believed that 1000 U.S. troops could be withdrawn by the end of 1963, while "the major part of the United States military task can be completed by the end of 1965."

The Generals' Coup Is On Again

On October 2, the same day that McNamara and Taylor delivered their report to President Kennedy, the Vietnamese generals told a CIA agent in Saigon that they were again planning to move ahead with the coup. Three days later, the American agent received a more detailed account of the coup plans from General Duong Van Minh, the leader. The generals had said earlier that they would regard a cutoff of U.S. aid to Diem as sufficient proof that the United States would not betray their plans. Once it became known that the United States was cutting back its aid program, people would automatically assume that Washington had decided to support a coup.

On October 5, the CIA station chief, John Richardson, was recalled from South Vietnam at the request of Ambassador Lodge. Although Richardson may have had private doubts about the course of action which Lodge and the administration were following, he cooperated fully with their effort to persuade Diem to get rid of Nhu. Nevertheless, the only way to prove to the Nhus and to the Vietnamese generals that the United States had ended its policy of unquestioning support of the Diem regime was to recall Richardson, who had worked closely with Nhu for several years.

On October 24, one of the Vietnamese generals finally passed the word to the U.S. Mission that, after several delays, their plans were firm at last and the coup would take place before November 2. He would not give any more detail except to say that U.S. officials would receive some warning and that the coup leaders were counting on the U.S. not to obstruct their plans. Lodge, who had been scheduled to return to Washington for consultations on October 31, decided against doing so when he heard that General Harkins would be in charge of the U.S. Mission during his absence.

The Events of November 1 and 2

On the morning of November 1, Lodge took the commander in chief of U.S. forces in the Pacific to make a previously scheduled courtesy call on Diem. At one point in the meeting, Diem made light of rumors that a coup was being planned, and his visitors revealed nothing. Whether Diem suspected the end was near is impossible to say; he had been living in the shadow of real or imagined coups for over nine years. At the end of the meeting, he told Lodge privately that he wanted to talk to him sometime about the various actions which the U.S. government wanted him to take.

At 1:30 P.M. that same afternoon, a large number of Vietnamese army troops began moving through the streets of Saigon. At 1:45 P.M., General Tran Van Don telephoned General Harkins' deputy and told him that a coup was under way and that all of the Vietnamese generals were together at the Joint General Staff Headquarters. Colonel Conein, the CIA agent in contact with the coup leaders from the start, was allowed to enter the headquarters building and to keep the American Embassy informed of developments by telephone. The Embassy, in turn, relayed the news to Washington by short wave radio.

After troops had occupied key positions throughout the city, the generals called President Diem's palace and asked Diem and Nhu to surrender. One by one, each general spoke to Diem to convince him of their unanimous opposition. Instead of surrendering, Diem invited the generals to the palace to discuss the situation. They refused, recognizing the tactic Diem had used during an earlier attempted coup to gain time for loyal forces to reach Saigon.

Diem called Ambassador Lodge at the American Embassy at 4:30 P.M., Saigon time, and their conversation was recorded by the Embassy:[6]

Diem: Some units have made a rebellion, and I want to know the attitude of the U.S.?

Lodge: I do not feel well enough informed to be able to tell you. I have heard the shooting, but am not acquainted with all the facts. Also it is 4:30 A.M. in Washington and the U.S. Government cannot possibly have a view.

Diem: But you must have general ideas. After all, I am a chief of state. I have tried to do my duty. I want to do now what duty and good sense require. I believe in duty above all.

Lodge: You have certainly done your duty. As I told you only this morning, I admire your courage and your great contributions to your country. No one can take away from you the credit for all you have done. Now I am worried about your physical safety. I have a report that those in charge of the current activity offer you and your brother safe conduct out of the country if you resign. Had you heard this?

Diem: No. (And then after a pause) You have my telephone number.

Lodge: Yes. If I can do anything for your physical safety, please call me.

Diem: I am trying to re-establish order.

The generals called the palace twice more during the next hour, but they failed to persuade Diem and Nhu to surrender. The two brothers spent much of the night calling different command posts around the country, in an unsuccessful effort to rally support. On November 2, when the attack on the palace began, they escaped by way of an underground tunnel sometime before 3:30 A.M.. At first, they hid in the home of a Chinese friend. When this hiding place was discovered, they fled to a nearby Catholic church. At dawn, Diem told the coup leaders on the telephone that he would accept their offer of safe conduct to the airport to leave the country. Diem and Nhu were picked up by army troops and were shot to death in an armored personnel carrier taking them to the Joint General Staff Headquarters.

Although the American government was not directly responsible for the murders of Diem and Nhu, it was deeply implicated in the plot to overthrow their regime. After nine years of almost blind devotion to the cause of keeping Diem in power, this sudden switch revealed the emptiness of U.S. policy. No abrupt changes were made, however. During the final weeks of the Kennedy administration, the main emphasis was on moving ahead with the war effort and on doing "business as usual" with the new military leaders in Saigon.

The Kennedy administration failed to find any solution to Vietnam's problems, perhaps because there were no answers that could be imposed by outsiders. Failure to achieve the impossible is not tragic—especially if it leads to greater understanding of what can be attained. The real tragedy of the Kennedy administration's failure in Vietnam is that the Johnson administration learned nothing from it.

Notes

1. Minutes of the August 31, 1963 National Security Council meeting, prepared by Major General Victor H. Krulak (special assistant to the Joint Chiefs of Staff), are included in *Pentagon Papers*, pp. 202-05.

2. Words in quotes are from General Krulak's minutes of the meeting.

3. *Pentagon Papers* pp. 158-233, contain excerpts or the full texts of a number of Ambassador Lodge's cables from Saigon.

4. Mecklin, *Mission in Torment*, pp. 207-211.

5. Excerpts from the report submitted to the President by McNamara and Taylor on October 2, 1963 are included in *Pentagon Papers*, pp. 210-213.

6. The U.S. Embassy's transcript of the conversation is reproduced in *Pentagon Papers*, p. 232.

CHAPTER TEN

LBJ
at the Helm

On November 22, 1963, President Kennedy was assassinated. With no warning, Vice-President Lyndon Johnson found himself presiding over one of the most difficult transitions of authority in U.S. history. His first task was to convey to the American people and to friends and potential enemies abroad a sense of steady, humane, and constructive purpose in U.S. policy, to ease the pain of tragedy and violence. In this, he was largely successful. The wheels of government continued to turn smoothly enough, aided by the practiced teamwork of the professional bureaucracy and a large number of Kennedy administration holdovers.

Apart from President Johnson's inner circle of advisors, few people suspected, during his first year in office, that there were basic differences in the way he and his predecessor viewed the U.S. role in Indochina. Only a handful of government officials had read Johnson's report on his 1961 trip to Vietnam, and even fewer knew that Johnson had expressed himself on Vietnam policy at an NSC meeting less than three months before Kennedy's assassination.

Johnson was completely unlike the eastern Ivy League stereotype of a foreign policy specialist. His folksy style, mediocre education, and long immersion in domestic politics caused many people to assume that he was relying on the advice of Rusk, McGeorge Bundy, and other seasoned specialists in foreign affairs. Johnson himself deliberately cultivated the impression that he was following well-established national objectives. But the senior officials of his administration soon realized that Johnson had very definite views on Indochina. Some of them adjusted to the new chief's outlook; others sooner or later returned to private life.[1]

On November 26, 1963, (five days after John Kennedy's death), the new President issued a secret memorandum with which he undoubtedly meant to place his personal stamp on Indochina policy.[2] The purpose of U.S. involvement in Vietnam, he said, was to assist "the people and government of that country to win their contest against the externally directed and supported Communist conspiracy." (This emphasis on "winning" in Vietnam, which seemed so completely natural and "American" to military officers and Senators of Johnson's generation, had very little in common with the more arcane efforts of Kennedy administration officials to "signal" political messages to Moscow by the movement of U.S. forces in or near Indochina.) Johnson's memorandum also stressed another theme that was to become familiar—the need for full support of existing policy by all U.S. officials particularly in their contacts with the press and foreign governments.

The memorandum ended by stating flatly that it was a "major interest of the United States government" to help the Saigon military junta consolidate its political position. For this purpose, Johnson requested that plans be prepared for clandestine warfare by the Saigon regime against North Vietnam and in the southern border areas of Laos. (This was a hint to U.S. military commanders in Saigon and Washington that the "political constraints" imposed by the previous administration would be somewhat relaxed.) The State Department was directed to support these efforts by producing a white paper to prove that the Viet Cong relied completely on Hanoi's guidance and material support. The assignment was typical of the sort of supporting role the State Department would be expected to play throughout the Johnson administration.

McNamara's New Assessment of the Situation

Secretary McNamara visited South Vietnam about a month after President Kennedy's assassination and found the situation far worse than it had seemed during his previous visit in October.[3] Unless "current trends" were reversed in two to three months, McNamara predicted, South Vietnam would turn neutral or fall under Communist control. The main problems, according to McNamara, were poor leadership by the new military junta in Saigon and ineffective coordination of the U.S. programs by Ambassador Lodge. McNamara also reported that 1000 to 1500 Viet Cong had infiltrated South Vietnam during the first nine months of 1963. He said they had made much greater gains during the year than he or other Pentagon officials had previously realized; he attributed his error to "distorted Vietnamese reporting" and proposed creating an independent American intelligence network by greatly increasing the number of U.S. military and civilian advisors. Although McNamara opposed cross-border operations into Laos, he reviewed plans for covert (unacknowledged) military pressures against North Vietnam and pronounced these "excellent."

An important reason for McNamara's visit was to emphasize that the Johnson administration strongly opposed a neutralist solution in South Vietnam. Antiwar sentiment had surfaced after the assassination of Diem and Nhu, and on November 17, 1963, Radio Hanoi broadcast a statement by the NLF which proposed that

> the parties concerned in South Vietnam negotiate with one another to reach a cease-fire and solve important problems of the nation, to stabilize the basic internal and external policies, with a view to reaching free general elections to elect state organs and to form a national coalition government composed of representatives of all forces, parties, tendencies, and strata of the South Vietnamese people.[4]

McNamara and General Duong Van Minh, the Saigon junta leader, exchanged promises to oppose the neutralization of Vietnam.

(McNamara also told Minh "in somewhat more general terms" that the United States was not willing to see this happen in Cambodia.) On McNamara's recommendation, President Johnson sent Minh a New Year's message, which said that as long as the Communist regime in North Vietnam persisted in its "aggressive policy,"

> neutralization would only be another name for a Communist take-over. . . . The United States will continue to furnish you and your people with the fullest measure of support in this bitter fight. . . . We shall maintain in Vietnam American personnel and material as needed to assist you in achieving victory.

On January 30, 1964, General Nguyen Khanh overthrew Minh's government claiming that he had acted because Minh was not strong-willed enough to halt the country's drift toward neutralism. Again, the NLF called for a negotiated end to the war, but Khanh said he was aligning himself firmly with the United States. Washington was dismayed by Minh's overthrow, but it lost no time in announcing that it would recognize and work with Khanh's regime. During the next year, there were almost monthly changes of government in which the armed forces played the main role. Khanh was involved in each of these regimes, although his influence diminished steadily.

It became commonplace for political generals (and civilian politicians supported by the military) to accuse their rivals of "neutralism" in the hope of depriving them of American backing. When it became apparent to the South Vietnamese people, particularly the Buddhists and students, that none of these short-lived regimes would fight corruption, implement land reform, or seek an end to the war through compromise, the euphoria that greeted the overthrow of Diem and Nhu evaporated.

Covert Attacks Begin

In February 1964, the U.S. and South Vietnamese governments began to execute the plans for covert military pressures against North Vietnam which had been ordered by Johnson in November and endorsed by McNamara in December 1963. At the outset, the attacks were to be on a scale that would merely harass the North Vietnamese regime by demonstrating that American and South Vietnamese forces could carry the war into their country. But the scale of the attacks was supposed to increase steadily until, by the end of 1964, targets "identified with North Vietnam's economic and industrial well-being" would be hit.[5] The program of attacks included small-scale commando raids and sabotage missions along the coast of North Vietnam, air operations over Laos, and destroyer patrols in the Tonkin Gulf.

On February 21, 1964, shortly after the covert attacks began, President Johnson delivered a speech in Los Angeles in which he warned those engaged in "external direction and supply" of the Communists fighting in South Vietnam that "this type of aggression is a deeply dangerous game." On February 24, the Defense Department announced that Secretary McNamara would visit South Vietnam again to assess the military situation; the announcement indicated that he would also hear suggestions for expanding the war effort.

Meanwhile, General Maxwell Taylor, Walt Rostow, and other leading figures in the administration were secretly urging that the United States bomb North Vietnam's "industrial complex" as a rapid means of winning the war.[6] There were flaws in their reasoning that were as obvious then as they would be later on. First, proponents of the bombing strategy somehow assumed that it would not produce many civilian casualties. Second, they ignored the fact that non-nuclear bombing did not cause the defeat of Great Britain, Germany, or Japan, during World War II. Third, they failed to take note of the fact that North Vietnam had almost no targets for strategic bombing, being a largely agrarian society. Fourth, they assumed that the aim of preventing the Saigon regime from being overrun by its enemies was so important to the United States that it was worth trying even such a brutal and unlikely means to achieve it. Fifth, many proponents of bombing North Vietnam assumed that the action would be regarded as heroic (or at least fully justified) by world public opinion. Finally, the concept of bombing the North into submission implied that the Hanoi regime was not willing to pay a high price to achieve its aims in South Vietnam, while the American people would make whatever sacrifice (in terms of men, money, or world prestige) their government told them it needed.

U.S. Contingency Planning for Expanded War

The Johnson administration saw no way of halting the rapid disintegration of Saigon's political and military position except by large-scale

U.S. intervention in the war. However, Johnson was unwilling to move openly in that direction until after the November 1964 election. Meanwhile, there was always hope that the situation would right itself before the end of the year, and that U.S. intervention would not be necessary. Thus, the spring of 1964 was a time for secret planning and debate within the small group of administration officials who had begun to call themselves the "Vietnam principals," because they were the only people allowed to see the main U.S. policy papers on Vietnam.[7]

In March 1964, on the advice of Secretary McNamara, President Johnson ordered the Defense and State Departments to prepare contingency plans for greatly increased U.S. involvement in the Vietnam war, including sustained bombing north of the seventeenth parallel. By May, a detailed "scenario" had been written, listing major political and military steps required to Americanize the war. Appended to the scenario was the draft of a joint congressional resolution similar to the one which Congress would be asked to adopt ten weeks later at the time of the Tonkin Gulf crisis.[8]

The Atmosphere Grows More Tense

By June 1964, the continued disintegration of the Saigon regime's position caused some leading American officials to start dropping public hints about direct U.S. intervention. In a background news briefing on June 19, Secretary Rusk told newsmen that if Communist aggression did not cease in Southeast Asia, China and North Vietnam might find themselves at war with the United States. The following day the Commander in chief of U.S. forces in the Pacific said publicly that the United States was willing to risk war with China but he doubted if the reverse was true.

On July 19, a few days after the Republicans chose Barry Goldwater as their Presidential nominee, Premier Khanh delivered a major speech in Saigon on the theme of *bac tien*—"march north." Khanh apparently saw hope for a more aggressive policy in Goldwater's nomination; he also needed to divert his people's attention from the poor performance of his own regime. Air Vice Marshal Nguyen Cao Ky went even further, threatening publicly to bomb Hanoi. Ky received a private reprimand from General Maxwell Taylor, who had just replaced Lodge as American Ambassador in Saigon.

However, on July 25, Taylor cabled Washington recommending that the United States avoid expressing unqualified opposition to the Saigon regime's "march north" campaign. He suggested that the United States begin joint contingency planning with Khanh's generals to allow them to let off steam and to force them to think more realistically about the problems involved in attacking North Vietnam. Joint contingency planning would also gain time to stabilize the regime, and it would provide a useful basis for future military action, if that course were adopted.[9]

Meanwhile on July 8, UN Secretary-General U Thant had strongly urged that the Geneva conference be reconvened to seek a political solution to the conflict. On July 23, President de Gaulle of France supported U Thant's initiative, calling for a return to the 1954 Geneva agreements and stressing that this meant no foreign intervention in Indochina. In a surprising show of unanimity (in view of the tense state of Sino-Soviet relations at the time), the Russian, Chinese, and North Vietnamese governments all issued statements supporting a new Geneva conference. France, Russia, and North Vietnam also sent individual messages to the nations that had taken part in the 1961-62 Geneva conference.

On July 24, President Johnson rejected de Gaulle's proposal with the brusque phrase "we do not believe in conferences called to ratify terror. . . ." Johnson also chose this moment to increase the U.S. military mission in South Vietnam from 16,000 to 21,000 men. One of his reasons for publicly adopting a more intransigent attitude was undoubtedly to avoid giving Senator Goldwater an opening to attack his policy from the right.

In addition to all of these signs that the United States might be considering more direct involvement in the war, there was also the steadily increasing program of covert pressures which had begun four months earlier. Peking Radio probably reflected the Chinese leaders' uneasiness in its constant warnings of impending U.S. "aggression" during the last days of July. It is quite possible that the North Vietnamese, Chinese, and other well-informed governments suspected these small-scale, unacknowledged attacks might be a prelude to much more serious U.S. intervention.

It will be recalled that the United States had begun using covert pressures—commando raids, air attacks, and patrols by U.S. destroyers in the Tonkin Gulf. Commando raids and sabotage missions were carried out by specially trained South Vietnamese personnel (and perhaps people of other nationalities). The air attacks were carried out by planes with Royal Lao Air Force markings, flown by American and Thai as well as Lao pilots against Pathet Lao and North Vietnamese installations in Laos.

The destroyer operations, code-named "DeSoto" patrols, were intended mainly as a show of force. The U.S. government claimed publicly that their purpose was to prevent infiltration of Communist troops and equipment by sea into South Vietnam. An apparently secondary aspect of their mission was to collect intelligence data on North Vietnamese radar and other shore installations. In light of events that took place during the next few days, a major controversy has centered on whether or not they were used deliberately to provoke an attack by North Vietnamese forces which would provide an excuse for U.S. intervention in the war.

Notes

1. Assistant Secretary of State Roger Hilsman delivered a speech on China policy a few days after President Kennedy's assassination (although it was written before that event). The speech was designed to test the political climate in the United States for abandoning the China containment policy. It might have served as a step toward disengagement from Vietnam. This episode partly explains why Johnson and Rusk decided to replace Hilsman with William Bundy a few weeks later.

2. Excerpts from National Security Action Memorandum 273, November 26, 1963, are included in *Pentagon Papers*, pp. 232-33.

3. For the text of Secretary McNamara's December 21, 1963 report on his visit, see *Pentagon Papers*, pp. 271-74.

4. Excerpts from the NLF statement (dated November 8, 1963) appear in Kahin and Lewis, *The United States in Vietnam*, pp. 399-402.

5. *Pentagon Papers*, p. 238, cites a January 2, 1964 report to the President by General Victor Krulak, special assistant to the JCS.

6. See Walt Rostow memo dated November 24, 1963 entitled "Some Observations as We Come to the Crunch in Southeast Asia," *Pentagon Papers*, pp. 419-23.

7. The group included the President, Special Assistant for National Security McGeorge Bundy (later succeeded by Walt Rostow), Secretary of State Rusk,

Undersecretary Ball, Assistant Secretary for Far Eastern Affairs William Bundy, Secretary of Defense McNamara, Assistant Secretary for International Security Affairs McNaughton, CIA Director McCone (later succeeded by Richard Helms), chairman of the Joint Chiefs of Staff Maxwell Taylor (succeeded by General Earle Wheeler), plus the American Ambassador and the U.S. military commander in Saigon. This group of "principals" was sometimes expanded or contracted in particular situations.

8. For a description of this contingency planning exercise and excerpts from many of the planning documents, see *Pentagon Papers*, pp. 234-306.

9. The text of General Taylor's July 25, 1964, cable to Washington appears on pp. 288-89 of *Pentagon Papers*.

CHAPTER ELEVEN

The Tonkin Gulf Incidents

During the night of July 30-31, South Vietnamese vessels bombarded two islands off North Vietnam—Hon Ngu (near the port of Vinh) and Hon Me, about thirty miles to the north. This was one of a series of commando operations, code-named "34-A," which were run by the U.S. Military Assistance Command in Vietnam. The next morning, July 31, the U.S. Navy destroyer *Maddox* arrived at the mouth of the Tonkin Gulf to begin the second "DeSoto" patrol of the year. (In denying, later, that these patrols were part of a coordinated effort to provoke a North Vietnamese attack, Defense Department officials pointed out that the *Maddox* was at least 120 miles from the scene of the 34-A attack when it took place on the night of July 30.) Captain John Herrick, who was in charge of this one-destroyer task force, and other officers on board the *Maddox* knew very little about the 34-A operations, including the one that had just taken place. They had been ordered to keep their ship away from a specific area where more 34-A operations would occur during the six days that the *Maddox* was scheduled to patrol the Tonkin Gulf.

The *Maddox* had on board a special communications unit equipped to intercept radio transmissions. American personnel who could speak Vietnamese were assigned to this unit. As the *Maddox* moved up the North Vietnamese coast on July 31, they heard much excited message traffic indicating that the North Vietnamese forces had been stirred up by the recent 34-A attack. The ship's electronic gear also told Captain Herrick that the North Vietnamese were tracking the *Maddox* by radar. Following his prescribed route, Captain Herrick kept the *Maddox* moving generally northward, looping around from time to time and approaching within eight miles of the North Vietnamese coast and within four miles of North Vietnamese islands (to show that the United States recognized only the traditional three mile limit of territorial waters, not twelve miles, as claimed by the DRV).

Meanwhile, the U.S. aircraft carrier *Ticonderoga* was stationed near the mouth of the Tonkin Gulf, and land-based fighter-bombers stepped up their attacks over Laos. There are indications that, on August 1, they accidentally bombed and strafed a North Vietnamese border post.[1] Hanoi leaders said later that they regarded this concentration of U.S. and South Vietnamese pressures as a "most serious step forward" in their efforts to intimidate the DRV. Even though the *Maddox* had been ordered to steer clear of the areas chosen for the 34-A attacks while they were occurring, it was ordered to patrol around these areas shortly afterward. Thus, it is hardly surprising that the DRV thought the commando raids and DeSoto patrols were part of a coordinated U.S. program, and there is considerable evidence to show that the United States government hoped Hanoi would reach just that conclusion.[2]

During the night of August 1, Captain Herrick suspected the possibility of an ambush by North Vietnamese craft and took the *Maddox* out into the middle of the Gulf. (His ship's communications unit was picking up messages to North Vietnamese PT boats in the area telling them to get ready for action.) Early in the morning of August 2, Captain Herrick sent two messages to his fleet commander, with copies to the Joint Chiefs of Staff in Washington. The first message said that he had indications of "possible hostile action" by the North Vietnamese. The second message said bluntly that he thought continuing the patrol presented an "unacceptable risk." A reply from the admiral commanding the U.S. Seventh Fleet authorized him to deviate from his route whenever he felt the risk was unacceptable, but ordered him to return to the prescribed course as soon as he considered it safe to do so. Thus, later in the morning of August 2, the *Maddox* was back on its patrol course, ten miles from the coast of North Vietnam.

Shortly after noon, three Soviet-made torpedo boats came out of the mouth of a river and disappeared behind Hon Me island (where the 34-A attack had occurred). On the *Maddox*, the communications unit intercepted a message ordering the PT boats to attack the U.S. destroyer as soon as they had refueled. Almost immediately, the PT boats came out from around the island. the *Maddox* put on speed and headed for the mouth of the Tonkin Gulf; she reached her maximum speed of thirty knots, but the PT boats, moving at fifty knots, began to close in rapidly. Herrick sent a message to the Pacific command describing the situation and saying he intended to open fire in self-defense if necessary. He also requested air cover from the *Ticonderoga*.

When the PT boats were five miles off, the *Maddox* fired two shots. There is some question about whether these were warning shots or aimed right at the torpedo boats. But the intercepted attack order and the fact that the boats had pursued the *Maddox* far out into the Gulf made it seem likely that they would fire their torpedos as soon as they were in position to do so.

As the PT boats came in at an angle from starboard, the *Maddox* opened fire with its five-inch guns; two of the boats fired one torpedo each when they were about a mile and half away. Both torpedos missed the Maddox, whose guns stopped the third boat dead in the water as it fired on the *Maddox* at a distance of about one mile. At this point, three jets from the *Ticonderoga* arrived and the remaining two PT boats were both damaged, either by rockets from the jets or the guns of the *Maddox*. Since one of the planes appeared to have been hit, the *Maddox* followed it back toward the mouth of the Gulf, where the destroyer was ordered to withdraw from the Gulf entirely.

On August 3, President Johnson ordered the *Maddox* reinforced by the destroyer *C. Turner Joy* and sent them back into the Gulf with orders not to approach closer than eleven nautical miles from the North Vietnamese coast. A second aircraft carrier, the *Constellation*, was ordered to join the *Ticonderoga* as quickly as possible. According to President Johnson, reinforcing the patrol would show that the United States was "determined not to be provocative, nor were we going to run away."[3] But during the night of August 3, while the two destroyers were sailing back into the Gulf, two more 34-A attacks were carried out by South Vietnamese PT boats. This was done with the knowledge of the destroyers' commanders, who changed course in order to steer clear of the areas where the attacks were taking place.

Although both sides agreed that DRV torpedo boats deliberately engaged the *Maddox* on August 2, there is no agreement about the incident that is alleged to have taken place on August 4. According to officials of the U.S. Defense Department, DRV torpedo boats launched a second attack against both the *Maddox* and *Turner Joy* during the night of August 4, about twenty-four hours after the second group of 34-A raids and at a time when the two destroyers were sixty-five miles from shore. Neither destroyer suffered any casualties or damage, and they drove off the attacking PT boats, possibly destroying two of them.[4] The Hanoi government has denied that any attack took place.

During the night of August 4, clouds covered the sky over the Tonkin Gulf. There was a high wind and thunderstorms were near the area where the U.S. ships were patrolling. On board the *Maddox* and *Turner Joy*, experienced seamen could see their own ships' wakes for only 100 yards or less. However, between the hours of 8 P.M. and midnight, they saw and heard things that convinced most of the officers and men that another PT boat attack was occurring.

The radar screen of the *Maddox* (but not that of the *Turner Joy*) showed "blips" that appeared to be small craft pursuing the two destroyers. When these seemed to be 4000 yards away, the *Turner Joy* opened fire at the rate of 30 rounds a minute. The *Maddox* fired star shells which burst above the low clouds and failed to light up the darkness around the destroyers. (At one point, the *Turner Joy* was nearly blasted out of the water by gunners on the *Maddox* when the *Joy* appeared on her sister ship's radar.)

Officers and men on the two ships also saw what seemed to be torpedo wakes in the water, and an astonishing total of twenty-two "torpedo noises" were heard by the sonarman on the *Maddox* during the course of the evening. Some observers also reported seeing such objects as a signal light, cockpit lights, and a column of black smoke. Visibility was so poor that men looking in the same direction at the same time often disagreed about what they saw, but all of this evidence of an attack was radioed to Washington while the incident was taking place.

Around midnight, the blips on the radar screen disappeared, and the ships stopped firing their guns. About this time, the communications unit on the *Maddox* intercepted a North Vietnamese message, which confirmed Captain Herrick's belief that North Vietnamese boats had attacked his ships and that two of them had been sunk. However, the officers of the *Maddox* also discovered the cause of most of the "torpedo" noises which they had reported to Washington during the evening: the sound of the *Maddox's* propellor had been reflecting off the rudder as the ship zigzagged to and fro to evade possible attackers. Nevertheless, Captain Herrick remained convinced that the early radar contacts with enemy boats were genuine and that at least two torpedoes had been fired at his destroyers. However, fearing that the radio messages he had sent during the heat of the incident gave a distorted impression, he sent the following message at about one o'clock in the morning of August 5:[5]

Review of action makes many reported contacts and torpedoes fired appear doubtful. Freak weather effects and overeager sonarman may have accounted for many reports. No actual visual sightings by *Maddox*. Suggest complete evaluation before any further action.

By the time Washington learned of this uncertainty about the validity of the August 4 incident, plans were already well advanced for U.S. retaliation. The Pentagon had received word that intercepted DRV radio messages indicated preparations for an attack on the U.S. destroyers at 9:30 A.M., August 4. A message from the U.S. destroyers reporting that the attack was actually under way reached Washington at about 11 A.M. (It was twelve hours earlier in Washington than in the Tonkin Gulf.)

Within minutes, McNamara was discussing the subject of retaliation with the Joint Chiefs, and they were quickly joined by Rusk and William Bundy from the State Department. At about 11:30, McNamara, Rusk, and Bundy left for an NSC meeting at the White House. There they recommended reprisal strikes to the President. While the President and his top advisors were at lunch, the director of the Joint Staff phoned McNamara to report that the reprisal targets had been chosen—four torpedo boat bases and an oil storage depot near Vinh, which held 10 percent of North Vietnam's oil supply.

At a second NSC meeting that afternoon, President Johnson ordered the reprisals and decided to ask Congress to pass a joint resolution giving him very broad powers to respond to Communist aggression in Southeast Asia. He also discussed with his advisors the deployment of U.S. forces to the region in preparation for a possible later bombing campaign against the DRV. (Contingency plans for this deployment, known as Operation Plan 37-64, had been approved by the Joint Chiefs in April.) President Johnson probably ordered the deployment of air force units later in the day, while army and marine units were instructed to be prepared to meet any Chinese or DRV retaliation for the bombing.

It was not until 4 P.M. that Secretary McNamara learned from Admiral Sharp at Honolulu of the doubt that existed about the second DRV attack. McNamara told Sharp that the reprisal order would remain in effect, but before launching the strikes the Admiral was to check and be certain that the attack had taken place. The order to execute the reprisal was sent to Honolulu at 4:49 P.M. (Washington time), before Admiral Sharp confirmed the validity of the attack. The planes which would carry out the punitive strike were ordered to take off from their carriers within two and a half hours. This would allow them to be over their targets at about 8:30 P.M., Washington time, when President Johnson wanted to make his announcement to the large East Coast television audience.

At 5:23 P.M., Admiral Sharp called the Pentagon and reported that, on the basis of information from the task group commander of the two destroyers, he was satisfied that the DRV attack had taken place. McNamara and the Joint Chiefs also stated afterward that they examined evidence of the attacks around this time and reached the same conclusion.

However, a complete evaluation of the evidence, such as Captain Herrick had urged, could not possibly have been made in the limited time which the administration allowed before launching reprisals against the DRV. Between President Johnson, Secretary McNamara, Admiral Sharp, and other high officials there was an unspoken understanding that if they all claimed the evidence of a North Vietnamese attack was solid, the case for retaliation would stand.

Captain Herrick, the task group commander, was certain that some form of attack had occurred, but he and other observers on the spot were by no means certain of the details.[6] It took great courage for them to say so, because their story did not fit the political needs of the moment. President Johnson could never announce that he was bombing a country because its ships had "possibly" attacked American warships—or even because they had "probably" done so. And this would certainly have been insufficient grounds for asking Congress to give him a free hand to commit U.S. forces to a land war in Asia. The President chose to believe an "incident" had taken place on August 4, because this provided an ideal opportunity to avoid an awkward political debate over the merits of full-scale U.S. intervention.

At 6:45 P.M., President Johnson met with congressional leaders from both parties and told them that because of a second attack on American destroyers, he had decided to launch reprisal air strikes and to ask for a joint Congressional resolution. Apparently he did not tell the congressmen that the United States was responsible for the commando raids against North Vietnam which helped to provoke the August 2 attack (and the possible attack on August 4). Nor did he indicate the element of doubt surrounding the August 4 incident.[7]

At 11:30 P.M., Secretary McNamara learned, after several phone calls to Admiral Sharp, that there had been delays in the launching of the reprisal strikes, but they had gotten off at 10:43 P.M. (Washington time). They would be over their targets in just under two hours. Although he had originally planned to announce the attacks just as they were taking place, the President decided not to delay his announcement any longer. At 11:36 P.M., he went before the television cameras and stated that "Air action is now in execution against gunboats and certain supporting facilities in North Vietnam which have been used in these hostile operations" against American forces.

The Tonkin Gulf Resolution

The President also announced that he had met with the congressional leaders of both parties and told them that he would immediately ask Congress to pass a resolution "making it clear that our government is united in its determination to take all necessary measures in support of freedom and in defense of peace in Southeast Asia." The congressmen had, he said, given him "encouraging assurance" that "such a resolution will be promptly introduced, freely and expeditiously debated, and passed with overwhelming support."

In a message to Congress the next day, President Johnson asked for speed in passing what came to be known as the Tonkin Gulf Resolution, because "we are entering on three months of political campaigning. Nations must understand that in such a period the United States will continue to protect its national interests, and that in these matters there is no division among us."

The resolution was introduced by the chairmen of the Senate Foreign Relations Committee and the House Committee on Foreign Affairs. It was similar to the draft prepared three months earlier as part of the administration's contingency plan for enlarging the war. The resolution was passed by a vote of 466-0 in the House and 88-2 in the Senate; only Senators Morse and Gruening opposed it. The operative sections authorized the President to take "all necessary measures to repel any armed attack against the forces of the United States and to prevent further aggression." The resolution also said that the United States was prepared

> as the President determines to take all necessary steps, including the use of armed force, to assist any member or protocol state of the Southeast Asia Collective Defense Treaty requesting assistance in defense of its freedom.

Thus, the administration made use of a crisis atmosphere, partly generated by its own covert war measures against North Vietnam, to obtain a broad grant of authority from Congress to make war in Southeast Asia whenever it saw fit. Congress and the American people were led to believe that the administration was seeking a moderate solution to the Vietnam problem when, in fact, it was carefully preparing to involve the United States in a major war after the November election. This devious leadership gradually undermined the support of Congress and the American public for President Johnson's Indochina policy by creating grave doubts about his truthfulness on the central issue of his administration.

Notes

1. See *Pentagon Papers*, pp. 302-306.

2. American officials denied at the time that there had been any shelling of North Vietnamese islands in the Tonkin Gulf and said they had no knowledge of any air attack on a North Vietnamese village (as claimed by Radio Hanoi). But on August 3, the United States sent a note to the Hanoi government, warning of the "grave consequences which would inevitably result from any further unprovoked offensive military action against United States forces." See Anthony Austin, *The President's War* (Philadelphia: Lippincott, 1971).

3. Johnson, *Vantage Point*, p. 112.

4. *Hearings Before the Committee on Foreign Relations, United States Senate, 90th Congress, Second Session (The Gulf of Tonkin, the 1964 Incidents)*, February 20, 1968 (Washington, D.C.: U.S. Government Printing Office, 1968).

5. Ibid., p. 54.

6. The main conclusion that has emerged from intensive studies of the alleged incident is that none of the evidence of an attack was solid enough to have justified retaliation. See Anthony Austin and Eugene G. Windchy, *Tonkin Gulf* (Garden City, New York: Doubleday, 1971).

7. See Johnson, *Vantage Point*, pp. 112-117. In this account of his August 4 decisions, Johnson seems to suggest that he was following Eisenhower's example in seeking the Tonkin Gulf resolution. Yet it was Eisenhower who refused to take the United States into the first Indochina war without a formal declaration of war.

CHAPTER TWELVE

A Secret Change of Course

The last thing Lyndon Johnson wanted was to have his domestic program sidetracked by a prolonged and unpopular war. He believed, however, that his government could not afford to let Saigon lose its struggle. This meant full-scale U.S. intervention, unless the Saigon generals managed to put their house in order and win some popular support, or unless their enemy abandoned its aim of controlling the South. Johnson and his advisors knew how slim the chances were that either of these conditions would be fulfilled. They also knew that it would be very difficult to persuade Congress and the American public to go to war to save South Vietnam— and foolhardy even to attempt such a move before the November election.

The Tonkin Gulf incident and the joint congressional

resolution greatly simplified the administration's political problems. But nevertheless, President Johnson decided to tread warily until after his expected electoral victory. The best time to use his congressional mandate for intervention would be around the start of the new year; this would allow a brief period *after* the election in which to prepare the people for another land war in Asia.

Charting the Next Moves After Tonkin Gulf

The political chaos in Saigon during the second half of 1964 was reason enough for the Johnson administration to proceed cautiously. In August, General Khanh tried and failed to make himself the dictator of South Vietnam. Demonstrations by Buddhists and students in the principal cities prevented him from achieving his aim. On August 24, an American spokesman warned that the United States would take "an extremely serious and negative view of any move to oust the regime of President Nguyen Khanh." But, if anything, this pressure only made the militant Buddhists more determined to push the Saigon government toward a neutralist position. On September 4, Khanh announced that he had accepted the Buddhists' demand that he transfer power to a civilian government within two months.

Meanwhile, at the start of the crisis, the U.S. Mission chiefs in Saigon had sent a lengthy appraisal of the situation to Washington, along with their recommendations. The most noteworthy was their proposal for "an orchestrated air attack against North Viet Nam" with January 1, 1965, "as a target D-Day." The Mission also recommended that, during the intervening four and a half months, the United States keep up pressure on North Vietnam by means of 34-A operations, DeSoto patrols, U-2 flights over North Vietnam, and air and ground strikes against infiltration routes in Laos. However, the Mission said that it did not consider reprisal strikes against North Vietnam (in response to specific Communist attacks) to be "desirable" before the start of 1965 (except in an "emergency"). But the Mission also proposed an alternative course of action in the same cable. It said that it might be desirable to begin a sustained air war against the North *immediately* to sustain the morale of the South Vietnamese people and to present international critics of a U.S. bombing policy with a fait accompli.[1]

The most obvious reason for this strange procedure of recommending two contradictory courses of action (labeled Course A and Course B) was that the Mission knew that the decision about bombing Vietnam would be made on political grounds. Thus, the Mission recommended bombing and thought it should begin no later than a few weeks after the U.S. election; and furthermore, it supplied the administration with a detailed rationale for whichever course it chose.

In a memorandum to Secretary McNamara on August 26, the Joint Chiefs of Staff took issue with the U.S. Mission in Saigon on the desirability of reprisal air attacks against North Vietnam. The Joint Chiefs argued that reprisal raids were needed to keep up the momentum begun by the August 4 retaliation strike.[2] Their disagreement with the U.S. Mission was due to the political turmoil which had begun in South Vietnam during the previous week. But it seems quite clear that the Joint Chiefs were concerned that the Mission's August 18 cable might pave the way for President Johnson to delay the start of bombing until the new year.

In Texas on August 29, President Johnson delivered a political speech in which he referred obliquely to the secret recommendations from the Joint Chiefs of Staff and from the U.S. Mission. "I have had advice," he said

... to load our planes with bombs, and to drop them on certain areas that I think would enlarge the war and escalate the war, and result in our committing a good many American boys to fighting a war that I think ought to be fought by the boys of Asia to help protect their own land. ...

[Our Vietnam policy is] to furnish advice, give counsel, express good judgment, give them trained counselors, and help them with equipment to help themselves ... we have tried very carefully to restrain ourselves and not to enlarge the war.

On September 3, Assistant Secretary of Defense McNaughton recommended to Secretary McNamara a strategy by which the DeSoto patrols, 34-A attacks, and other pressures would be used to provoke North Vietnamese attacks (such as the August 2 Tonkin Gulf incident) to give the United States an excuse for reprisal bombing. This may have been the first formal recommendation of its kind made within the administration. (As indicated in the previous chapter, U.S. officials probably did not expect the North Vietnamese to attack their destroyers, either on August 2 or on August 4.) McNaughton's September 3 proposal became known within the Johnson administration as the "provocation strategy." It amounted to doing what up to that time had been left to chance.

On September 7, an important meeting took place in Washington between Rusk, McNamara, Ambassador Taylor (who had flown home from Saigon), and General Earle Wheeler (Taylor's successor as Chairman of the Joint Chiefs). At this meeting, President Johnson's top advisers recommended *against* adopting McNaughton's provocation strategy. However, to maintain the morale of Khanh's government and the South Vietnamese people, they recommended adopting all of the interim measures (DeSoto patrols, etc.) which had been proposed by the Mission in Saigon for the remaining months of 1964. While they emphasized the need to avoid any provocation "initially" (by keeping the destroyer patrols at least twelve miles from North Vietnam's coast) they recommended reprisal strikes in case U.S. forces were attacked, as in the Tonkin Gulf incidents.

The main reason for their decision may have been a realization that the provocation strategy would undermine the President's whole effort to present himself to the electorate as the candidate of moderation and restraint. Another reason for the administration's decision to go slow at this stage may have been the fear that the Saigon regime would collapse completely if the war were suddenly intensified. Concern about upsetting the delicate situation in Laos probably also influenced the decision. And finally, Secretary Rusk and others in the administration were certainly aware that neither Congress nor the American public had been prepared for deeper U.S. involvement in the war.

Many administration officials expected, on the basis of the Korean experience, that there would be intensive pressure for negotiations from the U.S. public and from world public opinion very soon after any major escalation of the war. And the administration plainly felt that the balance of forces in Vietnam was so unfavorable to their side that negotiations would automatically produce a Communist victory. This was perhaps the main reason for concealing their plans to escalate the war. When U Thant proposed, in the early fall, that secret negotiations be held in Rangoon between the United States and North Vietnam, the United States insisted on postponing any such move until after the U.S. election.

To keep the pressure on North Vietnam, President Johnson decided to resume DeSoto destroyer patrols on September 12, and 34-A commando operations in early October. Air attacks on the infiltration routes in Laos would be carried out by South Vietnamese (and possibly by American) aircraft and pilots. But on the question of reprisal strikes against North Vietnam, Johnson retained full discretion to deal with incidents on a case-by-case basis. These orders, which he issued on September 10, postponed a decision on launching a full-scale air war against North Vietnam. The final paragraph read:

> These decisions are governed by a prevailing judgment that the first order of business at present is to take actions which will help to strengthen the fabric of the Government of South Vietnam; to the extent that the situation permits, such action should precede larger decisions. If such decisions are required at any time by a change in the situation, they will be taken.[3]

According to the Defense Department, the destroyers which entered the Tonkin Gulf on September 12, were attacked six days later forty-two miles from shore. There were no American casualties, so President Johnson rejected the Pentagon's advice that he order retaliatory strikes. Quite possibly, one reason for his action was to avoid controversy over whether or not the DeSoto patrols were "provocative," a question that some newsmen had already raised in connection with the various Tonkin Gulf incidents.

Indeed, correspondents had begun to note that members of the Johnson administration were talking openly about expanding the war. While the President was telling campaign audiences that "we don't want our American boys to do the fighting for Asian boys" or to "get tied down in a land war in Asia," Assistant Secretary Bundy during a speech in Tokyo declared:

> Expansion of the war outside South Vietnam, while not a course that we want or seek, could be forced upon us by the increased external pressures of the Communists, including the rising scale of infiltration.[4]

On October 14, Nikita Khrushchev's resignation as head of the Soviet Communist party and government was announced in Moscow.

Two days later, China extended "warm greetings" to the new Soviet leaders while announcing that it had exploded its first nuclear device. At almost the same moment, Harold Wilson became Prime Minister of Great Britain, ending thirteen years of Tory rule. Thus, within less than three days, there was a change in leadership of two of the major powers, and China joined the nuclear club.

John Kennedy or Richard Nixon might have felt that these major developments called for rethinking of U.S. aims and strategy in Indochina. But Lyndon Johnson only found it necessary to reassure the world, on October 18, that none of these events would in any way alter his Indochina policy. He also promised those "nations that do not seek national nuclear weapons" that "if they need our strong support against some threat of nuclear blackmail, then they will have it."

On November 1, (two days before the U.S. election), the Viet Cong staged a surprise raid on the U.S. air base at Bien Hoa, near Saigon, killing five Americans, wounding seventy-six, and damaging numerous aircraft. As in September, President Johnson resisted strong pressures from the Pentagon for retaliatory bombing. But with the election campaign nearly over, he appointed a secret interagency working group to draw up detailed plans for direct U.S. action against North Vietnam.

Options Chosen for President's Decision

The Vietnam interagency working group held its first meeting on November 3, the day of President Johnson's landslide victory over Barry Goldwater. Eight months earlier, Johnson had defined the minimum aim of the United States as an independent, non-Communist South Vietnam. This is probably why all of the choices produced by the working group called for indefinite U.S. involvement in the war and some form of bombing. The hard line taken by the working group may also have reflected a feeling within the administration that Johnson's overwhelming victory made it possible for him to do almost anything. The working group strongly recommended against beginning talks with the DRV until U.S. bombing of the North had made Hanoi willing to agree to the United States' minimum goals.

On November 24, Secretaries Rusk and McNamara, CIA Director McCone, General Wheeler (Chairman of the Joint Chiefs), McGeorge

Bundy (Special Assistant for National Security), and Undersecretary of State George Ball met to discuss three options which had been presented to them by the interagency working group:

Option A—Reprisal air strikes against the North whenever the Viet Cong carried out a fairly large action in South Vietnam, plus intensified 34-A operations, DeSoto destroyer patrols in the Tonkin Gulf, T-28 strikes against infiltration targets in Laos, and U.S. pressure for reforms in Saigon. (Only the reprisal strikes were essentially new.)

Option B—Sustained and fairly heavy bombing of North Vietnam until all U.S. demands were met. This might lead to unavoidable international pressure for negotiations before the Communists were willing to accept the minimum U.S. terms. If so, the U.S. would adopt such a stiff negotiating position that the Communists would be likely to break off the talks. (The working group probably opposed this option, which was worded in such a way as to make it unlikely that Johnson would agree to it.)

Option C—Air war first against Laos, then against North Vietnam, gradually increasing in intensity. This option also included possible deployment of large numbers of U.S. ground forces in the northern part of South Vietnam. (This choice was probably favored by the interagency working group.)

The senior administration officials were unable to agree on a clear majority recommendation to Johnson at their November 24 meeting. George Ball was alone in favoring Option A (only retaliatory bombing); he argued against the domino theory and expressed doubts about the effectiveness of bombing the North. Ball presented his own paper which proposed an international conference to work out a compromise political settlement for South Vietnam.

Secretary Rusk favored bombing North Vietnam. However, he disagreed with some of his colleagues who thought that even if the United States tried and failed to "save" South Vietnam by bombing, it would still win international credit for having tried. Rusk pointed out that under these circumstances, the United States would be blamed much more than if it did not bomb the North at all. General Wheeler argued for the Joint Chiefs' position that intensive bombing carried less risk of leading to a major conflict than gradual bombing pressure.

Ambassador Maxwell Taylor returned from Saigon and on November 27 told the President's senior advisors that he believed bombing the North would have a favorable effect in South Vietnam, although he was not sure it would be enough to improve the situation greatly. McNamara was more optimistic; he expressed the view that gradual bombing pressure (Option C) would strengthen Saigon's morale enough to buy time, possibly measured in years.

The Decision to Bomb the North

A majority of the administration leaders present at the November 27 meeting agreed to recommend to the President a two-phase strategy which Ambassador Taylor suggested. The first phase would consist of thirty days of actions listed under Option A: intensification of coastal raids on the North, air strikes by American jets at infiltration routes in Laos, and one or two reprisal bombing raids against the North. Meanwhile, Ambassador Taylor would seek promises of reform and political stability from South Vietnamese leaders. At the end of thirty days, Taylor was supposed to have obtained the necessary promises, and sustained bombing of the North would begin. This second phase would last from two to six months; Taylor and other top U.S. officials seem to have expected North Vietnam and the Viet Cong to abandon their efforts to dominate the South within that period.

This proposal was submitted to the President on December 1, as soon as he returned from his Thanksgiving holiday in Texas. An early draft of the position paper, prepared by William Bundy on November 29, included the idea that the President should make a major speech explaining the new direction which U.S. policy was taking. This highly important suggestion was deleted from the final version of the proposal given President Johnson on December 1. Also excluded was a recommendation that he brief "available congressional leaders" on new evidence of North Vietnamese infiltration into the South—which would have served as public justification for the air war.[5] These steps may have been omitted because of fear that the release of infiltration data would produce speculation about an impending change of policy.

Senior officials in the administration had reached a high degree of consensus on Ambassador Taylor's two-phase strategy and knew that this plan was likely to lead to sustained bombing of the North in early 1965. Apparently, however, no one in the administration considered it to be his responsibility to prepare public opinion for what was to come. At the same time, all the senior officials ignored the power of Congress to make and declare war. Finally, Johnson made one of the greatest mistakes an American President can make when he gambled on the hope that bombing would produce such quick results that in the end the public would support him.

On December 1, President Johnson met with Ambassador Taylor and his other top advisors and approved the first phase of their recommended program, code-named "Operation Barrel Roll." Because he did not issue a National Security Action Memorandum after this meeting, it is not clear whether the President approved "in principle" the second phase of the recommended program (sustained bombing) or whether he linked approval of this phase to the achievement of a more stable government in Saigon. By implementing phase one, however, he was creating a momentum which would be almost impossible to reverse when the time came to make the final decision about sustained bombing. After a year of step-by-step progress toward bombing, it is hard to believe that President Johnson and his advisors were not aware of this.

In the December 1 meeting it was noted that General Khanh (in his position as commander in chief of South Vietnamese forces) was intriguing against Saigon's new civilian government, while Marshall Ky, the head of the air force, was intriguing both for and against Khanh. The Buddhists were strongly opposed to the new civilian government, and some of the younger generals were angling for their support. President Johnson told his advisors that he regarded it as basic to anything the U.S. might do that South Vietnamese leaders be made to unite politically. He wondered out loud about the possibility of withholding aid unless they did so. However, Taylor advised that the U.S. government should not apply too much pressure; he probably viewed the Saigon regime as a legal façade for U.S. intervention rather than a viable government.

Turning to the question of allies, Johnson approved his advisors' plans to seek new support from Australia, New Zealand, Canada, the Philippines, and others. During a state visit to Washington the following week, the British Prime Minister, Harold Wilson, was given a thorough briefing on the new U.S. plan of action in Vietnam. Australia and New Zealand were also given full details of the new U.S. bombing policy.[6] The Canadians were told slighly less; and the Filipinos, Chinese Nationalists, and South Koreans were only told about the first phase—retaliation bombing.

What President Johnson told the other governments with interests in the area is not known. If he followed his advisors' suggestions, the governments of Laos and Thailand were informed only in general terms about the new strategy, although they were given specific details on aspects requiring their approval. (For example, Souvanna Phouma's permission was sought and obtained for intensified strikes at the Ho Chi Minh trail network.) President Johnson may also have followed his advisors' suggestion that he inform France, India, and a number of other friendly governments that the United States was deeply concerned about the situation, without revealing his specific plans. The President was advised to tell the Soviet Union of America's "grave concern" and to warn Russia against becoming involved in the Vietnam war.

Perhaps the main reason that President Johnson did not make a public announcement of his new Vietnam policy was his fear that it would lead to increased pressure for peace talks. At the end of the December 1 meeting, a statement was issued that barely hinted at the fateful matters which had been discussed. It said that "The President instructed Ambassador Taylor to consult urgently with the South Vietnamese government as to measures that should be taken to improve the situation in all its aspects." The statement also noted that the President had "reaffirmed the basic U.S. policy of providing all possible and useful assistance to the South Vietnamese people and Government in their struggle to defeat the externally supported insurgency and aggression being conducted against them."

Thus, the administration told the public that it was not changing the policy of relatively cautious intervention which it had been following for the past year—and which had just received an overwhelming vote of confidence from the electorate. Johnson's sudden popularity was based on the public's confidence that he would not lead the country into war in Asia. Yet that was exactly what he now planned to do.

According to the December 1 White House statement, the President's policy was "in accordance with the congressional joint resolution of August 10, 1964, which remains in full force and effect." One reason why the administration did not seek new authority for its policy from Congress was that it was concerned about opposition from lame-duck Republicans defeated in the November election.[7]

Notes

1. The U.S. Mission's August 18, 1964 cable is included in *Pentagon Papers*, pp. 349-352.

2. Excerpts from the Joint Chief's August 26 memo to Secretary McNamara are included in *Pentagon Papers*, pp. 354-55.

3. The full text of the September 10, 1964 National Security Action Memorandum is included in *Pentagon Papers*, pp. 359-360. "Larger decisions" appears to refer to air attacks on North Vietnam.

4. Both Johnson's and Bundy's statement were reported in *The New York Times*, October 2, 1964. President Johnson also said, in a September 28 speech in Manchester, N.H., that the U.S. was "not going north (in Vietnam) and drop bombs at this stage."

5. The November 29, 1964 position papers (including material that was later added or deleted) appears in *Pentagon Papers*, pp. 373-378. A recommendation by the Joint Chiefs for intensive bombing was also excluded; however, the Joint Chiefs could, and probably did, make their views known directly to the President.

6. The government of New Zealand expressed "grave doubts" (according to *Pentagon Papers*, p. 335) that bombing would break Hanoi's will; it predicted that bombing might lead to increased Communist infiltration into South Vietnam, as it did.

7. *Pentagon Papers*, pp. 363-64, includes a November 5, 1964 paper by Assistant Secretary Bundy on the problem of dealing with U.S. and world opinion.

CHAPTER THIRTEEN

America
Takes Over the War

Ambassador Taylor met with General Khanh and Premier Huong in Saigon on December 7 and 9, while U.S. envoys were briefing other allied governments. Taylor seems to have had no problem gaining the desired statements from the Saigon leaders in exchange for his government's promise to start sustained bombing in the near future. On December 11, the Saigon authorities issued in their own name a press release drafted by U.S. officials; it said that South Vietnam had accepted "additional assistance to improve the execution of the government's program and to restrain the mounting infiltration of men and equipment by the Hanoi regime in support of the Viet Cong."

On December 14, with Souvanna Phouma's approval, Operation Barrel Roll began with attacks by American jets on unprogrammed "targets of opportunity" along the Ho Chi Minh trail in eastern Laos. The U.S. National Security Council had agreed, two days earlier, not to acknowledge these attacks publicly unless a plane were lost, in which case the U.S. government would insist that its planes were merely escorting reconnaissance flights at the request of the Lao government. On December 18, the level of "Barrel Roll" attacks for the next thirty days was set at two missions of our aircraft each per week. T-28 fighter plane raids within Laos were also intensified.

On December 19, a group of South Vietnamese officers (including Marshal Ky and Generals Khanh, Thieu, and Tri) arrested most of the active members of the High National Council, which was supposed to be drawing up a constitution for a permanent civilian government. They also jailed the leading political opponents of Premier Huong and announced that they had done so because they trusted the premier and chief of state, but not the High National Council.

The following day, Ambassador Taylor summoned to the American Embassy the generals who had taken part in the coup. There he told them that they had made "a real mess of things" and that America was tired of coups. He warned that the United States could not support them forever if they did things like that. Marshal Ky and the other generals denied they had staged a coup, saying they had merely been trying to achieve unity by getting rid of divisive elements. They refused to restore the High National Council. General Khanh, temporarily supported by Ky, became head of a new Armed Forces Council.

On December 23, Secretary Rusk and Ambassador Taylor warned publicly that U.S. aid would be reduced unless South Vietnamese leaders set aside personal rivalries in the interest of unity.

Rusk was deeply troubled by the growing gap between the U.S. public's perception of the situation and the way in which the administration professed to see it. However, he seems to have been temperamentally incapable of playing a stronger role in bridging this dangerous chasm. Opinions vary as to whether or not he regarded the administration's new policy as basically sound. But he and the President seem to have been in full agreement on the need for secrecy.

On Christmas Eve, Rusk pointed out at a meeting of the National Security Council that the American people were troubled by the political chaos in Saigon and were questioning why U.S. aid should go to such a regime. After the meeting, Rusk sent a cable to Taylor in Saigon telling him to stop releasing information on Communist infiltration from North to South Vietnam because it might create speculation about a change in U.S. policy. (The data on infiltration was being compiled for the express purpose of making a public case for U.S. intervention.)

That same evening, the Viet Cong exploded a bomb in an American officers' billet in Saigon, killing two Americans and wounding fifty-eight others. But President Johnson decided against retaliation, in spite of vigorous protests from Ambassador Taylor and the Joint Chiefs. Again, Johnson's motive was to avoid encouraging speculation about a change in policy. He may also have been unwilling to add to the unsettling world news during his first Christmas season as an elected President.

On January 3, Secretary Rusk went on television in an effort to try to promote confidence in the administration's grasp of the situation. However, because of the administration's self-imposed ban on acknowledging its plans, Rusk found himself in the position of asking the public to support a policy which the administration had already discarded. He explicitly ruled out either a U.S. withdrawal or a major expansion of the war. His speech ended with the familiar homily that the South Vietnamese people could defeat insurgency by themselves if they combined internal unity, U.S. aid, and persistence.

Within the private councils of the administration, Rusk may also have argued, at this stage, that the consequences of either escalation or withdrawal would be so serious that the United States must make its old policy of limited involvement work. McGeorge Bundy reported this to President Johnson in a January 27 memorandum, adding that "This would be good if it was possible. Bob [McNamara] and I do not think it is." Bundy and McNamara believed that the old policy of limited involvement was leading toward "disastrous defeat," and that the administration must choose between escalation or negotiation: they were inclined to favor escalation, although they urged that both alternatives be studied and argued out in Johnson's presence.[1]

Power Struggle in Saigon

For the next two months, the political situation in Saigon was dominated by a three-way power struggle between the Buddhists, the Saigon generals, and the U.S. Mission, each attempting to impose its own form of unity on the country. Neither the Buddhists nor the Saigon military were sure of their aims or more than superficially unified for tactical purposes. The same could be said, to a lesser degree, of the various elements comprising the U.S. Mission. In general, the Mission feared that a Buddhist-dominated government would adopt a neutralist policy, but they were also anxious to restore at least a façade of civilian government and persuade the generals to go back to fighting the war.

Relations between Ambassador Taylor and General Khanh became more and more strained. On January 4, Premier Huong declared in an interview published in the *Indian Express* that this was the main reason for the political chaos in Saigon. The following day, the American Embassy issued a denial in a statement (approved in Washington) which said that the U.S. government and its representatives wanted to see "a stable government in place, able to speak for all its components, to carry out plans and execute decisions."

On January 9, the armed forces repeated their earlier promise to leave government in the hands of civilians. Ambassador Taylor called this "a promising step in the direction of establishing a stable and effective government." But two days later, Secretary Rusk instructed him "to avoid actions that would further commit the United States to any particular form of political solution" in Saigon. If another military regime emerged, Rusk said, "we might well have to swallow our pride and work with it."

On January 13, Huong announced that he intended to bring the military into his government and convene a national congress in March to cope with the political crisis. He gave portfolios to four generals (including Nguyen Van Thieu, who later became president) and removed two civilians who had been criticized by the Buddhists. However, this action only led to sharper criticism by the Buddhists of Huong and his American backers. In Saigon, the U.S. Information Service library was sacked, and in Hue a mob of 5000 demanded that Ambassador Taylor go home. Leading Buddhist monks of several major factions began a fast aimed at mobilizing public opinion against Premier Huong and American influence in Vietnam.

On January 27, General Khanh and his followers staged a successful coup against Premier Huong. The latter's third deputy premier, Nguyen Xuan Oanh, was named premier. By this time, Khanh was thoroughly at odds with the U.S. Mission in Saigon, and the militant Buddhists, led by Thich Tri Quang, were reported to have gained great influence following the latest coup. Washington plainly feared that the South Vietnamese government was moving toward neutralism, especially during the period of intense political infighting that lasted for several weeks.

Kosygin's Visit and Pleiku Reprisal

The Soviet Union chose this time of extreme political instability in the South to announce that the new Soviet premier, Aleksei Kosygin, would visit Hanoi. The trip seemed designed to underscore Russia's concern about American escalation of the Vietnam war and to bolster the pro-Soviet faction in the DRV Politburo. Kosygin received a cool reception in Peking, where he stopped on his way to Hanoi. Meanwhile, President Johnson accepted a month-old invitation to meet with Kosygin—probably to show that the United States' forthcoming escalation of the war was not meant to antagonize the USSR.

When McGeorge Bundy arrived in Saigon on February 4, he learned that the militant Buddhists were using their position of increased influence to press for a negotiated end to the war. Two days later, Kosygin arrived in Hanoi, accompanied by the chief of the Soviet air force, the minister of aviation, and the senior Soviet foreign aid specialist. Kosygin was publicly urged by Premier Pham Van Dong to bury the Sino-Soviet conflict. But within hours of the arrival of the Soviet officials in the North Vietnamese capital, the Viet Cong provided the act of provocation which led to the start of U.S. bombing.[2] Early in the morning of February 7 (Vietnam time), Viet Cong troops attacked a U.S. airfield and billeting area at Pleiku and two smaller installations, killing nine Americans and wounding over a hundred. Because of the time difference, news of the attack reached Washington at 2:30 P.M. on February 6.

Kosygin, obviously aware of the attack, told a mass rally in Hanoi some hours later that the Soviet Union would supply the DRV with "all necessary assistance if aggressors dare encroach upon [its] independence and sovereignty." He also warned the United States against carrying out "schemes to provoke acts of war against North Vietnam."

In spite of this warning, the United States reprisal raid was delivered in just fourteen hours (at 4:00 P.M. on February 7, Vietnam time). This was an even quicker reaction than the reprisal after the Tonkin Gulf incident; it showed the high state of readiness of U.S. forces, who had been preparing for further reprisals for six months. Forty-nine carrier-based U.S. jets dropped their bombs and rockets on DRV barracks and staging areas at Donghoi, forty miles north of the seventeenth parallel.

President Johnson has stated that his decision to launch the February 7 reprisal strike still left open the question of whether or not to begin sustained bombing against the North. He thought that "perhaps a sudden and effective air strike would convince the leaders of Hanoi that we were serious in our purpose and also that the North could not count on continued immunity if they persisted in aggression in the South."[3] However, nothing that North Vietnam or the Viet Cong had ever done before made this hope rational, and every important decision Johnson had made about Vietnam since he took office had brought him closer to the final decision to wage war. The President's advisors had recommended that his next move be sustained bombing, and Johnson appears to have agreed with them, at least in principle, when he approved the first phase of Taylor's strategy on December 1, 1964.

Johnson summoned his leading advisors to the cabinet room in the evening of February 6. (Rusk was recovering from influenza and McGeorge Bundy was still in Saigon.) Johnson had asked the Senate Majority Leader, Mike Mansfield, and House Speaker McCormack to attend. There was no disagreement among the administration members about the idea of a reprisal strike; McGeorge Bundy was reached by telephone and urged this course from Saigon. The one dissenting voice was that of Senator Mansfield, who spoke out strongly against the idea of a reprisal strike, fearing that it might lead to war with China or that it might heal the rift between Moscow and Peking. Johnson, after listening patiently, replied that he was concerned about the safety of the men he had sent to Vietnam; he would order the reprisals.

When the first reprisal strikes were announced on February 7, Johnson also indicated that he was evacuating 1800 American dependents from Vietnam because "it has become clear that Hanoi has undertaken a more aggressive course of action against both South Vietnamese and American installations." He added that he had ordered troop reinforcements and the deployment of Hawk ground-to-air missile battalions to South Vietnam. A White House statement, issued earlier the same day, said "we seek no wider war," but added that "whether or not this course can be maintained lies with the North Vietnamese aggressors." It was also announced that the Soviet government had been informed of the "limited" nature and intent of the U.S. air attacks. Llewellyn Thompson, twice U.S. Ambassador to Moscow, was among State Department officials deeply concerned about the risk of bombing North Vietnam while the Soviet premier was in the country.

Most members of Congress supported the February 1965 reprisals. Although Senator Mansfield had opposed the idea the evening before, he now closed ranks with the administration and told reporters that the President "did the only thing he could do. He had little choice in the matter." As in the case of the Tonkin Gulf incident, Senator Morse was one of the few dissenters; he pointed out that violations of treaties by the Communists could not "justify the United States committing the same wrongs."

Late at night on February 7, McGeorge Bundy and his party returned from Saigon. Bundy immediately drove to the White House and gave the President, a long memorandum recommending a program of "sustained reprisals," linking each U.S. bombing raid to a specific Viet Cong terrorist act in the South. The main advantage to this procedure, he believed, was that it would produce far less international pressure for negotiation than an air war not based on reprisals.[4]

Johnson had not allowed himself any way to back off from the final decision to launch a sustained air war. Bundy and others were now urging him to go ahead with it, in the hope that it would enable the U.S. government to demand in return better performance by the Saigon generals. While some of his advisors were possibly holding out the prospect of a quick, cheap war, Bundy's memorandum was more realistic:

> . . . At its very best the struggle in Vietnam will be long. It seems to us important that this fundamental fact be made clear and our understanding of it be made clear to our own people and to the people of Vietnam. Too often in the past we have conveyed the impression that we expect an early solution when those who live with this war know that no early solution is possible.[5]

Johnson read it before going to sleep, and on the morning of February 8 decided that no further purpose would be served by delay. He called a meeting of the National Security Council and invited the two leading Democrats and two Republican leaders of Congress to attend. (Committee chairmen concerned with foreign and defense affairs were not invited; the President had the joint resolution he needed, and his main interest was in preventing unwanted congressional initiatives.)

The meeting was designed to demonstrate the unanimity and serious-ness of the administration in its approach to the problem and to as-sociate the congressmen with the President's decision. First, McNamara briefed congressional leaders on the military effects of the reprisal. Because of Rusk's continued illness, Undersecretary Ball described the diplomatic situation. Then Johnson took over and explained to the congressional leaders that the idea of sustained bombing of the North had been considered several months earlier. Johnson apparently chose this moment to inform everyone present that he had decided "to go forward with the kind of program we had earlier studied and post-poned." Later in the day, he cabled Ambassador Taylor the news that he had decided to carry out a plan for "continuing action" against North Vietnam "with modifications up and down in tempo and scale in the light of your recommendations . . . and our own continuing review of the situation."[6]

On February 11, U.S. aircraft executed another reprisal raid (which was again clearly labeled as such) after the Viet Cong attacked a U.S. barracks in Qui Nhon, killing twenty-three Americans and seven Viet-namese and wounding twenty-one Americans. Vice-President Humph-rey, Undersecretary Ball and Ambassador Llewellyn Thompson all ex-pressed concern about striking before Kosygin finished his tour of the Far East. Johnson met them part way by eliminating a reprisal target that was close to Hanoi. On February 13, he sent Taylor a more de-tailed description of the strategy he planned to follow. This message also indicated that the United States would adopt a public posture of willingness to negotiate and that it would take its case against North Vietnam to the UN Security Council.[7]

Taylor replied that the President's decision had been received with much enthusiasm in Saigon.[8] Nevertheless, the political situation there remained chaotic. General Khanh, now openly at odds with the American Embassy, helped install a civilian government representing a fairly wide range of interests. This government, led by Phan Huy Quat, seemed to be toying with the idea of neutralism. However, it was weakened almost at once when Khanh himself was deposed as commander of the army and forced into exile. By the end of February, real power had passed into the hands of an armed forces council opposed to any sort of negotiation.

Meanwhile, leaders of the French, Soviet, and British governments reacted to the crisis by undertaking independent efforts to convene a new Geneva conference. On February 24, Secretary-General U Thant held a press conference. He described in general terms his earlier attempts to bring the United States and North Vietnam together in direct negotiations. He implied that the United States government had deliberately concealed from its people the fact that certain possibilities existed for a negotiated end to the war. "As you know," he said, "in times of war and of hostilities the first casualty is truth."[9] U Thant's remarks angered President Johnson. On the following day, the White House press secretary denied that there was any proposal by U Thant for negotiations currently "before the President."

On March 1, Premier Phan Huy Quat finally provided the United States with assurances that his government would not seek peace until "the communists end the war they have provoked and stop their infiltration." The next day, American aircraft carried out the first strike against the North which was not described as a reprisal for some Viet Cong attack in the South.

President Johnson had embarked upon an entirely open-ended war in Asia just four months after receiving a mandate for peace from the American voters. He made his moves and timed them with the instinctive care of a master politician. None of the major policy issues involved were raised or debated in Congress until after United States military prestige had been thoroughly committed to winning the war. By manipulating congressional as well as public opinion, instead of consulting them, President Johnson created a time bomb. Over the next three years, he would use all the power of the Presidency to prevent it from blowing up. But the longer he tried to suppress public debate of his war policy, the more likely it was that the eventual explosion would destroy not just his policy or even his legislative program, but that it would shake the confidence of the American public in the very institutions of government which he had sworn to defend.

Notes

1. President Johnson quotes from McGeorge Bundy's January 27, 1965 memorandum in *Vantage Point*, pp. 122-23.

2. The Johnson administration took the position that the Viet Cong attack was ordered by Hanoi for the purpose of testing the U.S. will. This was essential to rationalize a U.S. reprisal strike against North Vietnam. However, there is no way, at present, of knowing whether Hanoi leaders really did have advance knowledge of the attack and, if so, what their attitude toward it was. They might have known about it in advance or not known about it. They might have been for it or against it. They might have been primarily interested in the Soviet response, the American response, or that of other governments.

3. *Vantage Point*, p. 125.

4. The annex to Bundy's memo which outlined this strategy is included in *Pentagon Papers*, pp. 423-27. According to Johnson, it was largely drafted by Assistant Secretary John McNaughton, who accompanied Bundy. See *Vantage Point*, pp. 126-28, for excerpts from the covering memo.

5. *Vantage Point*, p. 127.

6. Ibid., p. 129.

7. *The Pentagon Papers*, pp. 423-27.

8. During the rest of February, there were no more U.S. air strikes, but on February 25, the U.S. government acknowledged for the first time that its planes and pilots were making air strikes in the South.

9. United Nations Press Services Note 3075, Feb. 24, 1965.

CHAPTER FOURTEEN

Stalemate
and Peace Initiatives

President Johnson repeated again and again that his aim
was not to widen the war and that the purpose of escalation was to apply just the right amount of force needed
to induce North Vietnam and the Viet Cong to give up
their aims in the South. During 1965, he increased the
United States' involvement in the ground and air wars
very sharply (although not nearly so sharply as his military experts advised). The President's statements, in this
period, implied that he expected the war to be brief and
relatively painless, as far as the United States was concerned.

The other side of the coin, barely mentioned by
Johnson in his public statements, was that the United
States government had no way of knowing how much
force would be needed—or for how long. It seemed to

the Johnson administration that massive force *had* to work, because nothing else had been successful. The President probably felt that neither Congress nor the American people would accept the unlimited risks and the cost of the policy he had adopted if he described the situation to them as he and his advisors saw it. He might be forced by public opinion to scale down his objectives and lose this particular contest with the Communist powers. The likely consequences—both for himself and for the nation—of losing in this way became more frightening each time he raised the stakes of U.S. involvement in the war.

By 1966, the failure of the President's colossal gamble on undeclared war had become apparent to at least some of the Vietnam principals. The same was true of many working-level officials (whose views on Indochina policy, unless optimistic, were usually ignored by Johnson). Outside the executive branch, there was growing opposition to escalation by congressmen, journalists, teachers, students, and other informed members of the public. But most people underestimated the difficulty of reversing the administration's policy. Peace initiatives by third countries seemed only to harden Johnson's commitment to the "slow squeeze."

The 1967 presidential election in Saigon, by providing a legal basis for the anti-Communist regime, offered an ideal chance to begin scaling down U.S. involvement, but the opportunity was allowed to slip by. The year ended with key military and civilian officials still professing to see "light at the end of the tunnel." However, the resignation of Secretary McNamara, who had played a major role in shaping U.S. Indochina policy under two Presidents, showed the degree of doubt which existed just beneath the surface in Washington.

The Decision to Take Over the Ground War

A coordinated strategy of bombing the North and sending American combat troops to South Vietnam had long been under discussion within the Johnson administration. On March 6, 1965 four days after the start of sustained bombing, the President ordered 3500 Marines to Da Nang to defend the United States base there. In doing so, he was merely following the "scenario" for escalation that had been taking shape for nearly a year. The marines arrived at Da Nang on March 8. The day before they landed, Secretary Rusk announced on television that their mission was solely to provide security for the U.S. air base. This undoubtedly helped explain the lack of public outcry about their deployment.

Meanwhile, when the bombing raids on the North failed to produce any immediate signs that Hanoi was ready to sue for peace, the administration began to adopt a new rationale for the air war. Henceforth, the aim would be to destroy North Vietnam's capabilities to support the war in the South—particularly by bombing the lines of communication in eastern Laos and the southern half of North Vietnam. Many military leaders, however, preferred a brief and violent bombing campaign, designed to knock out "strategic" targets in the North. Instead, the President decided in favor of a heavy but carefully controlled air war, which was supposed to intensify the pressure on North Vietnam to negotiate while keeping worldwide criticism of the United States at a tolerable level.

Although President Johnson told reporters on March 31 that he knew of no "far-reaching strategy that is being suggested or promulgated," he was about to order a major change in the role of American forces in Vietnam. After meeting with his chief advisors on April 1 and 2, he sent two more marine combat battalions to South Vietnam and issued orders allowing them to engage in offensive operations, without clearly defining their mission. He also increased American support forces by about 19,000 men; their exact role was left unspecified, allowing the military chiefs to use some of them to prepare for the arrival of two or three more divisions.

If the President's instructions were ambiguous about how these forces were to be used, they were absolutely precise about the public relations aspect of his decisions. The Vietnam principals were told that "premature publicity" should be "avoided by all possible precautions." The actions should be taken "as rapidly as practicable, but in ways that should minimize any appearance of sudden changes in policy." The President wanted the actions to be understood as "wholly consistent with existing policy."[1]

Although he was in favor of United States military intervention, Ambassador Taylor was concerned that the President might be sending too many troops too soon—and that the Pentagon was apparently thinking in terms of conventional warfare rather than counterinsurgency. He informed Washington that he planned to spell out his own interpretation of the marines' new role when he went to Premier Phan Huy Quat to seek approval for bringing them ashore. Taylor said that he would define the new mission as a "mobile counterinsurgency role in the vicinity of Da Nang for the improved protection of that base and also ... a strike role as a reserve in support of ARVN operations anywhere within 50 miles of the base" after they gained experience in counterinsurgency.[2] This definition of what was referred to as the "enclave" strategy was accepted by Washington, and these guidelines were followed for the next three months.

On April 14, 1965, the Joint Chiefs ordered the deployment of the 173rd Airborne brigade to Vietnam, at General Westmoreland's urgent request. When he learned of this order, Ambassador Taylor declared it went beyond his understanding of the agreement reached two weeks earlier in Washington—to experiment with the marines in a counterinsurgency role before sending in other U.S. contingents. A joint State and Defense Department cable, answering Taylor's message, said that the President thought "something new must be added in the South to achieve victory." The State and Defense departments recommended sending the 173rd Airborne brigade and using military-civilian affairs personnel in the U.S. aid effort. Taylor cabled McGeorge Bundy, protesting the "hasty and ill-conceived" proposals for sending U.S. forces and adding a personal note: "Mac, can't we be better protected from our friends? I know that everyone wants to help, but there's such a thing as killing with kindness."[3]

Since 1961, Ambassador Maxwell Taylor had been advocating the use of American ground forces to carry out specific combat functions and to raise the morale of the South Vietnamese army. Now, he was concerned with the political problems that were likely to arise if the United States tried to take charge of the ground war too quickly. However, it was virtually impossible for the Ambassador in Saigon to slow the momentum of the interventionists. On April 20, top-level U.S. officials from Washington and Saigon met in Honolulu and decided that a "victory strategy" would require an increase of U.S. forces to 82,000 men. Additional troops from allied countries totalling 7250 men would be sought. The meeting also discussed the possibility of doubling this force in the near future. President Johnson promptly approved his advisors' recommendations after the Viet Cong ended a lull in the ground war by launching a new offensive.

Westmoreland's Strategy and Rising Troop Levels

On June 7, 1965, General Westmoreland submitted a long and gloomy assessment of the military situation in which he asked for a total of 100,000 men, including thirty-five battalions of combat troops, and indicated that he might ask for nine more battalions later. (He had already been promised 77,000 troops, including four battalions from allied countries.) In reply to a somewhat belated query from the Joint Chiefs of Staff about how he planned to use his forces, Westmoreland sent a message on June 13, in which, for the first time, he spelled out the "search and destroy strategy." He indicated that Americans and other non-ARVN forces would be employed against the main-force units of the enemy in less populated areas, while ARVN forces would be largely responsible for "pacification" and protecting the South Vietnamese people.

"Search and destroy" was a far more time-consuming and perhaps costlier approach than invading North Vietnam or destroying its dikes and harbors from the air. But President Johnson held back from allowing these latter moves for fear of bringing China into the war. The search and destroy strategy amounted to fighting a war of attrition against an intensely dedicated government and people. (In addition, North Vietnam could field almost unlimited reserves of military manpower.) Given the enormous rate of civilian and military casualties produced by American firepower and bombing, together with the destruction of property and the very ecology of South Vietnam, Westmoreland's strategy was hardly calculated to enhance the Saigon regime's popularity.

It is difficult to see how any American president could have expected the American people to support such a strategy for the years or decades it might take to undermine Hanoi's will. President Johnson soon found himself in a highly contradictory position. On the one hand, he tried to reassure the country that the combination of pressures being exerted against the enemy was bringing the war closer to a satisfactory end. His statements tended to leave the impression that each major increase in the troop level represented some sort of ceiling. On the other hand, he felt it necessary to reassure the military chiefs and their supporters in Congress that he was giving General Westmoreland all that he asked for. But President Johnson relied on Secretary McNamara to bargain with the military to keep their demands as low as possible. At the same time, he never made public any long-range plans for troop increases. He and his leading advisors issued frequent optimistic assessments of the war, which were designed to refute press reports that it was settling into a stalemate.

Perhaps because of McNamara's skill as a negotiator, there was very little overt criticism of President Johnson's policy by American military leaders during his administration. General Westmoreland supported the President's strategy of gradual escalation—which made it possible to avoid calling up the reserves. "I stayed within the ballpark," he told an interviewer in 1970, "but I played it right up to the fence."[4] Thus, as soon as Johnson announced that he had approved Westmoreland's request for thirty-five battalions, the general sent in a fresh request for another 100,000 men. This was promptly approved, and in November 1965, Westmoreland asked that the troop level be raised to 375,000 men. Not until June 1966 (when he asked for 542,000 troops) did Westmoreland fail to have any of his requests fully approved by Secretary McNamara and the President.

At least two theories have been advanced to explain why General Westmoreland's estimates of the number of troops he needed rose so frequently. One explanation is that the U.S. military establishment calculated at least as early as 1964 that about one million American troops would be needed to prevent a Communist victory in South Vietnam. Since a request of this size would have been rejected out of hand by Congress, the military leaders may have decided to ask for it in installments and to condition Congress and the public gradually to their idea of needed force levels. The other explanation is that intelligence and planning staffs repeatedly failed to predict the number of troops the enemy could field by infiltration from the North and by recruitment in South Vietnam.

In fact, these two explanations are not mutually exclusive. Moreover, in the eyes of some Pentagon officials, even a war fought under extreme political constraints (as both the Korean and Indochina wars were) had certain undeniable advantages. Vietnam became a major testing ground for counter-guerrilla tactics and exotic military "hardware," such as electronic devices to count the number of troops passing over remote trails. An enormous number of civilian technicians were recruited by the Pentagon to carry out projects in military research and development, and for a time official Washington seemed to believe that virtually any problem involved in combating a Communist "war of liberation" could be quantified and solved by the application of large amounts of money and technical know-how.

Vietnam also provided a chance for the armed services to document their overall capabilities. In the eyes of army chiefs, one of the major lessons derived from Vietnam was that the United States could fight a large ground war on the other side of the globe just as easily as in Cuba. In the eyes of some officers, this disproved the classic dictum against becoming involved in land wars in Asia. The air force and navy were also interested in testing the capabilities of land- and sea-based air power, although the enemy almost completely lacked the kind of targets chosen for World War II strategic bombing.

Italian Mediation Effort and Johnson's Peace Offensive

In November 1965, Italian Foreign Minister Fanfani tried to mediate the struggle, which had reached a stalemate that offered no immediate prospect of victory to either side. The diplomatic effort was unsuccessful, but at least it illustrated some of the problems of finding peace in Indochina.

Hanoi had presented a four-point peace program in April 1965, which was endorsed by the NLF five months later. It called for: 1) withdrawal of U.S. forces from Vietnam and cancellation of U.S.-South Vietnamese military ties; 2) respect for the military provisions of the 1954 Geneva accords pending Vietnam's reunification; 3) settlement of South Vietnam's internal affairs in accordance with the NLF's program; and 4) no foreign involvement or interference in the reunification of Vietnam.

The acceptance of Hanoi's four-point program as one of the conditions for peace talks was reiterated in a message from Ho Chi Minh to Johnson. This message, which also called for a cease-fire in North and South Vietnam, had been received in Hanoi by two Italian professors. It came to President Johnson through Foreign Minister Fanfani, who was serving as President of the UN General Assembly. Fanfani interpreted the DRV's four points as simply a return to the 1954 Geneva agreements.

Secretary Rusk indicated in a letter to Fanfani that some aspects of what Hanoi proposed—notably point three in Hanoi's program—had no basis in the Geneva agreements. Rusk accused Hanoi of wanting a cease-fire that imposed restraints on South Vietnam and its allies while imposing none on the North. Nevertheless, he concluded by saying that Ambassador Arthur Goldberg would be available to discuss "further soundings" which the Italian intermediaries might make in Hanoi. Rusk's letter was sent to Hanoi on December 13 with a request for clarification of certain "ambiguous" points in Ho Chi Minh's message. Two days later, United States aircraft carried out their first attack on a major industrial center in North Vietnam, destroying a power plant fourteen miles from Haiphong.

On December 17, the day that newspapers broke the story of the peace feeler from North Vietnam, the United States government confirmed the fact that a message had been received through Italian intermediaries but denied that it had been rejected out of hand. As evidence, Washington released copies of Foreign Minister Fanfani's letter and Secretary Rusk's reply. The following day, Hanoi repudiated the alleged peace feeler as "sheer groundless fabrication." According to press reports, the Johnson administration had been made aware that Hanoi would disown the peace move if it was made public.

The administration was widely criticized for escalating its bombing raids and publishing confidential messages while the mediation effort was taking place. After Pope Paul expressed his hope that the NLF's offer of a twelve hour Christmas truce would be accepted, the United States and South Vietnam offered a thirty-hour Christmas truce. In the United States, political pressure immediately began to build up for an extension of the cease-fire to include the Vietnamese lunar New Year (Tet). A four-day Tet cease-fire was arranged in the ground war, and the United States prolonged its bombing halt through the end of January. Meanwhile, on December 30, the Johnson administration confirmed the fact that a major "peace offensive" was under way, with prominent U.S. officials journeying to more than a dozen capitals to talk with heads of government who had expressed interest in mediating the conflict. But four days later, Hanoi followed Peking's lead and denounced the peace campaign and bombing halt as a "trick."

On January 7, 1966, the U.S. government announced a list of fourteen principles which might contribute to a peace settlement. In brief, it described the 1954 and 1962 Geneva accords as an adequate basis for peace in Southeast Asia and welcomed the idea of a conference on Southeast Asia and "unconditional discussions". The United States was prepared to discuss a cease-fire and Hanoi's four points along with points proposed by other conference participants. The United States wanted no U.S. bases in Southeast Asia and did not want to retain U.S. troops in Vietnam once peace was assured. It also supported free elections in South Vietnam and felt that the question of reunifying Vietnam was for the Vietnamese people to determine.

The statement pointed out that the countries of Southeast Asia could opt for nonalignment or neutrality if they wanted to. The United States was still prepared to contribute at least $1 billion to regional development and allow North Vietnam to share in it. On one of the most critical issues, the United States said it saw no insurmountable problem in the Viet Cong having their views represented—once North Vietnam ceased its aggression. Finally, the United States declared that it could stop bombing North Vietnam as a step toward peace, but it wanted to know what the other side would do if the bombing stopped.

Even though the fourteen-point statement came close to Hanoi's four points in many ways, Ho Chi Minh rejected it because of its failure to grant the NLF the status of a principal combatant in the war. He also questioned the United States' sincerity, as Washington had increased its troop commitment during the bombing pause.

"An Escalating Military Stalemate"

By early 1966, some of the administration's strongest proponents of intervention were beginning to doubt the possibility of achieving their maximum aims with anything other than a totally disproportionate amount of U.S. military force. "We are in an escalating military stalemate," wrote Assistant Secretary of Defense John McNaughton in a memorandum, presumably to Secretary McNamara.[5] He described the ARVN as "tired, passive and accommodation-prone" and pointed out that the enemy was "effectively matching our deployments." The bombing might or might not be able to prevent infiltration, he thought. Pacification had stalled. And the Saigon government's administrative organization was "moribund and weaker than the VC infrastructure" in rural areas.

On the basis of these and other gloomy observations, McNaughton took the position that the United States should begin preparing the ground for a compromise settlement which might take months to produce. But he also pointed to a dilemma: " . . . it may be that while going for victory we have the strength for compromise, but if we go for compromise we have the strength only for defeat." Thus, McNaughton favored almost the same tactical moves, at this stage, as the proponents of military victory: more effort in the ground and air wars, in the pacification program, and in the effort to make the Saigon regime militarily and politically effective. The main point on which McNaughton and American military commanders differed, at this stage, was that he was against mining or destroying North Vietnam's ports—probably because it would interfere with diplomatic efforts to arrange a compromise settlement.

Secretary McNamara had begun to reach somewhat the same conclusions as McNaughton, who was one of his closest associates at the Pentagon. During 1966, McNamara became increasingly doubtful that the war could be brought to any sort of successful conclusion by means that the United States was prepared to use. But, like McNaughton, he saw no alternative to continuing and slowly increasing the pressure, while looking for ways to promote a compromise peace.

Thus, in June 1966, Secretary McNamara supported General Westmoreland's request for 391,000 U.S. troops by the end of 1966 and 431,000 by June 1967. However, while President Johnson was approving these deployments, another message arrived from General Westmoreland saying that he would need 542,588 troops in 1967. When the Joint Chiefs formally submitted this request to McNamara, he asked for a line-by-line analysis of new requirements "to determine that each is truly essential to the carrying out of our war plan." After the Joint Chiefs completed this task, McNamara, for the first time, did not recommend that the President approve all they had asked for. From then on, McNamara began to examine the military leaders' recommendations much more closely.

The failure of a much-heralded plan for strategic bombing raids on the North was one of the main reasons for McNamara's disenchantment with the war. As already noted, the administration realized after only a few weeks of sustained bombing in 1965 that this type of pressure would not, by itself, persuade North Vietnam to accept the United States' demands. Thereafter, the bombing was regarded by most high

U.S. officials as a useful and necessary form of pressure which could be halted at some later date in exchange for concessions by Hanoi. The main focus of the administration's strategy shifted to the ground war in South Vietnam; it was hoped that the war of attrition being fought there would prove to the enemy that it could not win a military victory.

Nevertheless, military leaders continued to press energetically for the expansion of the air war to include virtually all industrial and economic resources in the North as well as all lines of communication. American intelligence agencies consistently argued against this policy by pointing out that North Vietnam, having an agrarian economy, simply lacked the kind of strategic targets that would make it vulnerable to any conceivable bombing strategy—except one aimed at slaughtering the country's urban population. (Such was not the aim of the strategic bombing proponents. Generally, they seem to have been trying to prove that air power could make a major contribution in a war against this type of enemy. There is no reason to doubt that they believed their own claims that strategic bombing of the North could be carried out "surgically" without many civilian casualties.)

In early 1966, those who favored strategic bombing and those who opposed it focused their attention on a plan to wipe out most of North Vietnam's petroleum storage capacity. The group who favored the plan claimed it would "bring the enemy to the conference table or cause the insurgency to wither."[6] (Undersecretary Ball was one of the few senior officials who saw in advance that this was wishful thinking of the most grotesque sort.) The plan was approved in May 1966 by President Johnson and carried out in June.

In July, the Defense Intelligence Agency estimated that 70 percent of North Vietnam's petroleum storage capacity had been destroyed, but there was no appreciable effect on the enemy's war effort. North Vietnam still had enough small, dispersed fuel depots around the countryside, which were quickly supplied with more fuel in drums. It was impossible for allied forces to locate and destroy more than a few of these tiny depots.

Immediately after this fiasco, General Westmoreland's request for 542,000 troops arrived. As justification for his request, the field commander even cited the continued high rate of infiltration of men and supplies—which was unaffected by the strategic bombing raids. It was this sequence of events that finally caused Secretary McNamara to begin reexamining the basic tenets of the war plan.

Typically, he marshalled a strong technical brief for his new position. During the summer of 1966, he assembled a group of the country's leading weapons scientists and asked them to evaluate the main military problems in Vietnam. The scientists' conclusions undercut the predictions of victory at various force levels which were being made by highly placed officials. They pointed out that Hanoi's infiltration of men and materiel into the South had actually increased in the second year of intensified bombing. They stressed the fact that logic and experience in other wars showed that bombing tends to increase a people's will to resist rather than undermine it. In short, according to the scientists, there was no rational basis for determining if *any* force level would achieve the government's objectives.[7]

1966 Peace Efforts Follow Same Pattern

During the latter part of 1966, the tempo of the ground and air war steadily increased in spite of McNamara's doubts and his growing disenchantment with the administration's whole strategic concept. Hanoi's conditions for peace talks also grew stiffer. On October 6, the United States learned from a nonaligned government that North Vietnam would not begin peace talks on the basis of a temporary pause in the bombing; a permanent bombing halt would now be necessary. Four days later, Hanoi also rejected the UN Secretary-General's proposal for a de-escalation of the ground war. The hardening of North Vietnam's attitude probably also explains why Russia, on October 8, rejected a British proposal to reconvene the Geneva conference. The Soviets were unwilling to place themselves in a position of publicly counseling Hanoi to talk peace.

Nevertheless, a sign that negotiations might be in the offing emerged from the October 1966 conference in Manila of governments supporting Saigon's side in the war. The conference announced that allied forces would be withdrawn from Vietnam not later than six months after "the other side withdraws its forces to the North, ceases infiltration, and the level of violence thus subsides."

Behind the scenes, a number of individual officials and governments were trying to mediate the conflict. One of the most promising of these efforts was undertaken by the Polish representative to the International Control Commission in Vietnam. It was particularly attractive to the Johnson administration because it seemed to offer hope of face-to-face talks with North Vietnamese representatives without a prior bombing halt by the United States. After meeting with American and North Vietnamese officials a number of times during 1966, the Polish diplomat, Janusz Lewandowski, gave Ambassador Lodge (who began his second term as Ambassador in Saigon on July 8, 1965) a list of ten points which the DRV was willing to discuss.

On December 2, Lodge indicated to the Polish representative that his government had agreed to accept these points as a basis for discussion even though the United States had important reservations about the language and substance of some of the points. At Lewandowski's suggestion, Lodge then cabled Washington to see if talks could begin in Warsaw as early as December 6. However, on the same day (December 2), U.S. fighter-bombers carried out their first raid on targets in and around the city of Hanoi since the massive "strategic" raid on petroleum storage facilities the previous June.

Why did such a dramatic air attack take place at this exact time? And why was it followed by three additional strikes on Hanoi during the rest of December, when there still seemed a possibility of peace talks? These questions were asked by a small group of officials who knew of the Polish mediation effort—Poles, North Vietnamese, Americans, and Italians. (The latter had helped arrange the meetings between Lodge and Lewandowski in Saigon.) After the Polish government leaked the story of its abortive peace initiative to the press in January 1967, people all over the world began to question the aims of the U.S. government. And when it was learned that other mediation efforts had been upset by escalation in much the same way, Washington's credibility dropped to a new low.[8] The story behind the December bombing raids provides important insights into why the Johnson administration found it so extraordinarily difficult to take any action that might end the Vietnam war.

President Johnson authorized the bombing of targets five miles from the center of Hanoi on November 14, 1966 at a meeting of his "Tuesday luncheon group." This was the inner circle of the Johnson administration where most Vietnam policy decisions were made.[9] A great many of its sessions, as on November 14, were taken up with minutiae, such as the choosing of individual bombing targets. No one in this group was able to devote his full attention to Vietnam—and none of the lower-ranking officials who could devote full time to Vietnam were invited to meet regularly with the inner circle to participate in the formulation of policy. Indeed, the full-time specialists were not even informed of many politically sensitive decisions because of Johnson's fear of leaks to the press or Congress.

Although air strikes in the vicinity of Hanoi were authorized on November 14, the timing of the raids was left to the discretion of local United States commanders in Asia (who had no knowledge of the Polish peace initiative). They simply chose dates for which favorable weather conditions were predicted.

The President and his advisors either forgot that they had authorized the bombing raids or else failed to realise how this might destroy the peace initiative. Neither Johnson nor his advisors assumed responsibility for monitoring their decisions about targets to be sure that authorized air strikes would not interfere with diplomatic efforts. This responsibility was delegated to a few middle-grade State Department officers, who probably received copies on December 2 of secret messages indicating that the raids were about to begin, just when there seemed to be a chance of peace talks in Warsaw. However, they either failed to see the connection between the two events or else concluded that there was not enough time to go through all the procedures required to stop the raids. Clearly, a much higher priority was attached, within the Johnson administration, to maintaining military pressure against North Vietnam than to exploring the possibility that Hanoi might be ready to compromise—even though bringing Hanoi to the conference table was the avowed aim of the bombing.

The first raid on December 2 was followed by another on December 4. In a series of meetings that began on December 3, the Polish Foreign Minister repeatedly told the American Ambassador in Warsaw. John Gronouski (who had been designated to meet with the North Vietnamese), that the North Vietnamese were upset about the bombing and that there was uncertainty about whether they would go ahead with a meeting. Gronouski passed on this information to President Johnson, although his reports may have reflected his own unfounded optimism that the peace talks would actually take place. (The United States had never been specifically told that Hanoi agreed to a December 6 meeting.)

At any rate, Johnson and his advisors apparently decided that the peace initiative had little chance of succeeding—or that, if it were going to succeed, bombing would make no difference.[10] In any case, Johnson authorized additional raids on December 13 and 14 against the same targets in Hanoi that had been struck earlier in the month. One of these was a group of sheds in which twelve or fourteen battered trucks and buses were undergoing repairs.[11] It is hard to imagine that destroying such a target—and, incidentally, a high school that stood near it—produced any worthwhile military advantages. Rather, it is plain that these bombing raids were intended to force Hanoi to agree to a settlement on United States terms.

On December 15, the Polish Foreign Minister informed Ambassador Gronouski that the North Vietnamese had called off the talks because of the bombing. About one week later, Johnson ordered a suspension of bombing anywhere within a ten-mile radius of the center of Hanoi.[12] But by this time it was quite clear that the Polish peace initiative was dead.

Notes

1. National Security Action Memorandum 328, of April 6, 1965, is included in *Pentagon Papers*, pp. 442-43.

2. Ambassador Taylor's April 4 cable is cited on page 402 of *Pentagon Papers*.

3. This series of messages is cited in *Pentagon Papers*, pp. 403-405.

4. See John B. Henry II, "February, 1968," *Foreign Policy* (Fall 1971), p. 8.

5. The text of McNaughton's January 9, 1966 memorandum is included in *Pentagon Papers*, pp. 491-93.

6. Statement by Admiral U. S. Grant Sharp, Commander in Chief, Pacific, quoted in *Pentagon Papers*, p. 461.

7. Excerpts from the scientists' conclusions are given in *Pentagon Papers*, pp. 502-509.

8. World opinion was less aware of the fact that North Vietnam's position had grown steadily tougher between 1965 and 1967. Some people who did know this simply took it as further evidence that American policy was self-defeating and that the United States would have to make the first move because it had so much less at stake in the war than North Vietnam.

9. The Tuesday luncheon group consisted, on this occasion, of the President, Rusk, McNamara, Rostow, and William Moyers, the President's press secretary. This was the usual composition of the group. (Moyers was later succeeded as press secretary by George Reedy, who also attended the Tuesday luncheons.) In addition, CIA Director Richard Helms; General Earle Wheeler, Chairman of the JCS; and Assistant Secretary William Bundy sometimes attended.

10. See Johnson, *Vantage Point*, pp. 251-52. It was easier to adopt this attitude than to admit that the December bombing raids had been a huge and tragic mistake.

11. Harrison Salisbury of *The New York Times* visited some of the sites a few weeks later, including civilian structures that appeared to have been accidentally hit by stray bombs. His impressions are described in his book *Behind the Lines— Hanoi* (New York: Bantam, 1967).

12. The circumstances surrounding the Polish peace initiative are described by David Kraslow and Stuart H. Loory in their book *The Secret Search for Peace in Vietnam* (New York: Vintage, 1968).

CHAPTER FIFTEEN

The Inability
to Admit Mistakes

A full year had passed since John McNaughton wrote, "We are in a dilemma . . . it may be that while going for victory we have the strength for compromise, but if we go for compromise we have the strength only for defeat." All during 1966, the United States had been "going for victory," but the result was still "escalating military stalemate."[1]

By January 1967, the United States had demonstrated that it was much too strong to be pushed out of South Vietnam by force. General Westmoreland's war of attrition strategy was producing a very high rate of North Vietnamese and Viet Cong casualties, but the enemy was able to more than replace his losses through recruitment in the South and infiltration from the North.[2] South Vietnam could not be completely overrun by Communist forces as long as a foreign military occupation force was prepared to remain indefinitely in the South. However, there seemed to be no way of defeating North Vietnam short of invading and occupying it. President Johnson was quite unlikely to approve such a strategy for fear of provoking a direct clash with China or the Soviet Union.

The President had come to realize that the air war had little military value, but he still regarded it as a major diplomatic trump card—something which he could stop inflicting on North Vietnam when its leaders indicated they were ready to be "reasonable." In the meantime, it was also a way of silencing the hawks in Congress and in the Pentagon, whom Johnson regarded (until 1968) as the major source of criticism of his policy. Thus, much of President Johnson's time was devoted to planning air attacks, choosing targets, and rationalizing the need to continue and intensify the air war. During 1966 and 1967, this activity became an end in itself and bombing raids often were allowed to interfere with serious mediation efforts.[3]

Like the United States, North Vietnam had shown that it could not be driven out of the South by force. Hanoi had also indicated that it might be willing to explore the possibility of a negotiated settlement. As described earlier, Hanoi's bargaining position was very harsh, and seemed to be getting more so all the time. Undoubtedly, DRV leaders believed there was a limit to the price the American people would pay to "save" South Vietnam from communism. At some point, they felt, it would become clear to Congress and the American public that South Vietnam was far less important to the security and well-being of the United States than other foreign and domestic goals, which were being neglected because of the war. When that happened, there would be no need to negotiate.

It does not seem to have occurred to any senior Johnson administration officials that 1967 was the last year in which they could hope to negotiate a compromise without being forced to do so by election year pressures. It was the last year in which the United States had the "strength to compromise," in McNaughton's phrase, and the last year in which there might have been something for Hanoi to gain by negotiating with the U.S. instead of waiting for the eventual U.S. withdrawal. President Johnson and his advisors feared that if they gave any public sign of interest in compromise, the morale of the Saigon regime and of allied troops in Vietnam would plummet while the enemy's fighting spirit would soar. (Hanoi's leaders probably rationalized their own intransigence in the same manner.) Neither side wanted to take the first step to de-escalate the war, in part because this would have seemed like an admission that all the sacrifices they had demanded of their people had been in vain. An episode illustrating this point took place in February 1967.

On February 1, DRV Foreign Minister Trinh hinted publicly that a U.S. bombing halt "could" be followed by peace talks. The allied side announced that it would observe a four-day truce (including a bombing halt) during the lunar new year, from February 8 to 11, 1967. This announcement coincided with a visit to Great Britain by Premier Kosygin. Prime Minister Harold Wilson decided to make a major effort to move the Vietnam war to the conference table. He was authorized by President Johnson to present the U.S. position to Kosygin, although Johnson "doubted strongly" that the mediation effort would be successful.[4]

Five days before the bombing halt began, a White House staff member, Chester Cooper, arrived in London to brief Prime Minister Harold Wilson and Foreign Secretary George Brown on the current U.S. negotiating position in regard to Vietnam. (Cooper assisted Averell Harriman in trying to coordinate the various diplomatic efforts to end the war.) The peace plan which he described to the British leaders, to prepare them for the forthcoming visit by Kosygin, was the "Phase A-Phase B" plan.

Phase A of the plan would be a U.S. bombing halt. Phase B would involve some further act of de-escalation by each side—but there would be no Phase A until agreement had been reached in secret on Phase B. The United States was prepared to make the first overt move in both phases, and it was willing to negotiate about the particular acts of de-escalation to be carried out by the two sides as well as such important points as the time that could elapse between the bombing halt (Phase A) and Phase B. If enemy forces were particularly active and menacing U.S. or South Vietnamese positions, Washington would insist on Phase B going into effect simultaneously with the bombing halt or only a day or so later. If, however, the war situation were relatively quiet, the United States might agree to allow three weeks or more to elapse between the two phases.

Under Phase B, as the plan was presented to Wilson, North Vietnam would be allowed to resupply its forces in the South at a "normal" rate, because the aim of the plan was to cool off the war as a preliminary to negotiations without loss of face or military advantage to either side. This was the essential content of a draft letter to Ho Chi Minh from President Johnson, which Cooper was shown in Washington on February 2—the day before he left for London. On that same day, Johnson was reminded at a press conference that he had said he would suspend the bombing of the North "in exchange for some suitable step" by the other side. When asked what he would consider suitable, he replied, "just almost any step."

On February 5, two American journalists who had visited Hanoi and taken part in informal exchanges of views between Hanoi and Washington received clearance from State Department officials for the text of a letter which they sent to Ho Chi Minh that same day by airmail (in care of the DRV embassy in Phnom Penh). The journalists were Harry Ashmore and William Baggs. Their letter said that "senior officials of the State Department" had

> expressed particular interest in your suggestion to us that private talks could begin provided the U.S. stopped bombing your country, and ceased introducing additional U.S. troops into Viet-Nam. They expressed the opinion that some reciprocal restraint to indicate that neither side intended to use the occasion of the talks for military advantage would provide tangible evidence of the good faith of all parties in the prospects for a negotiated settlement.[5]

In short, the February 5 letter, which was cleared by Assistant Secretary William Bundy, reaffirmed the description of the U.S. negotiating position which Cooper had given to Prime Minister Wilson on February 3 (and which Wilson laid before Kosygin three days later).

However, early on February 8, President Johnson dispatched a letter over his own signature to Ho Chi Minh to be passed by the U.S. embassy in Moscow to the DRV embassy there. This letter said that Johnson was prepared to halt the bombing of North Vietnam and the augmentation of U.S. forces in the South "as soon as I am assured that infiltration [of North Vietnamese forces and material] in South Vietnam by land and by sea has stopped."[6]

Apparently none of the senior officials in Washington who were aware of President Johnson's February 8 letter thought to advise Prime Minister Wilson that the United States was changing its terms and demanding that Hanoi agree to stop infiltration completely (which would amount to crippling its military operations in South Vietnam) before the U.S. would order a bombing halt.

On February 10, Wilson and Cooper drafted a written statement of the Phase A-Phase B plan as it had been described to Cooper a week earlier, and Wilson gave it to Kosygin at the Soviet leader's request; Cooper cabled the text to Washington for the information of U.S. officials, believing it was an accurate statement of U.S. policy. Later that evening, however, the White House called Wilson's official residence and insisted that Kosygin be given a revised version of the statement he had been handed by Wilson. Johnson's explanation of the new sequence of steps is worth quoting at some length:

> Hanoi would first stop infiltration; we would then stop the bombing and, in addition, we would agree not to increase our troop strength in Vietnam. That is what I told Ho Chi Minh in my letter. I recognized, of course, that the new proposal altered the Phase A-Phase B plan we had discussed earlier with the British and had offered to Hanoi. Instead of asking the North Vietnamese to promise to take steps to reduce the fighting after the bombing ended, I wanted them to begin cutting down their actions against the South before we stopped the bombing. I felt strongly that this change was justified by the hard fact that during the bombing pause then underway very large southward movements of men and supplies were taking place in the area above the demilitarized zone. I refused to risk the safety of our men in I Corps by stopping air strikes before Ho Chi Minh had acted. On the other hand, I went further than ever before by proposing to freeze U.S. troop levels in the South.[7]

The leaders of the British government were deeply disappointed at having the terms of the American negotiating position altered at the last minute, when the chances of moving the war to the conference table seemed so good. On February 11, the Tet truce expired, but the United States did not immediately resume bombing (in deference to Wilson, who would thereby have suffered further political embarrassment).

Johnson agreed to let Wilson make one more attempt at mediation before Kosygin left the United Kingdom.

Wilson told Kosygin on behalf of the U.S. government that if Hanoi would agree to stop infiltration into the South by February 13, the bombing would not be resumed and the build-up of American forces would end. However, no response was received from Hanoi on February 13, and the United States started the bombing again. The first raid was made at night and under such poor weather conditions that its result could not be determined. Apparently the bombing was resumed not for the military reasons cited earlier by the President but as a political bargaining point. Johnson feared that prolonging the pause would only increase both political and domestic pressure for a permanent halt.

The United States was slowly being "polarized" in early 1967; antiwar sentiment was growing, particularly on college campuses and among urban black Americans. In March, the Reverend Martin Luther King proposed a merger of the civil rights and peace movements. But the great majority of Americans were unwilling to take any extreme action to oppose their government's policy. Ironically, the prowar group sprang up mainly in reaction to the demonstrations and activism of the peace movement.

On March 1, 1967, the Senate adopted its first policy statement on the Vietnam war since the Tonkin Gulf resolution. It was far milder than various texts proposed by a growing band of antiwar senators, including Robert Kennedy. It supported American fighting men abroad, but also endorsed the efforts of President Johnson and "other men of good will" to prevent expansion of the war and to reach a negotiated peace. The policy statement, which was offered as an amendment to the war appropriations bill, called for the convening of a new Geneva conference to bring the war to an "honorable conclusion." This could be interpreted as a gentle reproach to the Johnson administration for its reluctance to risk making the first move toward de-escalation. Its language was so bland, however, that most people probably read it as an unqualified endorsement of administration policy.

Nevertheless, Johnson was concerned about the mounting criticism of his policy in intellectual circles—where it was widely believed that the conflict was a stalemate and that further escalation risked plunging the world into a major war. When Hanoi made public the notes that

Johnson and Ho Chi Minh had exchanged in February, Senator Robert Kennedy and others criticized the President for stiffening his negotiating position. Administration leaders vehemently denied the charge; in April, the President brought General Westmoreland home to address a joint session of Congress to reassure doubters that the war would be won if the people stood behind their President and their fighting men.

But neither direct appeals to patriotism nor the administration's campaign to document the success of its pacification efforts in South Vietnam could close the "credibility gap." American news media, reacting to administration efforts to manage the news, began to emphasize stories that refuted the administration's "success" campaign. A foreign war was being brought into American homes, live and in color, on daily TV news programs for the first time in history. People tended to believe what they could see with their own eyes and to discount the statistical case presented by the White House.

To more sophisticated members of Congress and the public, Johnson's Indochina policy failed to take account of major opportunities and obvious dangers in the world situation. China was in the second turbulent year of its Cultural Revolution, and the Soviet Union was being vilified almost daily by the Peking government for "revisionism" and other "crimes." The correct policy to pursue in regard to the Vietnam war had become a major bone of contention between the two Communist giants. This placed Hanoi in an extremely awkward position. North Vietnam found it almost impossible to maintain close relations with both Russia and China, on whom she depended for economic and military aid. Experts on Soviet-American relations, such as George Kennan, urged the Johnson administration to try to widen the Sino-Soviet split by working for a peace settlement in Vietnam. Others, like the journalist Harrison Salisbury, pointed out that the Sino-Soviet conflict would make Hanoi more receptive to the idea of a negotiated settlement.

But the U.S. administration merely reaffirmed its hard line. It increased bombing raids on targets near the China border in North Vietnam; four American aircraft were reportedly shot down over Chinese territory in the first half of 1967.

When Kosygin met with President Johnson at Glassboro, New Jersey (June 23 to 25, 1967), the Soviet premier reiterated Hanoi's January statement that talks would begin if there were a bombing halt. After discussing this overture with his advisors for two days, Johnson told

Kosygin that the United States was ready to stop bombing the North—he assumed that discussions would begin immediately thereafter. Johnson also asked Kosygin to tell Hanoi that American and allied forces near the seventeenth parallel would not advance northward; he would expect Hanoi's forces near the seventeenth parallel not to move south either. Hanoi did not respond to this message, according to President Johnson.[8] Peking denounced the Glassboro talks on their final day, saying they were "first and foremost directed against the Chinese."

President Johnson's message to Hanoi possibly failed to produce results because the DRV leaders were afraid of seriously antagonizing China. Some officials within the Johnson administration were beginning to consider de-escalating the war without reaching a formal agreement with Hanoi on subsequent steps. The catalyst for this major reassessment was a request for 200,000 more troops which General Westmoreland submitted in March 1967.

In that month, American troop strength in Vietnam stood at 470,000 men. General Westmoreland claimed that he needed 100,000 more men by July 1968 to contain the enemy threat and maintain the tactical initiative. An additional 100,000 troops (bringing the total to 670,000) would be an "optimum force," Westmoreland said, enabling him to destroy or neutralize enemy main force units more quickly and deny them long-established safe havens in South Vietnam. The Joint Chiefs of Staff endorsed the request and urged the Johnson administration to mobilize reserve units in the United States, extend the ground war into the enemy's safe havens in adjoining countries (Laos, Cambodia, and possibly North Vietnam), mine the main ports in the North, and generally adopt a clear-cut policy of seeking military victory.

President Johnson discussed the new proposals with General Wheeler (Chairman of the JCS) and General Westmoreland when the latter came to Washington in late April. Westmoreland acknowledged that there was no danger of defeat if he did not get the additional troops, but without them he said it would be difficult to cope with the reinforcements the enemy was capable of providing. Johnson asked whether the enemy was capable of matching any reinforcements the U.S. sent. "If so," he asked, "where does it all end?"[9] Westmoreland answered that the enemy could probably deploy four more divisions in South Vietnam.

At the same meeting, Westmoreland warned that the war could drag on for five more years without the requested reinforcements. With

565,000 U.S. troops under his command, he predicted the war could go on for three years, while it might take two years if he had 665,000 men (the "optimum force" level). [10]

General Wheeler argued the need for a reserve call-up to be prepared for any challenge to American positions in such places as South Korea or Berlin. He also wanted to be prepared for the possibility that the United States might decide to expand the war into Cambodia, Laos, or North Vietnam. General Westmoreland pointed out that Laos could become a major battlefield in the current war.

Senior civilian officials were almost unanimous in opposing the Westmoreland-Wheeler troop request. The three most disturbing aspects of the plan were the call-up of reserves, the idea of attacking the port of Haiphong, and the expansion of the ground war into neighboring countries. The reserve call-up would lead to a major congressional debate on the war, which civilian leaders were anxious to avoid because it might provide a focal point for American antiwar sentiment. Attacking or mining the port of Haiphong would be a direct threat to Soviet and other foreign shipping; it could lead to the most serious political consequences (besides raising awkward questions in international law since the U.S. was fighting an undeclared war). Civilian officials were more firmly opposed to expanding the war into North Vietnam than into Laos or Cambodia, but in all three cases they were concerned about provoking Chinese intervention.

While these arguments were being mustered within the administration, there was also a growing feeling among Johnson's advisors that the bombing should be cut back to the twentieth parallel (south of the Red River delta), mainly to reduce the very high losses of U.S. pilots and planes that resulted from attacking the well-defended areas around Hanoi and Haiphong. [11] McNamara and McNaughton had been among the first senior officials to suggest a bombing cutback in October 1966. Now they were seeking specific changes in strategy and a basic change in the nation's war goal—from military victory to a compromise peace settlement.

On May 19, McNamara presented Johnson with a long memorandum reflecting the views of many disillusioned senior officials. McNamara's May 1967 memorandum proposed cutting back the bombing to the twentieth parallel and sending General Westmoreland 30,000 more troops instead of 200,000. The paper followed the general thrust of a May 6 memorandum by McNaughton, urging that

... the "philosophy" of the war should be fought out now so everyone will not be proceeding on their own major premises, and getting us in deeper and deeper; at the very least, the President should give General Westmoreland his limit (as President Truman did to General MacArthur). That is, if General Westmoreland is to get 550,000 men, he should be told, "That will be all, and we mean it."[12]

McNaughton, whose eighteen-year-old son was about to enter college, was more sensitive than most senior officials to the widespread public opposition to the war, particularly among young people. In the same memorandum, he wrote that

A feeling is widely and strongly held that "the Establishment" is out of its mind. The feeling is that we are trying to impose some U.S. image on distant peoples we cannot understand (any more than we can the younger generation here at home), and we are carrying the thing to absurd lengths.

Related to this feeling is the increased polarization that is taking place in the United States with seeds of the worst split in our people in more than a century. ...

However, there was plenty of sentiment in Washington, particularly among the military chiefs at the Pentagon, for intensifying the pressures on North Vietnam rather than cutting them back. In the past, President Johnson had often agreed to major policy statements on the war as soon as Secretary McNamara submitted them to him. He did not do so in the case of the May 19 memorandum because it did not represent an agreed position of his main civilian and military advisers. McNamara's job was to negotiate such agreed positions and keep the military from publicly opposing the administration's policy. Thus, when McNamara began to advocate a major policy change (and to reveal his doubts about past decisions), the military chiefs saw their opportunity to weaken the Secretary's iron grip on U.S. security policy.

A few days after McNamara submitted his May 19 memorandum to the President, the military (who had been shown a copy but were unaware that Johnson had seen it) attacked the Secretary's arguments. Some of the harshest criticism was contained in a May 31 paper which McNamara received from the Joint Chiefs. [13] According to this document, the "drastic changes" in U.S. policy proposed by McNamara "would undermine and no longer provide a complete rationale for our presence in South Vietnam or much of our efforts over the past two years."

This, of course, was exactly McNamara's point. But the Joint Chiefs saw no reason to change the existing policy, and they were "unable to find due cause for the degree of pessimism expressed" by McNamara about the war situation. Indeed, he had even ignored the basic dogma of the domino theory by failing "to appreciate the full implications for the free world of failure" in Vietnam. A cutback of the bombing, the Joint Chiefs predicted, was most unlikely to lead to negotiations; in fact, it was likely to have the opposite effect and might "result in the strengthening of the enemy's resolve to continue the war." Quite plainly, the Joint Chiefs did not concur in McNamara's proposal, and they urged him not to forward it to the President. Johnson's failure to act on McNamara's proposal suggests that he was already aware of the chiefs' position.

In a rare instance of the State Department taking the initiative on Vietnam policy, Undersecretary Katzenbach tried to find a compromise between the positions espoused by McNamara and the Joint Chiefs. According to Katzenbach's formula, the U.S. political objective should be to leave behind a stable, democratic Saigon regime by neutralizing the Viet Cong threat internally and persuading Hanoi to abandon the struggle. To achieve these aims, he proposed sending 30,000 more U.S. troops in small increments over an eighteen-month period. The bombing would avoid the Hanoi-Haiphong area, and concentrate on lines of communication all over the North (perhaps including roads and railroads near the China border).

However, it was one thing to propose a compromise and another thing to sell it to the main protagonists within the administration. Even though McNamara was now one of the protagonists, he must come to terms with the chiefs to maintain his effectiveness. Thus, in July, he flew to Saigon, as he had done so many times before, and hammered out an agreement with Westmoreland. There would be a 55,000 man troop increase; this was not the 200,000 Westmoreland had asked for, but it was not a trivial number either. From the political standpoint, it allowed the administration to delay a little longer the crucial decision of whether or not to call up the reserves. (McNaughton had pointed out that it would be far better to face that issue squarely in 1967 than to have it come up in an election year.)

On the question of a bombing halt or cutback, President Johnson responded to increased pressure from Congress. From July through September, he authorized strikes against most of the remaining targets requested by the Joint Chiefs, including many in the highly dangerous Hanoi-Haiphong area. Their purpose was to reduce the pressure for an all-or-nothing strategy in Vietnam, which was being generated by a series of hearings of the Senate Preparedness Subcommittee.

Secretary McNamara testified in secret before the Preparedness Subcommittee, presenting a devastating attack on the air war in which he had once believed so firmly. The bombing had destroyed $320 million worth of facilities in the North and had cost the United States $911 million in destroyed aircraft alone (not to mention lives lost). Only 2 percent of the troops Hanoi attempted to infiltrate south were killed by bombing, in spite of incredible concentrations of explosives dumped on eastern Laos. Over 8000 trucks had been destroyed or damaged, but traffic over the Ho Chi Minh road network had increased steadily. McNamara's testimony may have helped persuade certain hawkish senators (including Jackson of Washington and Symington of Missouri) that the United States should begin to withdraw from Vietnam.

McNamara's aim in discrediting the air war was to prepare congressional opinion for an important diplomatic initiative involving a public offer to stop the bombing. In the course of a speech at San Antonio on September 29, President Johnson said that the U.S. would stop bombing North Vietnam "when this will lead promptly to productive discussions." He added that "We of course assume that while discussions proceed, North Vietnam would not take advantage of the bombing cessation or limitation.' This "San Antonio formula" was much like the "Phase A-Phase B" plan which had been proposed by the United States (and then suddenly withdrawn) the previous February. The bombing was halted, or restricted to certain areas, several times before and after Johnson announced the San Antonio formula, but no face-to-face talks were begun with the North Vietnamese during the remainder of the year.

Meanwhile in South Vietnam, a presidential election was held in September 1967 under the country's newly proclaimed American-style constitution. General Thieu was elected president and—in a notable departure from the past practice of the Saigon generals—his main rival, Air Vice Marshal Ky, agreed to accept the vice-presidency instead of organizing a coup. The actual balloting was not tampered with by

Saigon's military rulers, although they refused to allow any neutralist candidates to run and took other special "precautions" to insure that their ticket won. Nevertheless, the restoration of at least a façade of legal and stable government in Saigon marked the achievement of one of the United States' main objectives. It seemed an ideal moment to announce the leveling off of American involvement and gradual withdrawal, but once again the opportunity was allowed to pass.

In the United States, antiwar demonstrations were growing in intensity in many parts of the country. In October 1967, they were climaxed by the march of 55,000 militants to the Pentagon. Large numbers of federal troops in battle dress ringed the building and were held in readiness throughout Washington. Although the march produced no serious violence, it emphasized the sharp decline in respect for law and established values, which some attributed to the government's example in prosecuting an undeclared war.

On November 30, 1967, Senator Eugene McCarthy entered the race for the Democratic nomination, asking the American people to back him as a peace candidate, rather than President Johnson. One of McCarthy's major aims was to take the antiwar movement out of the streets (where its disorderliness tended to frighten voters and create a prowar backlash) into established patterns of electoral politics. President Johnson had told very few people that he was considering not running for reelection, and it appeared at first that McCarthy's cause was hopeless. There were rumors that he was merely a stalking horse for Robert Kennedy, who held similar views on the war.

If he had decided to run again, President Johnson would no longer have at his side the man who, since 1961, had borne vast administrative responsibilities in connection with the Vietnam war and other national security problems. In spite of his immense dynamism, Robert McNamara now needed a change from the intense pressures of his office. He was also deeply disenchanted with the war policy and was perhaps aware that his influence was slipping, now that he was more the advocate of a change of policy than an impartial mediator. On November 1, 1967, he submitted a plan to phase out United States military involvement in Vietnam. It called for a bombing halt, an end to U.S. troop increases in the South, and the adoption of a less aggressive strategy to reduce American casualties and "Vietnamize" the war.

President Johnson sent the plan to eleven senior advisors, telling none of them that it came from McNamara. Secretary Rusk and Under-secretary Katzenbach were the only ones who partially approved the plan. Clark Clifford, a Washington lawyer and Johnson confidant, strongly advised against a bombing halt. Clifford was named McNamara's successor—and thus he entered the small circle of "Vietnam principals" on the eve of the most dramatic moment in the history of U.S. involvement in Indochina.

Notes

1. The words in quotation marks are from Assistant Secretary of Defense John McNaughton's memo dated Jan. 19, 1966, excerpts of which are included in *Pentagon Papers*, pp. 491-93.

2. U.S. figures showed an estimated 150,000 enemy troops had been killed in action by September 1966, compared with 5141 Americans. Yet the enemy's troop strength in South Vietnam rose steadily from 1961 to 1966, with infiltration running at an all-time high of 5000 men per month in the latter year. It was frequently impossible to tell whether a corpse lying on a Vietnamese battlefield represented a dead soldier or a dead civilian. But it appears likely that there were two civilian casualties for every Viet Cong casualty, according to Representative Clement J. Zablocki; see his "Report on Vietnam," U.S. Senate, *U.S. Policy with Respect to Mainland China* (Washington: Government Printing Office, 1965), p. 349.

3. This thesis is developed and documented by David Kraslow and Stuart H. Loory, two investigative reporters, in their book *The Secret Search for Peace in Vietnam* (New York: Vintage, 1968).

4. For President Johnson's account of this episode, see *Vantage Point*, pp. 253-55.

5. See Harry S. Ashmore and William C. Baggs, *Mission to Hanoi, a Chronicle of Double-Dealing in High Places* (New York: Putnam, 1968). The text of the February 5 letter is on pp. 70-71.

6. For the text of Johnson's February 8 letter and Ho Chi Minh's reply (dated February 15, 1967), see *Vantage Point*, pp. 592-95.

7. Ibid., pp. 253-54.

8. Ibid., pp. 256-57.

9. Notes of the meeting were kept by Assistant Secretary McNaughton and included in *Pentagon Papers*, pp. 567-69.

10. The Pentagon's systems analysis office produced an estimate that a 200,000-man U.S. troops increase would make it possible to raise the enemy's losses (at most) by 3700 per week. This would be 400 a week more than he could replace. At this rate, it would take ten years to destroy the enemy's forces by fighting a war of attrition in the South. See May 4, 1967 memo by Assistant Secretary of Defense Alain Enthoven, *Pentagon Papers*, pp. 572-73.

11. In a May 5, 1967 memorandum, Assistant Secretary McNaughton noted that the loss rate for American pilots over the Hanoi-Haiphong area was one pilot for every forty sorties. (A sortie is a mission flown by one aircraft.) He said this was six times as high as the loss rate over the rest of North Vietnam.

12. See *Pentagon Papers*, pp. 534-35. Just two months later, McNaughton, his wife, and their younger son were killed in a plane collision over North Carolina. McNaughton's death deprived McNamara of one of his most valued colleagues in the Pentagon just when they and others were struggling to change the administration's war policy.

13. Excerpts from this memo are included in *Pentagon Papers*, pp. 538-39.

CHAPTER SIXTEEN

The 1968
Tet Offensive

The climactic struggle for South Vietnam's cities in early 1968—and General Westmoreland's request for 206,000 more troops—made President Johnson's war of attrition policy untenable in the United States. By showing that they could still launch simultaneous attacks on towns and cities throughout South Vietnam, the Communists achieved their minimum aim of discrediting Washington's "success campaign" and undermining the American people's support for the war.

Hanoi's effort to ignite a general uprising in South Vietnam—its maximum goal—was however a complete failure. To many of the cautious and frightened people of the South, the fact that the Viet Cong were eventually driven out of all the towns and cities which they seized during Tet was highly instructive. It proved that the Viet Cong were no more infallible than ARVN or the Saigon regime. Because the most seasoned Viet Cong guerrillas (rather than North Vietnamese units) bore the brunt of the fighting on the Communist side, they were slaughtered by the thousands when they came up against superior allied firepower. As a result, the war became more nearly a North-South struggle (as Washington had always claimed it was) and less of a civil war between foreign-supported South Vietnamese factions. Beginning in April 1968, the odds which had favored Communist victory in the South started to move slowly (though not inexorably) in Saigon's direction.

The Offensive

By early 1967, the exodus of villagers from the war torn countryside of South Vietnam into the comparative safety of the towns and cities had begun to deprive the Viet Cong of recruits, supplies, and tax revenue. Therefore, Hanoi's leaders planned a general offensive against the cities of South Vietnam at the start of the next year; their aim was to promote antiwar feeling in the United States (as the earlier seige of Dien Bien Phu did in France) and to spark a general uprising which would lead to the reunification of Vietnam.[1] In July 1967, Viet Cong commanders in the South were told to begin preparing the general offensive, although most were not told when it would take place until the last possible moment. Extremely complex logistical, training, and intelligence tasks had to be carried out during the intervening months. At the same time, an intensive effort was made to lay the necessary groundwork for a general uprising in the cities, where the Communist organization was still relatively weak compared with rural areas.

Preparations on such a grandiose scale could not be hidden from thousands of South Vietnamese and allied intelligence agents who were operating all over the country. In fact, the Hanoi regime's written order for a major offensive and uprising was among the many captured documents which the U.S. Mission in Saigon routinely translated, mimeographed, and distributed to journalists.[2] As a result of this and other warnings, some American units were braced for attacks during the Tet truce. But no one really believed the enemy would try to carry out an offensive on the scale which the captured documents indicated. Allied forces had been placed frequently on alert for enemy action during the second half of 1967, and very few enemy attacks had materialized.

The Johnson administration rashly interpreted the lull in late 1967 as evidence that allied forces had almost destroyed the enemy's capability for large-unit action. (As described in the previous chapter, the administration was engaged at this time in a major "success offensive" to convince the increasingly skeptical American public that there really was "light at the end of the tunnel.") The lull in Communist-initiated actions simply meant that the enemy was preparing for the big offensive.

On December 30, 1967, North Vietnamese Foreign Minister Nguyen Duy Trinh announced that, if the United States halted its bombing unconditionally, North Vietnam would hold talks with the United States on relevant questions.[3] Previously, Hanoi had not clarified what it would do if the United States stopped the bombing, and Trinh's December 30 statement was evidently designed to place the American government in a dilemma. There was a growing array of evidence that Communist forces were preparing some spectacular military action. (High officials in Washington thought it might be a seige of the remote Khesanh base on the pattern of Dien Bien Phu.) Was Hanoi trying to trick the United States into a bombing halt that would allow a rapid build-up of supplies near Khesanh?

Administration leaders could however hardly ignore Trinh's statement because for months they had said they were looking for a signal that Hanoi was ready to negotiate. At Washington's request, the deputy foreign minister of Rumania flew to Hanoi to seek clarification of the DRV's position. While he was there, the United States placed Hanoi and Haiphong off limits to bombing. But the Rumanian diplomat was still waiting for final answers to his questions when the Tet offensive began.

On the night of January 30 (possibly through an error in timing), the enemy attacked seven cities in the northern half of South Vietnam. As fighting continued the next day, Viet Cong political agents passed out leaflets calling for a general uprising against the Saigon regime. Even with these warnings that they were in for a major offensive, the Saigon government did not make any nationwide effort to recall to duty ARVN officers and men who were on leave for the Tet holidays.

During the night of January 31, the map of South Vietnam was lit up like a pinball machine by separate enemy attacks all over the metropolitan area of Saigon (where 3.2 million people were concentrated) and by attacks against every major city and most of the larger towns throughout the country. The nature and size of the attacks and the effectiveness with which they were carried out varied from place to place. Most involved small numbers of specially trained Viet Cong troops, many of whom were infiltrated into the target areas well beforehand. Their main hope of success lay in a general uprising (which did not take place) and in large-scale reinforcements, which they were told to expect but which generally did not materialize.

In Saigon, commando groups were assigned to execute key officials, such as President Thieu and Ambassador Bunker, but these attempts all failed. Communist efforts to seize strategic facilities, such as airfields and radio stations, were also beaten back by allied forces, although in some cases the attackers came extremely close to achieving their objectives. The allies' counter attack to expel an estimated 1000 Viet Cong from the Saigon area lasted three weeks and resulted in massive destruction and many civilian casualties, particularly in Cholon, the Chinese section. In most cases, the psychological effects of the Viet Cong offensive were much more important than the military consequences. For example, a small band of nineteen Viet Cong commandos blasted their way into the American Embassy compound and managed to hold out for six hours against U.S. marine guards and paratroopers, who were landed by helicopter on the embassy roof. The battle, featured on the major U.S. television networks, was to many Americans one of the most dramatic episodes of the whole Tet offensive.

Hue, the old imperial capital, is the only city which the Communists held long enough to begin trying to alter the political and social system. As the religious center of South Vietnam, Hue contained many of the country's architectural treasures. It is associated with a Confucian official class who gained its position through academic accomplishment rather than wealth. For many Vietnamese, Hue is the heart of Vietnam, as Kyoto is the heart of Japan.

An estimated one thousand Viet Cong troops occupied large areas of this city for more than three weeks. During that time, they killed at least 2800 local notables and pro-government Vietnamese as well as most of the foreign residents whom they took prisoner. Allied forces reoccupied the city after bombarding it with heavy-weapons fire and after some of the most intensive street fighting of the war. Many civilians were killed in the process, and well over half of the buildings in the city were destroyed or badly damaged. The Johnson administration cited the mass graves of Viet Cong victims in Hue as a foretaste of what would happen if the Communists won the war. American opponents of the war pointed out that the only way of "saving" South Vietnam seemed to be to destroy it.

By mid-February (when most of the larger actions had ended), the U.S. Mission in Saigon estimated that 33,000 enemy soldiers had been killed and 6700 captured. The number of allied soldiers killed in action was put at 3400 (including 1000 Americans). Of the 12,000 allied troops wounded, American G.I.s accounted for 5500. Most reporters estimated that civilian casualties were even higher than military. One of the most horrifying examples of deliberate civilian bloodshed involving U.S. forces was the My Lai massacre, which took place on March 16, 1968, about a hundred miles south of Hue. A platoon of U.S. Army troops under the command of Lieutenant William L. Calley, Jr. entered the hamlet and killed several hundred unarmed civilians; Calley later testified at his court martial that he believed they were concealing Viet Cong soldiers.[4]

President Out of Touch With the People

The Tet offensive, as portrayed by U.S. news media, convinced many Americans that their government had been lying to them. Instead of leading to military victory in the fairly near future, the war of attrition strategy seemed to be leading to a steadily increasing commitment of troops and money, rising casualty rates, and the danger of all-out war with Russia or China. Long angered and disgusted by the U.S. government's effort to manage the news of a war they regarded as immoral, American newsmen hammered away at what seemed to be the basic lesson of the grim offensive: South Vietnam was further away than ever from being able to stand on its own as a non-Communist nation.

For once, television cameramen had no difficulty zeroing in on what seemed to be the "big picture" of history in the making in Vietnam—the attacks on the American Embassy and the presidential palace, the street-by-street liberation and destruction of Hue, the cold-blooded shooting of a Viet Cong suspect by South Vietnam's police chief. Unquestionably, the media exaggerated the Viet Cong's military success in the first weeks of the offensive and so contributed to their psychological victory. But the Johnson administration had set the stage with its elaborate "success campaign" in 1967.

At his press conference on February 2 (just after the start of the Tet offensive), President Johnson declared that militarily the enemy had suffered a "complete failure." Although this was true, it hardly squared with what people were reading in their newspapers or watching on television. (And because they felt they had been deceived in the past, an unusually high percentage of Americans were prepared to believe the media and doubt the President's claims.) President Johnson also indicated that there were no plans for any substantial increase in the number of U.S. troops in Vietnam beyond the already approved level of 525,000 men. Nor did he foresee "any change of great consequence" in the existing strategy. He predicted that the enemy would "fail and fail again, because we Americans will never yield." He warned however that the enemy's second objective was to achieve a psychological victory, and he implied that "some unknowing people here at home" were associating themselves with that aim.

The President was trying to prevent his critics on both the left and right from gaining the initiative. As far as the antiwar critics were concerned, his press conference statement amounted to calling them defeatists and unwitting dupes of Communist propaganda. But he was also telling his critics on the right—those who favored general mobilization and a more risky offensive strategy in the war—that the Tet offensive did not provide a rationale for what they were seeking.

In speeches and statements all during February, President Johnson hammered away at the idea that a unified America could overcome all threats from the Communist world. Borrowing themes from Churchill's wartime speeches, he compared Hanoi's aggression with that of Hitler and likened the Saigon regime to an embattled democracy. He reminded friend and foe alike that no slackening of the U.S. military effort could be considered until the aggressors had been put to rout. Apparently at this stage, Johnson believed that only a small, unrepresentative minority of the American people was opposed to his policy.[5]

By the end of February, the news media were beginning to give the public a somewhat less apocalyptic view of the military situation in Vietnam (just when the military chiefs were prophesying a dire "emergency," requiring the mobilization of reserve units in the United States). According to the newsmen, it now appeared that there had been no winners, only losers; in fact, the enemy had lost just as heavily as the allies, and quite likely even more so. However, the administration and its critics continued to disagree concerning the impact of the Tet offensive on the rural pacification program. President Johnson believed U.S. Mission reports which claimed the program had survived largely unscathed in most areas. His critics on the other hand felt that the unexpected scale of the Tet offensive proved that no one in Saigon really knew what was going on in the country—and that the U.S. Mission was a victim of its own "success" propaganda.

Neither Congress nor the American public was very interested in the precise degree of damage caused by the Tet offensive. What they wanted to know was when the United States commitment would end, how the administration planned to disengage from the war, and whether or not the administration's answers to these questions could be believed.

The Wheeler-Westmoreland Troop Request

President Johnson was wrestling with the problem of an involvement that seemed to be growing larger instead of smaller. Since 1965, he had rejected all proposals by his military advisors for mobilizing the reserves and National Guard units to replace forces sent to Vietnam. To disturb the country's normal peacetime routine as little as possible, he decided to rely entirely on the draft and voluntary enlistment to increase the size of the armed forces. This decision had made it necessary to adopt the policy of "graduated response," and the troop build-up in Vietnam had been much slower than the military chiefs recommended. But within these broad limits, President Johnson had done all in his power to make it impossible for the Joint Chiefs of Staff to blame him for American military failures in Indochina.

The President's reluctance to resort to mobilization also meant that strategic reserve forces (which might be needed at home or to implement NATO defense plans) were robbed of more than half their effective strength between 1965 and 1968. All over the world—in Korea, Germany, the Mediterranean, and elsewhere—U.S. forces were considered to be stretched too thin to cope with a possible emergency. In the eyes of the Joint Chiefs, the Tet offensive offered a rationale for sharply raising the force level in Vietnam—and if the President agreed to this, he would have no choice except to mobilize the reserves.

Beginning shortly after the start of the Tet offensive, General

Wheeler (Chairman of the JCS) sent a series of messages to General Westmoreland hinting that he should marshal a case for a large-scale reinforcement of his command. (President Johnson, at the same time, was emphasizing in public statements that Westmoreland had all the troops he had said he needed and that there was no likelihood of exceeding the current 525,000 man ceiling.) In mid-February, perhaps partly to reduce the pressure for major reinforcements, Johnson ordered 10,500 combat troops to Vietnam. But he stressed the fact that they were going out on "temporary duty," and he did not mobilize any reserve units to replace them.

As allied forces began to regain control of most of the towns attacked by the enemy, General Wheeler went to Saigon with instructions from President Johnson "to find out what else Westmoreland might need." Wheeler evidently took this to mean that Westmoreland had carte blanche to request large-scale reinforcements.

After consulting with General Westmoreland and pointing out the critical need—and opportunity—to augment U.S. military manpower around the world, General Wheeler cabled from Saigon, on February 26, saying that Westmoreland required 206,756 more men. (Back in Washington, Secretary McNamara promptly calculated that this would mean mobilizing about half a million reservists and raising the defense budget to $100 billion.) General Westmoreland welcomed the prospect of having additional troops under his command because this would make it possible for him to undertake a more aggressive strategy, including an amphibious assault on North Vietnam and attacks across the borders of Laos and Cambodia to cut the enemy's supply routes and clean out his sanctuaries.

General Wheeler's report in late February indicated the 206,000 additional troops were needed in three installments: 108,000 by the first of May; 42,000 by September 1; and 55,000 by the end of December. However, the two generals had an understanding that only the first 108,000 men would actually be sent to Vietnam; the rest would be added to the strategic reserve and would be sent to Vietnam only if the military situation became exceedingly grave.[6]

Generals Wheeler and Westmoreland also agreed that, from a tactical viewpoint, they should first obtain approval from civilian leaders in Washington for additional troops and *then* broach the question of adopting a more offensive strategy. General Westmoreland was shocked, however, when he learned that his recommendation for additional troops had been portrayed by General Wheeler as an "urgent" request designed to meet the threat of a renewed communist offensive.[7] Westmoreland and his staff knew that the rationale for this was inaccurate and self-serving. But they gradually became more attuned to the realities of bureaucratic politics in Washington. (For example, they revised their original low estimates of the enemy's post-Tet strength so as to leave Hanoi with enough troops to provide a "credible" threat.) Westmoreland's optimism about the military situation and his candor in reporting it to Washington undercut General Wheeler's effort to base his troop request on a "dire emergency."[8]

In Washington, many civilian officials were appalled by the Wheeler-Westmoreland request for a 40 percent troop increase. At a meeting of the Vietnam principals on February 27, McNamara (who was leaving the government in three more days) said that the proper number of additional troops to send was zero.[9] As an alternative, McNamara suggested that the United States might combine a smaller military increase with a new peace initiative. Rusk said that if a peace proposal were made, it should be specific; for example, the U.S. might stop the bombing north of the twentieth parallel (where most of North Vietnam's people live) or halt the bombing entirely if Hanoi would withdraw its troops from the area just south of the demilitarized zone.[10]

President Johnson was in Texas, and Walt Rostow sent him a teletype summary of the February 27 meeting. Rostow reported that the "only firm agreement" reached by the Vietnam principals was that the troop issue "raised many questions to which you ought to have clear answers before making a final decision." Rostow also suggested making Clark Clifford chairman of a working group to "staff out the alternatives and their implications."[11]

The President returned to Washington in the early hours of February 28 and met the Vietnam principals at a White House breakfast, where General Wheeler, just back from Vietnam, presented an oral briefing on the situation. Wheeler told the group that the Tet offensive had narrowly missed achieving its aims, and that 206,000 more troops were needed on an emergency basis to head off a possible second offensive. The reaction of the civilian leaders assembled in the family dining room of the White House was one of deep concern, bordering on fear, that the war might be getting out of control.

Notes

1. The idea of launching a major offensive to produce a general uprising had long been a central element of the Indochina Communist party's strategy. The device was first tried against the French in the early 1930s, with disastrous results for the ICP. The August 1945 uprising, in which the ICP managed to gain the initiative before the French returned in force, was much more successful—although France refused to accept the fait accompli without eight and a half years of war.

2. Don Oberdorfer, *Tet!* (Garden City, N.Y.; Doubleday, 1971), pp. 117-121. The text of the U.S. mission's press release describing the order for the offensive as well as the key paragraph of the document itself are given on pp. 118-19 of Oberdorfer's book. The press release was dated January 5, 1968, twenty-five days before the start of the offensive.

3. This gesture was patterned closely on Ho Chi Minh's November 1953 offer to negotiate with the French; on this occasion, the DRV had just decided to accept General Navarre's challenge for a set-piece battle at Dien Bien Phu. Fighting and negotiating would thus proceed at the same time.

4. Seymour M. Hersh, *My Lai 4* (New York: Random House, 1970).

5. Before long, the polls began to tell a different story. Just before President Johnson's major speech about Vietnam on March 31, the Gallup poll showed that only 26 percent of the public approved his conduct of the war, 36 percent approved his overall performance as President, while 52 percent disapproved. The rest were undecided.

6. John B. Henry II, "February, 1968," *Foreign Policy*, Fall 1971, pp. 16-17.

7. Ibid., pp. 17-20.

8. Oberdorfer, *Tet!* p. 290.

9. Townsend Hoopes, *The Limits of Intervention* (New York: McKay, 1969), pp. 162-65, speculates that if McNamara had made the trip to Saigon instead of Wheeler, he would have persuaded Westmoreland to reduce his troop request to about 50,000 men—and that this more modest figure would not have touched off a major debate on the administration's policy the way the 206,000 figure did. Hoopes was serving as Undersecretary of the air force at the time, and it was he who told the press that the administration was deeply divided on the issue of sending more troops.

10. *Vantage Point*, pp. 389-90. President Johnson gives Secretary Rusk full credit for influencing the bombing halt decision.

11. Ibid., p. 390.

CHAPTER SEVENTEEN

A Presidential Victim

After General Wheeler's briefing on the morning of February 28, a profoundly worried President Johnson asked Clark Clifford to serve as chairman of a special working group on Vietnam, as Rostow had suggested. Clifford was regarded at the time as a "hawk" on Vietnam. In November 1967, he had recommended emphatically that President Johnson not accept McNamara's bombing halt proposal. Chosen to succeed McNamara as Secretary of Defense, he met regularly with the Vietnam principals all during February 1968, McNamara's last month in office. Clifford had no personal identification with existing policy; he brought to the inner circle of the Johnson administration the perspective of an outsider in close touch with influential leaders of public opinion. But he also had an insider's instinctive knack for influencing the decision-making process.

After talking with the President on the morning of February 28, Clifford had the impression that Johnson wanted the working group on Vietnam to deal primarily with the political and other problems that would arise if the 206,000-man request were implemented. At some point, President Johnson sent the Vietnam principals a directive (in draft, so that their ideas could be added). It called for "recommendations in response to the situation presented to us by General Wheeler and his preliminary proposals. I wish alternatives examined," the directive stated, "and, if possible, agreed recommendations to emerge which reconcile the military, diplomatic, economic, and public opinion problems involved."[1]

Johnson may have spelled out a broader mandate for the working group in his directive than he did in his oral statement to Clifford on the morning of February 28. The working group held its first meeting later that same day, and it is quite possible that Clifford broadened the scope of its inquiry on his own initiative, before seeing the President's directive. At any rate, the meetings were an education for the new Secretary of Defense. He was amazed to discover that he could not find out when the war was going to end, or how it was going to end, or whether the new requests for men and equipment were going to be enough, or when the South Vietnamese forces would be ready to take over. "All I had," he recalled later, "was the statement, given with too little self-assurance to be comforting, that if we persisted for an indeterminate length of time, the enemy would choose not to go on."[2]

The degree to which other key Pentagon civilians were disenchanted with administration policy also came to light in the Vietnam working group meetings. The solution Deputy Secretary Paul Nitze proposed was that the United States reduce its objectives in Vietnam to fit the resources which could reasonably be made available. Specifically, he thought that the United States' limited stake in South Vietnam made it worth committing up to 50,000 more men before June 30, to enable Westmoreland to cope with the uncertainties of the situation. But he also proposed that Westmoreland be instructed to lower his sights and concentrate on protecting populated areas and on such other tasks as he could perform without a drastic increase in manpower. Nitze recommended stopping the bombing of North Vietnam completely, because by almost any yardstick it seemed to cost the United States more than it cost the enemy.[3]

Phil Goulding, in charge of the Pentagon's office of Public Affairs, argued that the American people were totally unprepared for a large-scale mobilization and that there was no national emergency which would justify such a move. He predicted the direst political consequences if the government, after claiming to have thrown back the enemy's offensive, suddenly called up 250,000 or more reservists for active duty.

Paul Warnke, head of the Pentagon's office of International Security Affairs, believed that the war was a stalemate; he argued that the United States should reduce its casualties and other costs, transfer as much as possible of the burden of South Vietnam's defense to the Vietnamese themselves, and search for a long-term strategy which the American people would support. He fully agreed with Nitze that the bombing should be stopped and that there should be a major reorientation of U.S. military strategy toward the protection of populated areas of South Vietnam. General Wheeler attacked this approach, known as the "enclave" strategy; he said it would allow the enemy to mass its forces closer to the cities, and would result in more civilian casualties than "search and destroy."

The Vietnam working group's March 4 report to the President recommended deployment of 23,000 more troops, a call-up of 45,000 reservists, and "further study" of the question of deploying the other 183,000 troops requested by Westmoreland. It recommended against any new peace initiative, but advised study of possible new "political and strategic guidance" for U.S. operations in Vietnam. Finally, it informed the President that his advisors disagreed about the bombing. One group, including General Wheeler, wanted to extend aerial bombing closer to the center of Hanoi and Haiphong, with naval bombardment close to the Chinese border. Another group favored intensification of the bombing as weather permitted, but without adding any new targets.

Clifford indicated when he gave the President the working group's report that he was still uncertain of his own views. At the March 4 meeting of the Vietnam principals, Paul Nitze suggested making a new peace initiative no later than May or June, when the allied military position should have righted itself. (This apparently represented the views of a group of senior officials at the deputy and assistant secretary level—including Harriman and Katzenbach—who favored a political settlement rather than military victory.)

Nitze's suggestion, as described by Johnson, seemed to prompt Rusk to say that they could stop most of the bombing of North Vietnam during the rainy season without too much military risk. Johnson asked Rusk to pursue the idea. At the end of the meeting, it was agreed to inform Westmoreland that 22,000 combat and support troops would be sent by June 1 and that this was "all we can give at the moment." Westmoreland had just cut the ground from under his 206,000 man request with his latest report indicating that the ARVN had nearly recovered its pre-Tet strength.[4]

On March 5, Johnson, Rusk, and Clifford discussed Rusk's partial bombing halt idea. Although the President was interested, he was not yet ready to commit himself to a specific course of action. He allowed Clifford to give a copy of Rusk's proposal (which was in writing by this time) to General Wheeler for consideration by the Joint Chiefs of Staff. But on March 6, when Rusk prepared a cable to Ambassador Bunker on the subject, Johnson decided to hold it back for the moment. He may have felt that sending the plan to Bunker to solicit the Saigon leaders' views would increase the possibility of a leak.[5] Rusk was due to testify in public before the Senate Foreign Relations Committee on March 11. If the senators learned that a bombing cutback was being considered, they could make it much harder for Rusk to avoid committing the administration to this approach.

On March 11 and 12, Secretary Rusk spent a total of eleven hours in the witness chair while the Senate Foreign Relations Committee questioned him about administration policy on live television. His position was made all the more uncomfortable by the fact that, on March 10, *The New York Times* broke the story that General Westmoreland had asked for 206,000 more troops. The *Times* said the request had "touched off a divisive internal debate within high levels of the Johnson Administration."

The Foreign Relations Committee had known for several days about General Westmoreland's large troop request.[6] They did not know (and probably did not suspect) that Rusk and Johnson were considering announcing a partial bombing halt by the end of the month. The Committee wanted the Secretary to commit himself then and there to a de-escalation of the war. Rusk politely declined to "speculate about decisions that have not been made and conclusions that have not been reached."

The New Hampshire primary—traditionally the first in the nation each election year—was held on March 12, the second day of Rusk's televised ordeal. A write-in campaign had been organized for President Johnson, but his name did not appear on the ballot. Johnson's main challenger was Senator Eugene McCarthy of Minnesota, who advocated disengagement from the war. Pro-Johnson radio ads warned that "the Communists in Vietnam are watching the New Hampshire primary." McCarthy's radio commercials called upon the voters to "change the course of American politics" by voting against Johnson.

Although few professionals thought McCarthy stood a chance, he received 42.2 percent of the Democratic votes to Johnson's 49.4 percent. When Republican write-in votes were added, McCarthy was only 330 votes short of Johnson's total—a stunning moral victory which tended to obscure the fact that Johnson actually won the primary.

McCarthy's success was followed almost immediately by Senator Robert Kennedy's announcement of his candidacy. On March 14, Kennedy and Theodore Sorensen (former special counsel to President John Kennedy) met with Clark Clifford and proposed that President Johnson appoint a commission to reevaluate U.S. policy in Vietnam and report their findings to the President and to the American people. The commission would include eight or ten prominent liberal educators, lawyers, retired generals, and senators, including Robert Kennedy. It was implied, but not stated in so many words, that under these conditions, Kennedy would not become a candidate.[7]

When he was told of the proposal, President Johnson said it would mean handing over the powers of the President to a committee. Not surprisingly, Johnson found it unacceptable that a committee chosen by Robert Kennedy would sit in public judgment on his policy, with Kennedy himself playing a major role in the proceedings. He rejected the idea out of hand, and Kennedy announced his candidacy on March 16. (Johnson's strong dislike for Robert Kennedy went back to the 1960 Democratic convention, where the latter opposed his nomination for Vice-President.)

When Clark Clifford proposed a few days later to assemble a group of "elder statesmen" for a private discussion of his policy, the President readily agreed to the idea. The group, which included Dean Acheson and other distinguished former cabinet officers and generals, had met from time to time and had always endorsed Johnson's Vietnam policy.

After the Tet offensive, however, Johnson had asked Acheson for his views, and Acheson told him he was not sure he had a useful opinion because he had lost faith in the objectivity of the officials who were sent to brief him from time to time. "With all due respect, Mr. President," Acheson was quoted as saying, "the Joint Chiefs of Staff don't know what they're talking about." Johnson said that was a shocking statement, and Acheson said that if it were, perhaps the President ought to be shocked by it.[8] At Johnson's request, Acheson then spent several weeks reviewing the post-Tet situation with briefing officers from State, Defense, and CIA whom he selected and cross-examined at his home in Georgetown. On March 15, Acheson gave the President his findings at a somewhat hurried private lunch at the White House. The former Secretary told the President that

> he was being led down a garden path by the JCS, that what Westmoreland was attempting in Vietnam was simply not possible—without the application of totally unlimited resources "and maybe five years." He told the President that his recent speeches were quite unrealistic and believed by no one, either at home or abroad. He added the judgment that the country was no longer supporting the war.[9]

Acheson advised the President to revise his ground strategy, halt or at least greatly reduce the bombing, and liquidate U.S. involvement in the war with the least possible damage to the United States. Johnson listened to Acheson and did not argue with him. (He had to cut the luncheon meeting short to attend an emergency conference with his financial advisors on the worldwide dollar crisis which followed the report of Westmoreland's 206,000 troop request.) There is at least a suggestion in Johnson's memoirs, however, that he felt Acheson did not understand the situation.

On the same day, Arthur Goldberg, Ambassador to the UN, sent the President a memorandum urging a complete bombing halt. Johnson was angered by this suggestion. But those who knew him tended to discount his first reactions when faced with a difficult decision. As it happened, Goldberg's arguments for a full bombing halt and Rusk's case for a partial cessation were summarized in a telegram sent to Ambassador Bunker in Saigon on March 16, without identifying the authors of the two proposals. Bunker responded that he was opposed to a full bombing halt but that a cutback to the twentieth parallel would probably be acceptable to the Thieu regime, especially if accompanied by a U.S. troop increase.[10]

On March 20, Johnson told Clifford that he had decided to be a "peace candidate," but said he needed a proposal for a "Churchill peace, not a Chamberlain peace." Two days later, he announced that he was recalling General Westmoreland from Saigon and appointing him Chief of Staff of the Army. Pentagon officials took this as a signal that Johnson had decided against any major escalation of the ground war, such as Westmoreland had proposed. Admiral Sharp, who had also advocated enlargement of the war and a policy of military victory, was retiring as commander in chief in the Pacific. Thus, Johnson had maximum control at this point over decisions relating to military aspects of the war.

By the time the "elder statemen" met with senior administration officials on March 25-26,[11] President Johnson had probably ruled out all but a very small troop increase. He was also considering the idea of a bombing cutback but was apparently not willing to face the idea of U.S. disengagement without a military victory. He believed that both the allied military situation and the Saigon regime's effectiveness were improving steadily. But he was dismayed to learn that all of the outside advisors, except Murphy, Bradley, Taylor, and Fortas, favored some form of reduction of the U.S. commitment.

President Johnson was shaken to find that so many of these distinguished men had changed their opinion of his policy since their last meeting four months earlier. He had sought reassurance, and he received instead a resounding vote of no confidence. His first reaction was that those who had briefed the elder statesmen must have told them something they had not told him. But whether he agreed with the verdict or not, the meeting helped drive home the fact that public opinion was no longer with him and a change of course was necessary.

On March 28, Rusk, Clifford, Rostow, William Bundy, and Harry McPherson (a White House speech writer) met to work on the Vietnam policy speech that President Johnson was scheduled to deliver three days later. The working draft made no mention of a bombing halt; it still had the defiant, uncompromising ring of speeches Johnson had been giving over the past year. Clark Clifford argued for a more conciliatory position on the basis of internal political considerations in the United States, the military situation in Vietnam, and U.S. commitments around the world. Rusk also agreed that a more conciliatory draft should be prepared for the President to compare with the old one. Johnson looked at both drafts that same evening; but for fear of a press leak, he would not even comment on them in the presence of the whole group of Vietnam principals.[12]

When he was alone with Rusk, just after the meeting, Johnson approved the Secretary's draft cable to Saigon asking Bunker to clear the partial bombing halt with President Thieu. Rusk also told Johnson that he would see to it that the governments whose troops had fought on Saigon's side were informed of the partial bombing halt decision. The message Rusk sent to American embassies for transmission to allied governments on March 30 had a deliberately pessimistic tone about it. The American ambassadors were authorized to tell allied leaders that Hanoi was "most likely to denounce" the U.S. peace offer

and thus free our hand after a short period. Nonetheless, we might wish to continue the limitation even after a formal denunciation, in order to reinforce its sincerity and put the monkey firmly on Hanoi's back for whatever follows. Of course, any major military change could compel full-scale resumption at any time.[13]

In Washington, the President's outlook was beginning to brighten. After his private talk with Rusk on the night of March 28, Johnson recalls

I began to feel the pressure lifting. It had been quite a month, but now the wheels were turning; decisions had been made. Only the announcement of those decisions remained. Work continued on the draft of my speech, but it was largely a matter of refinement of language. George Christian and Tom Johnson were polishing the draft of my personal statement on politics.[14]

When he finally went before the television cameras on the night of March 31, to deliver the most important speech of his career, and the most dramatic speech he or any other U.S. President had ever made about Indochina, Johnson was able to savor the fact that of the millions of people who tuned in to the broadcast, almost none had guessed what he was going to say.

After describing his past efforts to find a basis for peace, the President announced that he was stopping the bombing in areas inhabited by "almost ninety percent" of the North Vietnamese people; bombing would continue only in areas where the enemy buildup threatened allied forward positions. President Johnson called on President Ho Chi Minh to "respond positively, and favorably, to this new step toward peace."

Johnson then told his listeners obliquely that the long period of rising U.S. commitments to the ground war was ending. He would send only a tenth of the troops Westmoreland had requested. Meanwhile, the Saigon regime would mobilize 135,000 more men, and the re-equipment of ARVN would be speeded up to enable them to assume more responsiblity for the defense of their country. Finally, President Johnson delivered his carefully written peroration:

> With America's sons in the fields far away, with America's future under challenge right here at home, with our hopes and the world's hopes for peace in the balance every day, I do not believe that I should devote an hour or a day of my time to any personal partisan causes or to any duties other than the awesome duties of this office—the Presidency of your country.
>
> Accordingly, I shall not seek, and I will not accept, the nomination of my party for another term as your President. . . .

Notes

1. *Vantage Point*, pp. 392-94. Johnson summarizes the rest of the directive and indicates that the working group modified it only by adding a question about the Communist powers' reaction. The directive was then signed by him and sent to McNamara, Rusk, and Clifford for their records. Clifford and McNamara decided not to circulate the draft directive to all the people working on the problem, Johnson recalls. Instead, Assistant Secretary Bundy prepared a summary of its essential assignments for lower level officers; according to Johnson, the first item listed in Bundy's memo was "What alternative courses of action are available to the U.S.?"

2. Quoted by Oberdorfer in *Tet!* pp. 287-88.

3. Ibid., p. 286; and John B. Henry II, "February, 1968," *Foreign Policy* (Fall 1971), pp. 27-28.

4. *Vantage Point*, pp. 397-99; and Oberdorfer, pp. 291-92. Rusk had, that morning, sent over to the President a peace proposal which had been submitted by a group of British intellectuals through British government channels. The proposal (signed by Barbara Ward and others) urged the United States to stop the bombing of the North, mobilize more men for Vietnam, and launch a major peace offensive.

5. *Vantage Point*, pp. 399-401. As indicated, Rusk's proposal was sent to Bunker along with Goldberg's plan for a total bombing halt on March 16.

6. Oberdorfer, *Tet!* pp. 266-71. Early in March, President Johnson asked Clifford and Wheeler to sound out the committee chairmen and other leaders of Congress whose support would be needed should he agree to large-scale mobilization and reinforcement of Westmoreland's command. They found that Senators Russell, Stennis, Jackson, and other key members of the Armed Services Committee were strongly opposed to a large troop increase or mobilization, particularly without a major change in the strategy which Westmoreland was pursuing.

7. Oberdorfer, *Tet!* p. 294.

8. Townsend Hoopes, *The Limits of Power* (New York: McKay, 1969), pp. 204-05.

9. Ibid., p. 205.

10. *Vantage Point*, pp. 408 and 411. Bunker's reply was received March 20.

11. The twelve persons from outside the Johnson administration who took part in the meeting were: Dean Acheson, former Secretary of State; George Ball, former Undersecretary of State; General Omar Bradley, former Chairman of the JCS; McGeorge Bundy, former Special Assistant for National Security Affairs; Arthur Dean, Korean truce negotiator; Douglas Dillon, former Secretary of the Treasury and Ambassador to France; Abe Fortas, Associate Justice of the Supreme Court; Henry Cabot Lodge, former senator and Ambassador to South Vietnam; Robert Murphy, former Ambassador to Japan and senior foreign service officer; General Matthew Ridgway, former Chief of Staff of the Army; General Maxwell Taylor, former Chairman of the JCS and Ambassador to South Vietnam; and Cyrus Vance, former Deputy Secretary of Defense.

12. *Vantage Point*, pp. 420-21. Most of the Vietnam advisors knew by March 29 that Johnson was using the "peace draft" as the basis of his speech, because he began calling them up and asking their reaction to various points.

13. Excerpts from the cable to U.S. ambassadors in allied countries are included in *Pentagon Papers*, pp. 622-23.

14. *Vantage Point*, p. 421.

CHAPTER EIGHTEEN

Start of the Paris Peace Talks

President Johnson undoubtedly would have liked to reach a peace agreement with Hanoi during his last ten months in office. But he was not prepared to relinquish any major aim which his administration had set itself in Indochina. As he groped his way through the nightmare final year of his presidency—the year of the Tet offensive, the murders of Martin Luther King and Bobby Kennedy, smoldering riots and troops in Washington, a mangled Democratic convention in Chicago, and the widening gap between himself and the public—much of Johnson's concern focused on preserving the dignity of the office he was about to relinquish. He was also determined, as he told many of his advisors, to pass on to his successor the best possible battlefield position, as a means of achieving a peace settlement that would not damage U.S. prestige.

On April 3, 1968, the North Vietnamese leaders responded to Johnson's offer by agreeing to hold face-to-face talks; they stipulated that the only topic they would discuss was how and when the air war would be entirely ended. The speed with which Hanoi responded apparently took the Johnson administration by surprise—judging by the way it fumbled the largely procedural question of where to hold the talks.

Washington first proposed Geneva as the site; Hanoi countered by suggesting Phnom Penh. The administration decided against the Cambodian capital because there was no American embassy there at the time and hence no established U.S. communication facilities. Instead, the U.S. government suggested four other neutral Asian capitals—Vientiane, Rangoon, Djarkarta, and New Delhi (all of which had American embassies). Hanoi found none of these sites acceptable and proposed Warsaw, where both sides had embassies.

Even though the United States had been holding talks at the ambassadorial level with the Chinese in Warsaw for many years, Johnson rejected this offer. He felt that negotiations in a Communist capital would be disadvantageous to the United States. He then proposed ten other European and Asian capitals: Brussels, Colombo, Helsinki, Kabul, Katmandu, Kuala Lumpur, Rawalpindi, Rome, Tokyo, or Vienna. Some were neutral and some pro-West, but none had North Vietnamese embassies.

After almost a month of petty quibbling, President Johnson (who had often said he would meet the other side "any time, any place") was being ridiculed by the world press; people could not understand why the leader of the most powerful country on earth had to be so inflexible. Finally, Hanoi proposed Paris on May 3, and the United States accepted. It is not known whether the President's inner circle shared his belief that this tedious exercise had been worth the trouble.

The talks finally began in Paris on May 13, 1968. The basic U.S. objective had been defined over a month earlier:

To make arrangements with the North Vietnamese representatives for prompt and serious substantive talks looking towards peace in Vietnam, in the course of which an understanding may be reached on a cessation of bombing in the North under circumstances which would not be militarily disadvantageous.[1]

President Johnson instructed the U.S. delegation, led by Averell Harriman, to avoid any agreement that would make it difficult for the United States to carry out reconnaissance flights over North Vietnam after the bombing ended. (This rather extraordinary condition was apparently demanded by the Joint Chiefs of Staff.) Harriman was also told to insist on the "reestablishment of the demilitarized zone between North and South Vietnam as provided in the 1954 Geneva agreements," and to make clear that "any talks on the future of South Vietnam had to involve the legal government of the Republic of Vietnam." At some point during the summer of 1968, the U.S. delegation was also instructed to emphasize that a bombing pause would not continue if there were large-scale attacks by the enemy on South Vietnam's cities.[2]

North Vietnam's basic position was that they would be willing to discuss other matters as soon as the United States had stopped the bombing completely. In public and private sessions (as far as the record shows at present), they held to the letter of this position. For months, they even refused to say what they would do once the United States had announced a full bombing halt. The two sides seemed to be engaged in a public display of rigid willpower. In Mid-August, Johnson told the Veterans of Foreign Wars convention that:

We have made a reasonable offer and we have taken a major first step. That offer has not been accepted. This administration does not intend to move further until it has good reason to believe that the other side intends seriously to join us in de-escalating the war and moving seriously toward peace. . . .[3]

During the second half of 1968, General Abrams (Westmoreland's successor) concentrated more on protecting urban centers and less on "search and destroy" missions. But the latter approach was by no means abandoned and U.S. casualty figures remained very high throughout the year. Johnson's critics claimed that he was still pursuing the vain hope of military victory—by means that blocked the search for diplomatic settlement in Paris. Johnson and his advisors knew, however, that a major turning point in the United States' involvement in the war had been reached. The President's announced decision to retire from politics made it next to impossible for him to contemplate any bold new military moves, particularly when a powerful group within his administration (Clifford, Harriman, Nitze, Katzenbach, Ball, and apparently also Rusk and William Bundy) were urging him to stabilize or reduce the level of U.S. involvement. The decision in March to send 13,500 more troops was the last increase in U.S. forces, even though the phasing out of U.S. involvement in the ground war did not begin until 1969. The administration also realized that resuming the bombing raids above the twentieth parallel would be extremely difficult because of public opinion in the United States.[4]

On September 17, Harriman returned to Washington to report to President Johnson on the talks and to propose that a full bombing halt be considered on the basis of Hanoi's implicit acceptance of Washington's conditions—continued U.S. reconnaissance flights, restoration of the demilitarized zone, no major attacks on South Vietnam's cities, and the involvement of Saigon's government in any talks about the future of South Vietnam.

Ambassador Harriman was anxious to end the senseless killing and begin withdrawing U.S. forces from South Vietnam. He told the President that he thought the North Vietnamese understood the U.S. position and that they were serious about making progress. Harriman doubted, however, that Hanoi would ever agree explicitly to the U.S. demands, because they wanted to be able to say that a bombing halt was unconditional. Over the next few weeks, Harriman and Cyrus Vance urged Johnson to think seriously about accepting an implicit agreement with Hanoi instead of specific assurances.

Preliminary Agreement Begins to Take Shape

On October 11, The North Vietnamese asked privately whether the United States would stop the bombing if their government agreed to South Vietnam's participation in the next stage of the talks. After rapid consultations with President Thieu and allied governments fighting in Vietnam, the United States offered a full bombing halt, to be followed within twenty-four hours by "serious" talks in which representatives of the Saigon government would take part.

It was two weeks before the American delegation in Paris obtained a satisfactory response from the North Vietnamese. First of all, Hanoi wanted the U.S. government to sign a document certifying that its bombing halt was "unconditional." Then they said that the U.S. must agree to a conference of "four parties" rather than "two sides." They also wanted a period of "weeks" to elapse between the full bombing halt and the first meeting of the expanded conference. Undoubtedly, the North Vietnamese leaders were playing for time while they reached a consensus among themselves and cleared it with the National Liberation Front. Eventually, the DRV delegates in Paris dropped the idea of a written agreement; then they shortened the period between the bombing halt and the first meeting to three days; finally, they accepted the fact that the United States would regard the meetings as "two-sided."

On October 28, President Thieu in Saigon told Ambassador Bunker that he considered the terms of the agreement reasonable. The next day, however, he asked for more time before announcing the agreement jointly with President Johnson; he also wanted assurances that his representatives could deal with Hanoi rather than the Liberation Front.

The U.S. government was nonplused by these last-minute conditions. Bunker was instructed to tell Thieu that the United States could not control the way in which Hanoi and the Liberation Front would deal with Saigon's representatives in Paris. President Johnson knew that Thieu faced political problems, but he also suspected that he might be stalling. The United States had agreed with the DRV to announce the full bombing halt and other terms of the understanding on October 31. The consensus among Johnson's advisors was that they should follow through, even though the Saigon regime had far more at stake than the United States.

According to President Johnson, North Vietnam had agreed, before the bombing halt was announced, that representatives of the South Vietnamese government could take part in the Paris talks. The American delegates had spelled out their other basic conditions—respect for the demilitarized zone and no major attacks on cities—in twelve separate sessions of the talks. Hanoi's representatives, while refusing to agree explicitly, had said that if the bombing were stopped, they would "know what to do." In regard to U.S. aerial reconnaissance flights over their country, the North Vietnamese had demanded since the start of the talks that the United States stop all bombing of the North and "all other acts of war." Since military reconnaissance flights are clearly an act of war, the United States had proposed the formula "all acts involving the use of force." In October, the DRV agreed to this formula, which implicitly allowed for the possibility of reconnaissance flights.[5]

It goes without saying that the North Vietnamese were not allowed to make similar flights over South Vietnam.

In spite of intensive efforts, Bunker failed to persuade Thieu to announce the agreement jointly with President Johnson by the end of October. Johnson, who had been conferring with his advisors almost non-stop for several days, decided to go ahead without Thieu. He went on the air the night of October 31 and announced that he had ordered all U.S. air, naval, and artillery bombardment of North Vietnam to cease as of 8 A.M. Washington time, Friday, November 1. He also announced that a regular session of the peace talks would be held the following week and that "representatives of the government of South Vietnam are free to participate." President Johnson said that he had been told by Hanoi that representatives of the National Liberation Front would also be present. However, almost a month was to pass before the Saigon government sent a delegate to Paris.

Vietnam and the U.S. Election

The war in Vietnam and the political contest in America pulled and tugged at each other throughout 1968. The Tet offensive was probably designed to produce political pressure in the United States for military withdrawal from Indochina. It undoubtedly had this effect, and it confirmed President Johnson's personal decision not to seek reelection by making it obvious that to do so would further divide the country. Johnson's withdrawal made both the North and South Vietnamese governments wary of taking decisive action until they knew who his successor would be and what policies he would seek to implement. At the time they were nominated, in the summer of 1968, Nixon and Humphrey seemed more or less alike in their vague and centrist positions on the war.

Nixon frequently reminded the voters that Eisenhower had ended the Korean stalemate shortly after taking office, and he indicated that he had a plan to end the Vietnam war "with honor." One reason for his vagueness was that he knew he had an excellent chance of winning the election, and wanted to keep his options open for future negotiations. Nixon also believed, personally, that the strongest political issue he had was the antiwar issue; people no longer trusted the Johnson administration to cope with Vietnam. Over and over, he told cheering crowds that

" . . . after 25,000 dead, and 200,000 casualties, America needs new leadership."

When Vice-President Hubert Humphrey began his quest for the Presidency in the spring of 1968, he was closely identified with Johnson's war policies. Johnson may have given Humphrey important behind-the-scenes backing at this stage, in the belief that he would maintain essentially the same policies, while Kennedy or McCarthy would repudiate them. (Johnson's personal antipathy for Robert Kennedy was mentioned in the previous chapter.) Kennedy's assassination on June 5, 1968 deprived the Democratic party of its leading peace candidate and opened the way for Humphrey's nomination.

But the Democratic party was deeply divided and demoralized by the violence of its Chicago convention—with groups on the radical left goading the police to violence on live television. This spectacle repelled large groups of normally Democratic voters, and Humphrey began the campaign as an almost hopeless underdog, without the support of many liberal leaders, with almost no funds to pay for media time, and with mobs of student hecklers denying him the right to speak at outdoor meetings.

Humphrey first attempted to deal with the war issue by describing the administration's position on bombing and de-escalation as essentially flexible. This was coldly repudiated by Johnson and Rusk, leading to speculation that the President was indifferent to Humphrey's cause.[6] Not until Humphrey's Salt Lake City speech on September 30—when he sketched out his own position for "de-Americanizing" the war—did he begin to show his usual self-confidence and start to draw the active support of leading Democratic liberals. By mid-October, Humphrey had begun to overtake Nixon in the polls and was rapidly reassembling the Democratic coalition which had elected four of the last five Presidents.

After reaching a tacit agreement with the North Vietnamese in October on de-escalation of the war, Johnson asked the three candidates (Nixon, Humphrey, and Wallace) to refrain from partisan statements on the Vietnam issue. This helped Humphrey by making it very difficult for Nixon to claim that he would approach the problem differently from the Democrats. If the Johnson administration had been able to reach a tacit agreement with the North Vietnamese and declare a full bombing halt in August or September instead of late October, it is entirely possible that the outcome of the election might have been changed. As it happened, both Hanoi and Saigon exercised considerable leverage on the American political situation during those months.[7]

It is quite likely that President Johnson was more concerned with the Vietnam situation than with the election, as he claimed. But a great many senior Democrats in the administration, such as Clark Clifford and Averell Harriman, saw the two matters as closely interrelated. They were determined not to let the Saigon regime stall the announcement of the bombing halt, both because it would disrupt the chances for serious peace talks and because it would aid Nixon's chances of election. Clifford, Harriman, and others worked frantically to achieve a breakthrough in Paris almost to the day the Johnson administration left office, but their efforts produced only an agreement on procedures for the expanded talks. This included the point that the conference table would be round—to avoid a controversy over whether the meetings were "two sided" (Hanoi and the NLF versus the United States and Saigon) or "four-sided" with all parties taking part separately.

When the Nixon administration took office, the days of U.S. military involvement in Indochina seemed sharply limited. Vietnamese leaders, with one eye on U.S. public opinion, were looking beyond the time when either a Democratic or a Republican administration would be in position to fight Saigon's battles or to block Hanoi's aims. One of President Nixon's first initiatives was to seek to reopen contact with the Peking regime and to relax some of the pressures of the China containment policy. In this, and in seeking a more equal relationship with Japan, the new adminstration began to change the context in which previous Presidents had grappled with the Indochina problem.

Notes

1. *Vantage Point*, p. 501.

2. Ibid., p. 501. The other four U.S. delegates to the peace talks were: Cyrus Vance (deputy to Mr. Harriman), General Andrew Goodpaster (military member), Philip Habib (political officer), and William Jorden (press spokesman).

3. Ibid., p. 513.

4. In his March 31 speech, Johnson defined the area of North Vietnam in which he would continue the bombing as the area "north of the demilitarized zone

where the continuing enemy build-up directly threatens allied forward positions and where the movement of their troops and supplies are clearly related to that threat." He had decided at the last moment that it would be more graphic to use this language than to refer specifically to the twentieth parallel. But many people who heard the President's speech assumed that the bombing raids would be confined to the area immediately north of the demilitarized zone. Thus, Johnson was severely criticized for "misleading" the public when U.S. planes attacked North Vietnam just below the twentieth parallel on April 1.

5. *Vantage Point*, pp. 516-19. Mr. Johnson indicates that the Joint Chiefs agreed on October 14, 1968 to the idea of a total bombing halt of North Vietnam— "provided that we continued aerial reconnaissance over the North and would resume bombing if Hanoi grossly violated the understanding."

6. Johnson's comment on this was: "Politically, I was not overly partisan in the campaign, because I had promised the nation in my speech on March 31 that I would keep the Presidency out of politics, and because that obviously was what the Humphrey organization preferred." See *Vantage Point*, p. 548.

7. President Johnson indicates in *Vantage Point* (p. 521) that "We had received information that people who claimed to speak for the Republican candidate were . . . trying to influence the South Vietnamese to drag their feet on the peace talks. Their argument was: Nixon is going to win; a Nixon administration will be more friendly to Saigon than the Democrats will be; stick with us and we will stick with you."

It is, of course, quite possible that the Saigon leaders conducted delaying tactics to help Nixon without the idea being suggested to them by any American source.

CHAPTER NINETEEN

Vietnamization and
the War in Cambodia

In the 1968 election campaign, Nixon had said only that he had a "plan" to end U.S. involvement in Indochina. As President, he announced that it would be the main theme of his administration's foreign policy to move "from an era of confrontation to an era of negotiation." Although some of his advisors thought this would be impossible without a rapid withdrawal from Indochina, Nixon chose "Vietnamization"—an orderly transfer to South Vietnamese forces of full military responsibility within their country—as the basis of his policy in that region.[1]

On the diplomatic level, Nixon instructed U.S. representatives in Paris to adopt a hard bargaining line while waiting for Saigon's position to improve. Hanoi responded with an equally tough line, obviously believing that this would generate new anti-war pressure in the United States. With the semi-public talks in stalemate, Nixon's Special Advisor on National Security, Henry Kissinger, began a series of secret meetings with Le Duc Tho, a member of the North Vietnamese Politburo, and Xuan Tuy, Hanoi's chief negotiator at the Paris peace talks.[2]

During a trip to the Far East in 1969, the President proclaimed the "Nixon doctrine." He indicated that the United States would henceforth support only those governments which were willing and able to help themselves. This would allow the United States to make a long-term contribution to Asia's stability and economic development while avoiding direct military intervention as in Vietnam. This sensible doctrine was not immediately applied to Vietnam, however. President Nixon was evidently afraid that U.S. prestige would suffer a grievous blow if he withdrew under conditions which could be described as a major defeat for our original objectives in Vietnam.

This strategy was an immense gamble. Saigon's political and military situation might get worse instead of better. Congress and the American people would only support the President as long as they believed he was really ending U.S. involvement. If the Nixon strategy failed, U.S. prestige would plummet to a new low, and there would be no hope of reducing world tensions through an "era of negotiations" with the Soviet Union.

President Nixon decided to insure against possible failure by disowning the China containment policy, thus eliminating the very purpose of our Indochina venture. Overtures toward China also increased the chance that Hanoi leaders would agree to negotiate, because they could not count on continued Chinese support if relations between Washington and Peking were visibly improving. And if U.S. relations with Moscow grew more cordial at the same time, the Vietnamese were sure to brood about the fact that they had been "sold out" at the first Geneva conference.

By the end of 1969, about one fifth of U.S. forces which were in Vietnam at the start of the year had been withdrawn; the types of military operations which had produced heavy American casualties in the past had also been sharply curtailed. At the same time, ARVN forces were greatly increasing their pressure on Communist units and taking a correspondingly higher rate of casualties.

In Congress, a number of Democrats and a few Republicans began to criticize the strategy of Vietnamization, claiming that it was not a policy for ending the war but a means of stretching out indefinitely the withdrawal of American forces. These critics argued that the Saigon regime was not being forced to broaden its political base or even to improve its military performance. But antiwar sentiment in America fell off sharply because of the reduced U.S. casualty rates.

During February 1970, North Vietnam generated a crisis in Laos, apparently hoping to induce the United States to agree to an Indochina settlement on its own terms. This touched off the first major debate in the U.S. Senate over the Nixon administration's aims and strategy in Indochina. But even before the Laotian affair had run its course, it was overshadowed by the events surrounding the overthrow of Prince Sihanouk and the outbreak of war in Cambodia.

War Comes to Cambodia

The United States and Cambodia had agreed, in June 1969, to resume diplomatic relations after a four year rupture. The move seemed to herald Prince Sihanouk's growing confidence that a balance of Communist and non-Communist interests in Southeast Asia might again be feasible. But later in the year a major internal crisis broke out between Sihanouk and most of the Khmer political elite. Prime Minister Lon Nol (who was also the leading Cambodian general) publicly criticized Sihanouk for allowing 35,000 to 40,000 Vietnamese Communists to encroach on Cambodian territory. He claimed the problem was much worse than Sihanouk had ever admitted. Before this issue was resolved, the Deputy Premier got into a bitter argument with Sihanouk (his cousin) on the subject of economic planning. Debates in the National Assembly showed that Sihanouk was no longer regarded by educated Cambodians as able to cope with the key problems of security and economic development.

In February 1970, while Sihanouk was in France, Lon Nol's government encouraged anti-Viet Cong demonstrations. These got out of hand and led to student attacks on the Viet Cong and North Vietnamese embassies in Phnom Penh, with many demonstrators carrying anti-Sihanouk placards. As relations between the Vietnamese Communists and Lon Nol's government neared the breaking point, Sihanouk flew first to Moscow and then Peking to beg for help in ejecting the Viet

Cong from Cambodia. He was politely refused in both capitals. At about the same time, Lon Nol gave the Vietnamese Communists an ultimatum to remove their troops in three days.

When it was clear that neither Sihanouk's diplomacy nor Lon Nol's ultimatum would succeed, Lon Nol deposed Sihanouk as Chief of State in a bloodless coup on March 18, 1970. Most of the Cambodian army supported him; the few small pro-Sihanouk uprisings that occurred were soon suppressed. Apparently to rally public support, Lon Nol's government played on the Cambodians' strong anti-Vietnamese prejudices, branding the country's entire Vietnamese minority (numbering between 300,000 and 400,000) as potential Viet Cong supporters. Hundreds, perhaps thousands, of Vietnamese residents were murdered, and many thousand more were herded into "refugee" camps after being dispossessed of all their belongings.

In the final week of March, North Vietnamese and Viet Cong forces began to move westward from the Vietnam border sanctuaries into the center of Cambodia. It seems likely that this movement was designed to throw the Lon Nol government off balance and prevent Khmer troops from harassing the lightly fortified Communist border sanctuaries. The invaders may also have wanted to create insecurity on South Vietnam's western flank, but their most logical concern was to protect their extensive base network and supply lines in the eastern half of Cambodia.

By early April 1970, the South Vietnamese army (ARVN) was also conducting cross-border operations in Cambodia. Whether South Vietnamese officials hoped to shift the main battleground of the war to Cambodia at this stage, it is impossible to say. Nor can anyone tell whether the ARVN incursions provoked the North Vietnamese and Viet Cong to move still deeper into Cambodia. But the steady increase in the scale of fighting was undoubtedly due to actions by all four parties: North and South Vietnamese armies, the Viet Cong, and the Cambodians. Some of the North and South Vietnamese forces who entered Cambodia took revenge on unarmed Khmer civilians for the recent massacres of Vietnamese residents there.

Nixon Reacts to Cambodian Crisis

Officials close to President Nixon knew that he had been anxious, since the start of 1970, to find a way of showing Communist leaders around the world that his hands were not tied by anti-war opinion in the

United States and that he was able to meet force with force when necessary. Among the circumstances contributing to the President's mood of frustration were the Laotian crisis, the discovery that Soviet pilots were flying Egyptian aircraft in the Middle East, the continued probing actions by North Korea against South Korea, the failure of the North Vietnamese to begin serious negotiations in Paris, and the Senate's rejection of two of his nominees for the Supreme Court.

At the end of March, in response to a White House request, General Creighton Abrams in Saigon outlined several alternative plans for military action in Cambodia by ARVN troops alone and with American forces. (Since the late 1950s, South Vietnamese and American generals in Saigon had longed to attack these base areas; but Washington had always refused to allow it, because the turmoil it would produce would be a much greater problem than the bases.) As these and other plans were prepared, an interagency committee known as the Washington Special Action Group (WASAG) was given the task of assembling and refining all of the contingency plans, assessing their consequences, and managing the execution of presidential orders.

Among the President's leading advisors, Secretary of Defense Laird opposed the idea of cross-border operations in Cambodia in the second week of April, because their potential military advantages seemed far outweighed by the likelihood that they would produce large numbers of U.S. casualties. (The estimate was 400 to 800 Americans killed in the first week of an invasion.) This would have undermined public support for the strategy of Vietnamization and deepened political divisions in the country. Secretary of State Rogers also opposed cross-border operations because they would have upset a number of diplomatic efforts which were under way in early April.[3]

Around the middle of April, General Abrams asked the President to delay the next withdrawal of American combat forces from Vietnam for sixty days. Circumstances were beginning to make it seem highly attractive, from a military viewpoint, to attack the Cambodian sanctuaries. Thousands of Vietnamese Communist forces stationed in the sanctuaries had begun to move westward into districts closer to Phnom Penh. This meant that there would be far fewer U.S. casualties if an invasion were carried out immediately. One of the two American divisions in the area near the Cambodian sanctuaries was scheduled to go home soon. The rainy season, due to begin in late May, would gradually turn most of eastern Cambodia into a shallow lake and reduce the mobility of foot soldiers as well as vehicles. In addition, many American officials expected Lon Nol's government to collapse before the end of the rainy season; they feared that a Communist takeover of Cambodia would disrupt the orderly disengagement of U.S. forces from Vietnam.

President Nixon decided to announce a whole year's troop withdrawals in a major speech scheduled for April 20. Thus, he was able to comply with Abrams' request for a delay without creating new doubts among the American people about his long-range commitment to disengagement. In the same speech, the President also expressed his terms for a political settlement in Indochina more flexibly than he had ever done before. He warned that he might feel compelled to take "strong and effective measures" in the event of increased enemy actions in Indochina. But the optimistic tone of the speech conveyed a feeling that the administration planned to push ahead with disengagement in spite of the threatening pattern of Communist military moves in Laos, Cambodia, and South Vietnam.

Decision to Intervene in Cambodia

Just after the April 20 speech, General Abrams sent the President an urgent message, insisting that enemy sanctuaries in Cambodia must be destroyed if he were to assure the safety of his men and still meet the announced twelve-month withdrawal schedule. Abrams recommended an American attack into the "fishhook" area of Kompong Cham province, a densely wooded area bordering South Vietnam. Secretary Laird endorsed Abrams' recommendation, probably because the general claimed that the invasion would produce benefits for the Vietnamization program and that U.S. casualties would be low.

As Communist guerrillas attacked in many different parts of Cambodia over the next few days, the State and Defense Departments and U.S. military authorities in Saigon all drew different conclusions about the Communists' objectives. State Department officials believed that the guerrillas were carrying out hit-and-run attacks in relatively small numbers to create a climate of insecurity throughout the country and give the impression of widespread opposition to Lon Nol's rule. Defense Department specialists thought the Communist attacks were aimed at surrounding Phnom Penh and either cutting off its supplies or actually seizing the city. The President reportedly considered this view more persuasive than that of the State Department.

In Saigon, while some U.S. military officers also believed that the Communists were trying to coerce or overthrow the Lon Nol regime, others took the view that the main objective of the enemy was to expand and improve their string of base areas in Cambodia. Still another group of U.S. military officials felt that the Communists expected an American or South Vietnamese attack on their base areas and were redeploying their forces into Cambodia for defensive purposes.

The National Security Council considered the various contingency plans that had been drawn up for U.S. and South Vietnamese operations in Cambodia on April 22. The main subject discussed was a possible South Vietnamese attack on the Parrot's Beak portion of Svay Rieng province, but an American attack on the Fishhook portion of Kompong Cham was also discussed. On the morning of April 23, WASAG was ordered by the President to produce operational plans for the Parrot's Beak attack (using South Vietnamese forces).[4]

A White House spokesman gave an oblique warning that an important move was coming when, on April 24, he called the North Vietnamese and Viet Cong offensive in Cambodia a "foreign invasion of a neutral country which cannot be considered in any way a pretense of a civil war." On that day, Nixon asked to have operational plans for the Fishhook attack (using U.S. ground forces) delivered to him within twenty-four hours.

A crucial debate over whether or not to invade the sanctuaries was held at an April 26 meeting of the National Security Council. Those who attended were President Nixon, Secretaries Rogers and Laird, Attorney General Mitchell, General Wheeler, CIA Director Richard Helms, and Dr. Kissinger. Rogers spoke out most strongly against the invasion plans because of the risk of substantial damage to the U.S. position abroad and of serious domestic turmoil. Laird and Wheeler replied that the Communists were trying either to overthrow the Lon Nol government or to establish a safe supply route to the sea in eastern Cambodia. In either case, they asserted, the safety of American forces in South Vietnam would be jeopardized—as would the plans for their withdrawal.

Secretary Rogers pointed out that there was a grave risk of the

United States becoming trapped indefinitely in using its forces to prevent Lon Nol's defeat. The President might also forfeit the widespread support he had won in the United States with his strategy of Vietnamization and gradual withdrawal of U.S. forces. However, Rogers sensed that Nixon was determined to "do something." Thus, he began to argue for an attack on the sanctuaries using South Vietnamese forces alone. This would avoid the serious political dangers of sending in U.S. ground troops.

Laird and Wheeler said that U.S. air and logistical support would be needed, even if the only ground forces used were South Vietnamese. Thus, it would be impossible to describe such an operation to the American public as one in which the United States was not involved. Moreover, President Thieu was apparently reluctant to send his troops into Cambodia without American "advisors" to spread political responsibility for the attack.

President Nixon came away from the April 26 NSC meeting feeling that if he ordered either the Parrot's Beak or the Fishhook operation the United States would be deeply involved. Time was running out, and he felt that he must do something. But sending military aid to Lon Nol's regime would have only a symbolic effect, while inaction by the U.S. might tempt Hanoi to install a puppet regime in Phnom Penh. If both sides refrained from decisive action, time would favor the Communists. On the other hand, the President realized that sending in large numbers of U.S. forces would once again divide the American people and might provoke the Communists to launch a major attack or cause them to withdraw from the Paris peace talks.

On April 27, Secretary Rogers testified at a closed meeting of the Senate Foreign Relations Committee. He said that there had been several North Vietnamese incursions into Cambodia which had been "fairly successful," and that a Communist take-over in Cambodia would endanger the U.S. policy of withdrawing troops from South Vietnam. Without saying that an American attack on the sanctuaries was being considered by the administration, Rogers possibly tried to hint that a decision to attack could be expected at any time.

If this was so, none of the senators realized the full significance of his remarks. The reason may have been that they were intent on impressing Rogers with their concern about possible American involvement in Cambodia. The majority of senators probably believed that the only type of intervention then being considered by the administration was some form of military aid, with the President using contingency funds available to him for the purpose.

Although Rogers gave Nixon a detailed report that evening on his meeting with the senators, the President did not in fact consult the Senate before making his final decision to invade the sanctuaries. As a result, the net effect of Rogers' appearance before the committee may have been to make many senators even more aware that their views had been igrnored by the President and that he was bent on overriding the war-making powers of Congress. This broad constitutional issue concerned them more deeply than the specific question of U.S. intervention in Cambodia.

The next morning, April 28, President Nixon authorized U.S. forces to attack the Fishhook area and to accompany South Vietnamese forces into the Parrot's Beak. In addition, he ordered several other consecutive strikes at enemy bases, as well as four bombing raids against North Vietnam. The Parrot's Beak attack began on April 28, and the Fishhook operation on April 30, two hours before President Nixon went on television to explain his decision.

Effects of U.S.-ARVN Incursion

To improve conditions for continued U.S. military withdrawal from South Vietnam (the announced aim of the attacks), Cambodia was turned into a major battleground of the Vietnam war. In the name of "disengagement," a nation of 7 million people became almost totally dependent on U.S. military and economic aid for their survival.[5] No one knows how many Cambodian civilians and soldiers were killed or wounded, but much of the fighting took place in well-populated areas and without regard for civilian casualties. During 1970, more than a million Cambodians fled from the embattled countryside, swelling the populations of all the main towns.

During May and June, 339 Americans, 866 South Vietnamese, and 14,488 North Vietnamese and Viet Cong forces were killed in the fighting in Cambodia, according to official reports; in addition, 1500 American and 3724 South Vietnamese soldiers were wounded, and 1427 North Vietnamese and Viet Cong troops were captured. At the end of the two-month incursion, it was reported that 29,627 weapons had been captured or destroyed by U.S. and ARVN forces, as well as 11,000 tons of other types of munitions and 8500 tons of rice. In an effort to prevent the enemy from replacing these supplies, U.S. and South Vietnamese air operations were greatly intensified over Laos and Cambodia, and this produced continued high levels of civilian casualties, particularly in the more densely populated areas of Cambodia. The country's economy—based on the export of surplus rice, rubber, corn, and a few other agricultural products—was in ruins by the summer of 1970.

Protest Against the Incursion: The Cooper-Church Amendment

President Nixon's Cambodia decision produced a far greater shock wave of public protest than any of President Johnson's decisions leading to open-ended escalation of the war. Meetings and demonstrations protesting the incursion took place in towns and cities across the United States. The reaction abroad was also generally unfavorable.[6] Congressmen found their offices jammed with students, lawyers, veterans, and other groups urging them to reverse the President's decision by legislative action. The killing of four student demonstrators by National Guardsmen at Kent State College and two students at Jackson State College brought thousands more onto the streets. In response to this extraordinary public outcry, President Nixon announced on May 6 that all U.S. ground forces would be out of Cambodia by June 30 and that they would not go further than twenty-one miles into Cambodia.

On May 13, Senators John Sherman Cooper and Frank Church introduced a bill forbidding the use of funds for military operations in Cambodia beyond the limits of time and space which the President had announced. The bill had twenty-eight co-sponsors and took the form of an amendment to the Foreign Military Sales Act. On June 30, the date U.S. ground forces were withdrawn from Cambodia, the Senate passed the Cooper-Church amendment by a vote of 75 to 20. It was the first time the Senate had ever voted to restrict the spending of funds for military purposes while the United States was at war.

During the debate on Indochina, many senators indicated that they were less concerned about the incursion into Cambodia than about the broader issue which it symbolized: encroachment by the executive branch on powers granted to Congress under the Constitution to "make and declare war." In the course of the debate, the Senate voted to repeal the 1964 Tonkin Gulf resolution, which the Johnson administration had regarded as a "functional declaration of war."

President Nixon and his top advisors took issue with their critics in Congress on this basic constitutional question; they maintained that the President, as commander in chief, had an overriding responsibility to protect the lives of American servicemen. The antiwar senators replied that better protection would be provided by ending U.S. military involvement in Indochina rather than expanding it. But the Cooper-Church amendment was not a motion to censure President Nixon, as indicated by its opening phrase, "In concert with the declared objectives of the President. . . ." This was the reason the amendment was passed on June 30, President Nixon's self-imposed deadline for ending the incursion.[7]

On the grounds that the lives of U.S. troops in Vietnam might be at stake, administration officials refused to rule out future military action in Cambodia, Laos, or even North Vietnam.[8] They also indicated that they regarded the Cooper-Church amendment as a statement of principle not legally binding on the President. During the rest of 1970, the administration observed some of its restrictions and quietly ignored others. No American combat forces were retained in Cambodia, and efforts to transfer an American-subsidized Thai unit from Vietnam to Cambodia were abandoned. However, thousands of U.S.-supported ARVN troops continued to operate in Cambodia, while the bombing of suspected enemy concentrations continued without provoking any major challenge from Congress.

Neither the Nixon administration nor Congress recognized any moral obligation to assist Cambodia for its own sake. In a report to Congress in February 1971, President Nixon said "the objective of our activities related to Cambodia remains constant: to bar the reestablishment of secure communist base areas that could jeopardize allied forces in Vietnam." The 1970 incursion had helped transform a struggle for control of Cambodia's border areas into a war in which Cambodia's survival was at stake. North and South Vietnamese armies were vying for the right to "Vietnamize" Cambodia, a fate which the Cambodian people had been resisting for centuries. Nevertheless, in November 1971, President Nixon told a press conference that he considered U.S. operations in Cambodia to be the "purest example" of the Nixon doctrine in action.

Notes

1. On January 21, 1969, the day after he took office, President Nixon ordered a study of the Vietnam situation to be coordinated by the National Security Council. A summary of questions posed by the NSC and responses received from various U.S. agencies was compiled shortly thereafter; it was published on April 25, 1972 by the *Washington Post*, pp. A18 and A19.

2. The secret talks began in August 1969. For details of their results, see Chapter 20. Kissinger originally broached the idea of the secret talks to Jean Sainteny, who had been the chief Free French representative in China and North Vietnam in 1945. (Kissinger and Sainteny met when Madame Sainteny was Kissinger's student at Harvard.) Sainteny set up the first meeting between Kissinger and Xuan Tuy, loaned his apartment for the occasion, and introduced the principals; he then left them to talk privately with only their interpreters present.

3. The United States was aware that secret contacts had taken place between the Lon Nol government and Vietnamese Communists, and the United States tried to inform the Hanoi regime that it would abide by whatever agreement it might reach with the new Cambodian leaders.

4. Most of the actual drafting of these plans was carried out by General Abrams' headquarters in Saigon; but WASAG was kept busy communicating requirements from the President and other top officials to Saigon, putting the plans prepared in Saigon in final form, and briefing the key decision-makers (who had to cope with other major problems besides Cambodia during this period).

5. During the year ending June 1971, the United States provided Cambodia with $255 million in military and economic aid. In 1972, the Agency for International Development expected to fund $120 million out of a total flow of $140 million in essential imports for the Cambodian economy.

6. According to *The New York Times*, August 10, 1970, a secret USIA poll of public opinion was taken in five Asian and five Western European countries after the Cambodia incursion. It showed that public confidence in the United States declined significantly in most of these countries as a result of events in Indochina.

7. For a transcript of the historic Cambodia debate, adapted from the *Congressional Record*, see Eugene P. Dvorkin (editor), *The Senate's War Powers* (Chicago: Markham, 1970).

8. A raid by helicopter-borne U.S. troops on a prison camp in North Vietnam was carried out in the fall of 1970, but it failed to accomplish its aim of locating and releasing American prisoners of war. In February 1971, a large-scale ARVN incursion into eastern Laos took place with U.S. air and logistical support.

CHAPTER TWENTY

Conclusion: Vietnam and the China Containment Policy

Why did the United States become so deeply mired in the affairs of Indochina? Why fight to protect a regime that seemed to lack the support of its own people? The China containment policy, which successive American Presidents felt compelled to support, provides one of the main answers to the riddle.

In the mid-1940s, the U.S government received a number of overtures from Asian Communist leaders for support in their respective causes. American officials on the scene tended to be sympathetic, but U.S. resources were already stretched thin in other parts of the world. Thus, the Truman administration tried to avoid direct entanglement in both the Chinese civil war and the struggle between France and the Viet Minh for control of Indochina. However, Washington feared that if France were not allowed to regain her former colonies and prosperity, the French Communist Party might win control of the government. Thus, the United States gave France economic aid in the early postwar years, knowing this would help finance her colonial war in Vietnam.

At the same time, the United States provided modest sums of aid to Chiang Kai-shek, which the right-wing "China bloc" in Congress chose to construe as a commitment to Chiang's anti-Communist struggle.[1] The collapse of Chiang's forces in 1949 put the Truman administration on the political defensive; McCarthy and other right-wing congressmen tried to pin the blame on the Democrats for the massive Communist victory in China. The response of liberal internationalists in both the Truman and Eisenhower administrations was to adopt a policy of confrontation with China—which became known as the China containment policy—in the hope that this would prevent a dangerous stalemate between the Executive branch and Congress.

The French government saw its chance to shift most of the cost of its colonial war to the United States by rechristening it a war against communism. After the outbreak of the Korean conflict, Secretary of State Acheson stopped urging France to relinquish power to a Vietnamese national government. Instead, France was pledged not to make a separate peace with the Viet Minh.

The Eisenhower administration inherited and greatly expanded the program of aiding the French war effort in Indochina. During the climactic seige of Dien Bien Phu, the U.S. government teetered on the brink of intervention. Although France managed to strike a bargain with its erstwhile opponents at the Geneva conference, Secretary Dulles was ready to take up the burden of making Indochina a bastion of anti-Communism. SEATO may have helped to delay temporarily the resumption of war in Vietnam. But President Ngo Dinh Diem in Saigon failed to use the respite to build democratic support for his regime.

After John Foster Dulles' death in 1959, the China containment policy lost whatever coherence he had managed to give it. There followed three chaotic years in which American agencies engaged in freewheeling competition to influence U.S. policy in Indochina.

President Kennedy and some of his advisors doubted the wisdom of the China containment policy, which they recognized as the basis of U.S. involvement in Indochina. But the Kennedy administration lacked the political strength and self-confidence to risk a show-down with U.S.

military and congressional hard-liners. Thus, when Diem's government and army began to crumble under Communist pressure, they greatly increased American aid to Diem and, for the first time, involved American ground and air forces in the Vietnam war.

During President Kennedy's final year in office, the Buddhist crisis underlined the despotic character of Diem's regime, a fact which now became obvious to the U.S. public. President Kennedy seized this chance to disengage from Diem (as he had felt unable to do in the case of Chiang Kai-shek) by providing thinly veiled support to his assassins. However, this approach was strongly opposed within the administration (not least by Vice-President Johnson).

The murder of Diem and Nhu in November 1963 marked the end of an Indochina policy which the United States had followed for nine years—using limited American force to keep Diem in power in Saigon and thereby to prevent the expansion of China's influence. Some American officials believed the effort had proved self-defeating and that the logical alternative was to seek better relations with China. But John F. Kennedy's assassination brought to the White House the only President who ever fully believed that confronting China and seeking "victory" over the Viet Cong were major U.S. interests.

During his first year in office, President Johnson clearly indicated to his top advisors that he was not prepared to disengage from Vietnam short of victory and that he would use whatever force he deemed necessary to achieve this aim. But in spite of massive bombing of North Vietnam and the introduction of half a million U.S. troops in the South, Johnson's strategy merely produced escalating military stalemate. As U.S. involvement rose, the rationale of the China containment policy was more and more frequently invoked by Johnson and his associates. By the late 1960's, the struggle for control of South Vietnam had spread into neighboring countries and seemed to be leading toward a full-scale war with China.

The 1968 Tet offensive revealed the emptiness of President Johnson's claim of steady progress in South Vietnam. It left him little choice except to scale down the air war and try to get peace talks started. But Johnson never came to grips with the fact that his whole approach to Indochina had been fundamentally unsound. Thus, he left office with his domestic program in disarray, a major financial crisis brewing (because of war expenditures), and with the American people more divided than at any time in the past century.

President Nixon chose to prolong disengagement during his first four years in office to give the Saigon regime a better chance to take over its own defense. While U.S. combat forces were slowly withdrawn, the war was shifted westward into Cambodia, and U.S. 'bombing of most parts of Indochina was sharply increased. Except for the invasion of Cambodia, this process of "Vietnamization" was also designed to reduce public hostility to the war in the United States. By such means, President Nixon hoped to persuade Hanoi's leaders to negotiate seriously and accept less than their maximum aims.

On the diplomatic level, Nixon instructed U.S. representatives at the semi-public peace talks in Paris to adopt a hard bargaining line while waiting for Saigon's position to improve. Meanwhile, Nixon's Special Advisor on National Security Affairs, Henry Kissinger, began a series of secret meetings with Le Duc Tho and Xuan Tuy, representatives of the Hanoi government.

Realizing that none of these lines of action might produce results before domestic political pressure forced him to concede defeat, Nixon also began to make overtures for better relations with China in 1969. By disowning the China containment policy, Nixon limited the damage to U.S. prestige that might result from failure of his Vietnamization strategy.

During 1969, the Nixon strategy gained time, but produced little sign of improvement in ARVN or the Saigon regime. Over the next year, the U.S. invasion of Cambodia produced major civil unrest in America, and Peking suspended ambassadorial talks between the two countries. The Pentagon claimed that Vietnamization had been aided by the incursion, but Cambodia became a major battleground for North and South Vietnamese armies to destroy.

In 1971, the tempo of change in U.S.-China relations quickened, and helped to dampen criticism of Nixon's rigid posture at the Paris peace talks. In a speech in February 1971, which coincided with a major and unsuccessful ARVN incursion into Laos, President Nixon created a flurry of comment just by using the term "Peoples Republic of China" for the first time. Shortly after this, the State Department removed all restrictions on the use of American passports for travel to China and ended the long-standing embargo on trade with the mainland. The friendly reception given a U.S. table tennis team, which toured China in April, produced hints from both sides of more substantial moves to come. But even so, world opinion was stunned by the news, in July

1971, that President Nixon had accepted an invitation from Premier Chou En-lai to visit China early the next year. This sensational announcement made it easier for Nixon to ignore a North Vietnamese offer, less than a month earlier, to free all U.S. prisoners in exchange for the complete withdrawal of U.S. forces by the end of the year.[2]

Chou En-lai repeatedly stated that there could be no improvement in Sino-American relations before the United States withdrew its troops from Indochina. Nevertheless, the announcement of President Nixon's forthcoming visit weakened Hanoi's position by creating the impression that Chou was anxious for better U.S. relations to counter Soviet pressure. While the North Vietnamese found it hard to conceal their dismay, Saigon professed to be pleased with the prospect of the summit meeting. Undoubtedly Thieu and his advisors were astute enough to see that Nixon had been strengthened politically by the announcement, and thus could stretch out the process of Vietnamization.

President Nixon repeatedly urged the public not to expect an Indochina settlement to result from his visit to Peking (thus perhaps unintentionally playing on the hopes of his friends and the fears of his enemies). In fact, however, there was no indication, after the February 1972 summit, that Indochina had been a major topic of discussion. The joint communique issued at the close of the visit showed no change in either side's position on this issue. But the summit meeting itself had drastically altered the political situation throughout Asia. Chou En-lai met personally with Premier Pham Van Dong to reassure the Hanoi regime. Nixon sent Assistant Secretary of State Marshall Green to meet with Thieu and other Asian leaders.

After his trip to China, President Nixon ordered U.S. delegates at the Paris peace talks to stop attending regular weekly sessions until the Communists gave signs of being ready to engage in "serious" negotiations. Saigon adopted the same tough attitude. By denying North Vietnam and the Viet Cong a major propaganda forum during the U.S. election campaign, Nixon seemed to gain more freedom to complete the disengagement of U.S. troops in a way and at a time of his own choosing.

In April 1972, Hanoi launched a conventional military invasion across the demilitarized zone: this was supported by North Vietnamese and Viet Cong attacks elsewhere in the South. While the offensive was clearly designed to discredit the Thieu regime and President Nixon's

Vietnamization strategy, many observers were puzzled by its timing. The attack began only two months before the end of the dry season and not long before all U.S. troops were scheduled to be out of Vietnam. The fact that it came a month after President Nixon's visit to China and seven weeks before his scheduled summit meeting in Moscow suggested that Hanoi might be nervous about a "sellout' and was trying to force its major allies to reaffirm their support.

President Nixon reacted to the new situation by ordering massive B-52 bombing raids over much of North Vietnam and by mining Haiphong and other North Vietnamese ports. Though the Soviet leaders protested vigorously, they avoided a direct clash with the United States. President Nixon was able to carry out his planned visit to Moscow, and progress was achieved on limiting strategic arms and on trade between the superpowers.[3]

Meanwhile, heavy fighting in South Vietnam continued to test the ARVN's effectiveness. One South Vietnamese division fell apart and allowed DRV regulars to seize Quang Tri province. Elsewhere, see-saw battles produced heavy casualties on both sides. But by midsummer, it was clear that most ARVN units had stood up well and managed to blunt the DRV offensive. Improved ARVN leadership, training, morale, and equipment were probably more important factors than American air power or mines in winning a crucial campaign, which forced the DRV to alter their strategy.

The October Agreement

On October 8, 1972, a major breakthrough took place in the secret talks that Henry Kissinger had been carrying on since 1969 with North Vietnamese representatives Le Duc Tho and Xuan Tuy.[4] The DRV delegates tabled a draft agreement which they described as "new and extremely important." The key concession they offered was the elimination of an earlier demand that a coalition government be formed in South Vietnam prior to a cease-fire and general military settlement.

The United States responded by conceding that Thieu's regime was not the sole legitimate administration in South Vietnam. This opened the way for settling lesser issues that concerned the United States and the DRV. In a few days of intensive bargaining, a broad agreement was reached, and some of its terms were published by Hanoi in late

October. (However, the United States insisted on one more round of meetings to try to deal with certain objections raised by President Thieu. Thus, what both sides described as a "final" session began in Paris on November 21, 1972.)

In the October agreement, Hanoi accepted the idea that a cease-fire would take place in South Vietnam twenty-four hours after the accord had been signed. The United States agreed that all "acts of war" against North Vietnam would end at the same time (but there was no mention of a cease-fire in Laos or Cambodia).

The truce was to be followed by negotiations between the various South Vietnamese political groups for the purpose of arranging new general elections in the South. A "National Council of Reconciliation and National Concord" would be formed for this purpose, with the Viet Cong Provisional Revolutionary Government (PRG) taking part on a basis of equality with the Saigon regime and neutralist forces. No timetable was set for the elections under the October agreement.

From the standpoint of U.S. interests, one of the most important features of the October agreement was that it provided for the release of all military prisoners and all foreign civilians within the same sixty-day period in which U.S. troop withdrawals would take place.

When and if the October 1972 agreement was put into effect, the Thieu regime and the Viet Cong PRG would each administer those parts of South Vietnam that were under their control until elections were held and a new national government had been formed. Presumably, if no elections were held, this divided administration might continue indefinitely. There was no provision in the October agreement for withdrawal of the estimated 145,000 troops which North Vietnam had stationed in the South. Both the United States and North Vietnam were forbidden, under the agreement, to send armaments into the South except as replacements for arms which they had sent in before the agreement had been signed.

Some aspects of the October agreement were to be supervised by teams composed of representatives of North Vietnam, the Viet Cong, Saigon, and the United States. At least partial agreement had also reportedly been reached, by November 1972, on the creation of an international peace-keeping force to be composed of 1250 officers and men from each of four countries: Canada, Hungary, Indonesia, and Poland. There were also reportedly plans for convening a conference of countries interested in the area, similar to the 1954 and 1962 Geneva conferences.

Like the 1954 Geneva accords, the October 1972 agreement left unresolved many important aspects of relations between the countries of Indochina. President Thieu in Saigon immediately pressed for amendment of the agreement in four areas. First, he demanded that North Vietnam publicly commit itself to withdraw all its troops from the South (even if they remained beyond the sixty days allowed for U.S. withdrawal). Second, Thieu insisted that the cease-fire go into effect simultaneously in all parts of Indochina, not just in Vietnam.

Thieu's third demand was that the demilitarized zone, the line separating North and South Vietnam, be recognized in the cease-fire agreement. And finally, he called for clarification of the role of the "National Council of Reconciliation and National Concord.' Thieu wanted it to be on the record that this Council was not an embryonic government but merely an administrative unit with the sole function of arranging for elections.

Nixon Conciliates Thieu

In spite of having cabled Premier Pham Van Dong in Hanoi to say the agreement was "complete" in October, President Nixon insisted on reopening the negotiations to try to obtain further concessions for President Thieu. A number of countries, probably including China and Russia, put pressure on Hanoi to reopen the accord. Thus, Kissinger and Le Duc Tho began another round of secret talks in Paris on November 21.

We may never know precisely what took place in these talks. But according to press reports (which seem to have been borne out by subsequent events), Kissinger placed the United States' maximum demands on the table, in effect withdrawing the main concessions the United States had made a month earlier. Kissinger allegedly told some friends that he hoped it was clear to Le Duc Tho that he was doing this "for the record" (i.e., to prove to Thieu that no better agreement could be obtained). Kissinger may have hinted to Tho that the U.S. government would settle for minor "clarifications" of the October agreement.[5]

However, the North Vietnamese were obviously greatly disturbed by the U.S. government's newly stated position, whether or not they interpreted it as a charade to satisfy Thieu. Le Duc Tho responded in kind by withdrawing the main concessions he had made in October. No longer was Hanoi willing to release American prisoners of war in return for the withdrawal of U.S. forces. Tho said that U.S. prisoners would only be released if Saigon set free the tens of thousands of civilian political prisoners it was holding. (Their release was a major aim of the Viet Cong.) Le Duc Tho also appears to have sought the right for Hanoi to move its troops back and forth freely across the line between North and South Vietnam.

While adopting this tough stand in the private November talks, Hanoi continued to demand publicly that the United States sign the October agreement as it stood. This, in effect, told Washington that Hanoi was prepared to forget (or reduce) its new demands if the United States did likewise.

Nevertheless, President Nixon ordered his Special Assistant to break off the talks. Returning to Washington, Kissinger told a press conference that Hanoi had reopened major points on which agreement had previously been reached, and that President Nixon had therefore ordered a resumption of heavy bombing of North Vietnam. Whether Dr. Kissinger or President Nixon really believed that Hanoi had changed its position was not known. Rumors circulated at the time that Kissinger disagreed sharply with the President's decision to resume the bombing.

However, no further explanation was offered by the Nixon administration for its decision. President Nixon responded to the public's widespread dismay, confusion, and angry criticism of his action with icy silence. With the election behind him and with Congress unlikely to take any firm countermeasures until February at the earliest, he may have concluded that he was free to exert maximum pressure on North Vietnam for a brief period and that the result might be a more "honorable" American exit from the war.

The use of unabashed terror tactics to achieve a relatively minor aim raised once more the question of why one man should be allowed sole power to make such sweeping decisions. Leaders of both parties in Congress and of most governments that are normally friendly to the United States called for an end to the carpet bombing of North Vietnamese cities which, according to all reports, was far more indiscriminate and destructive of civilian life than any previous phase of the air war.

Throughout December, Washington and Hanoi remained in contact, and when President Nixon decided that Hanoi would make some further changes in the October accord, he ordered the bombing cut back to the twentieth parallel. Once again, there were reports of Chinese and Russian influence being exerted to make Hanoi swallow its pride and return to the bargaining table. On January 3, meetings resumed in Paris on technical aspects of a cease-fire. And on January 8, Kissinger and Le Duc Tho got down to serious bargaining.

The result of two final weeks of meetings was a cease-fire agreement that Le Duc Tho called "virtually the same" as the October accord and "a great victory for the Vietnamese people." Dr. Kissinger claimed "substantial improvement" on points that concerned President Thieu; and President Nixon, in a brief public statement, declared that the accord had brought "peace with honor." In spite of these brave statements, there were probably very few people in North or South Vietnam who had not lost at least one close relative in the long struggle and who believed the war had served any good purpose.

It was impossible to make any definite comparisons between the October and January versions of the cease-fire agreement, because the full text of the October agreement had not been made public at time of writing. However, its general outlines were revealed by Hanoi on October 20, 1972, and Dr. Kissinger publicly acknowledged that this summary was accurate. The January version apparently corrected a few oversights of the October draft and spelled out various technical aspects in much greater detail.

For example, there was no reference in the earlier agreement to the demilitarized zone (DMZ) or to any boundary line between North and South Vietnam. This may have been an oversight by the American negotiators. The January agreement included references to the DMZ, which gave some legal standing to Saigon's claim that South Vietnam was a "sovereign" entity. But the language Hanoi accepted was no stronger than that of the 1954 Geneva accords (which Hanoi had always accepted). And in a sense, the January 1973 accord was less emphatic than the 1954 agreement about maintaining the DMZ, because it raised the possibility of future consultation between North and South Vietnam on allowing civilian traffic to cross the zone.

On the prisoner-of-war issue, the January agreement appeared to favor Hanoi slightly more than the October version did. The United States was obliged, under the January version, to help promote the release of Viet Cong prisoners in Saigon jails. Americans were supposed to participate in mixed commissions on the prisoner issue until all prisoners had been released.

There were a number of other less important differences between the October and January agreements. But it is hard to believe that any of the changes that were made were worth the sacrifices of human life and the flaunting of established norms of civilized conduct that took place in December 1972. Hanoi made no important further concessions as a result of the December bombing raids. Indeed, the United States made some minor concessions to Hanoi in the January agreement. And there was no evidence that the minor concessions which Hanoi made were the result of the bombing rather than the patient efforts of Dr. Kissinger and his colleagues in Paris.

One of the many important issues left unresolved at time of writing was the question of cease-fire throughout Indochina. There was a chance that the DRV might decide to halt its military operations in Laos (which seemed to be designed mainly to protect its supply line) after a truce had been arranged in Vietnam. This would open the way to a political settlement between the competing Lao factions on the basis of the 1962 Geneva agreement. In Cambodia, the prospects for a political settlement between the many competing factions were unclear, even assuming that North Vietnamese troops followed the letter of the January accord and left the country.

In short, while U.S. involvement was ending in the long and bloody second phase of the Indochina war, only the haziest outlines of a settlement of the region's key political problems had emerged by the end of President Nixon's first term in office. Few people believed that the meager results summarized by the cease-fire agreement justified the slaughter of over a million human beings, including 50,000 Americans and other foreigners to the region. Other hundreds of thousands of people had been injured, millions had been made homeless, and large areas of one of the most fertile and beautiful lands in the world had been reduced to charred rubble. The United States would have to spend many years atoning for its unprecedented "experiments" with weapons of mass destruction, carried out against a population whose aims and interests we have never understood.

No one can say how much American intervention added to the suffering of a people already at war among themselves. Nor can we assess the damage to American society, the cleavages between class and race and generation that were deepened by an unfair apportionment of war's sacrifice. More than any national experience since our own Civil War, the Indochina struggle disrupted our habits of civility, catered to our national penchant for violence, and all but destroyed our sense of common national purpose.

Epilogue

With U.S. military involvement ending (and other powers unlikely to copy our example for at least a generation), the social and political forces of Indochina will be left to find their own level. The October agreement would leave the Saigon regime in control of the South's main population centers, with North Vietnam and the Viet Cong dominant in large rural areas of the country. This arrangement appears so impractical that some form of adjustment will be necessary. If elections do take place in South Vietnam, however, they will probably only be for the sake of ratifying a division of power that has been agreed to privately by the main political groups.

Ethnic and cultural differences between the North and South Vietnamese peoples will remain a potent force—one that may even inhibit full peacetime cooperation between Hanoi and the Viet Cong PRG. Between Communist Northerners and non-Communist Southerners, ideology will reinforce ethnic differences. Thus, full political unification of the North and South seems unlikely. North Vietnam might withdraw its forces from the South partly to avoid friction with the Viet Cong, when it concludes that they are strong enough to carry on by themselves. The DRV might then settle for some type of federal tie between the North and South which would allow for free exchange of goods and people between the two regions.

Even deeper ethnic antagonism will cause the Cambodian and Lao peoples to resist as they have in the past, being absorbed by either a unitary or federal Vietnam. However, the Lao and Khmer will have to find some way of living with their much more dynamic eastern neighbors. Conceivably, the Vietnamese may be wise enough to realize the value of these buffer states between themselves and Thailand. They may also see that the only way to discourage Chinese meddling in the affairs of Laos and Cambodia is to restrict their own meddling. Undoubtedly, Cambodian and Lao leaders will do whatever they can to make these lessons clear to the Vietnamese.

Thailand may choose to remain associated with the United States, while resuming its traditional friendly (but cautious) relations with China. The Thais will be natural allies of the Khmer and Lao people in limiting Vietnam's westward expansion. Fortunately, the Indochina war has spared Thai society the profound disruptions which it caused her neighbors. Politically, socially, and economically, Thailand is the mainland state that can contribute most to Southeast Asia's development. If the United States hopes to play a part in rebuilding the states of Indochina, it can perhaps best do so through regional organizations, of which Thailand will be a leading member.

Notes

1. Secretary of State Marshall was convinced by 1947 that Chiang Kai-shek was on the road to disaster, but Marshall needed the support of pro-Chiang congressmen for his program to aid the recovery of Western Europe. Hence, he delayed disengaging American aid (and prestige) from Chiang long after he believed that no amount of foreign aid would save him.

2. Reports of the North Vietnamese peace offer were circulating just before Nixon announced that he would visit China. The North Vietnamese originally made the offer as part of a secret nine-point proposal on June 26, 1971; they published the full proposal on January 31, 1972. This was in response to President Nixon's defiant gesture of making public his own latest proposal on January 24, 1972 (on the eve of his actual visit to China).

3. Perhaps Soviet leaders felt there was no need to go out of their way to support Hanoi at this stage because the Vietnamese Communists were virtually certain to obtain most of their aims in South Vietnam. In President Nixon's May 8 speech (in which he announed the mining of Haiphong), he offered to "stop all acts of force throughout Indochina" if Hanoi agreed to an "internationally supervised cease-fire throughout Indochina" and the return of all American prisoners. These terms, which foreshadowed the agreement of October 1972, failed to even mention President Thieu.

4. The session which began on October 8, 1972 was the nineteenth secret meeting between Kissinger and the North Vietnamese since August 1969.

5. See Flora Lewis, "How Compromise Was Reached," *New York Times*

January 25, 1973. In addition to supporting Thieu's four basic objections, Kissinger also probably tried to clarify the supervisory procedures for the truce and to have the English text of the agreement given the same official status as the Vietnamese text. Thieu was probably less concerned about the latter points.

For the text of the final agreement, which was signed January 27, 1973, see *New York Times* January 25, 1973.

Bibliographical Note

The literature on U.S. involvement in Indochina, already vast, will certainly continue to grow for many years to come. However, since the Library of Congress and other institutions update their bibliographies on the subject at fairly regular intervals, I will only mention the works which I have found most helpful.

The Pentagon Papers, the name commonly applied to a secret Defense Department study which was made public in 1971, is the most ambitious effort thus far to describe and analyze the main decisions by the United States government in regard to Indochina.[1] It summarizes events from the outbreak of World War II until President Johnson's decision to cut back the bombing of North Vietnam.

The Pentagon study was prepared at Secretary McNamara's initiative by a team of thirty-six government and private writers under the leadership of Leslie H. Gelb, who served in the Defense Department's Bureau of International Security Affairs during the Johnson administration. The team members were drawn from the military services, the State and Defense departments, defense research contractors, and other organizations. They worked on the project for an average of only four months each.

The Pentagon study is divided into separate monographs on particular events and decisions. Most of the monographs begin with a summary and analysis (written by Gelb) and a chronology of the main events discussed in the text. Appended to the study are several thousand pages of classified documents and unclassified statements by officials in support of U.S. policy in Indochina.

Work on the Pentagon study was begun in June 1967, after Secretary McNamara had developed strong misgivings about the Johnson administration's policy; it was completed only a few days before President Nixon took office. The research team was given unlimited access to the files of the office of the Secretary of Defense; they were also allowed to examine some reports prepared by the Central Intelligence Agency and some State Department cables and memoranda. They had no access to White House files. Unfortunately, their terms of reference (set by Secretary McNamara) also prevented them from interviewing any of the "Vietnam principals." (This may have been intended to minimize the chance that high officials might try to influence the team's conclusions.)

As a result of the restrictions under which the study team operated, *The Pentagon Papers* gives a distorted impression of the Defense Department's importance in the policy-making process, while adding very little to our knowledge of the roles played by the Presidents, White House staff officials, the State Department, or CIA.[2] Nevertheless, it is a rich store of documentation for the writing of an "interim" history until such time as researchers are allowed more complete access to government files.

The three public versions of *The Pentagon Papers* all have certain advantages and disadvantages. None of them gives the complete text of the study that was prepared for limited distribution to government officials.[3] The section of the original study which concerns negotiations with foreign governments has not as yet been made public. The publishers of the Gravel version state that it includes about 2900 pages of the original 3000 page narrative, as well as about a quarter of the 4000 pages of documents which were included in the original.

The GPO and Gravel versions include much the same portions of the original Pentagon study, although there are many differences in matters of detail. The most striking difference is the fact that, while the Gravel version has been somewhat rearranged and set in type, the GPO version is a facsimile reproduction of the Pentagon's original report. Many of the documents in the GPO version appear to have been xeroxed for the second, third, or fourth time, and portions of them are illegible. (The publishers of the Gravel version omitted the sections of the original that were illegible.) The Gravel version was published in extreme haste and contains some serious printing errors, but it does have a good Table of Contents, and the text is far less difficult to read than the GPO version. Although the researcher will find some advantages in using facsimiles of original documents, he will also encounter a certain amount of censorship in the GPO version.

The NYT version is highly condensed. It consists of short summaries of the narrative portions of the original Pentagon study prepared by a team of *New York Times* reporters. Added to this is a much smaller selection of original documents than that contained in either the Gravel or GPO versions. The summaries in the NYT version are of uneven quality (which is also true of the Pentagon original). But on the whole, the NYT summaries are faithful to the Pentagon study.

The NYT writers make very little reference to unclassified sources, and they provide the readers with inadequate chronologies. There is little effort to place the main events in U.S. relations with Indochina in a broader historical perspective. The NYT version is therefore the least balanced but also the most compact and readable of the three public versions. The moderate length and price of the NYT version make it likely to be preferred by the average student or general reader. It also contains a number of classified documents that were not included in either the original Pentagon study or the GPO version (although they are in the Gravel version). In Footnotes to the present volume, I have referred the reader to the NYT version of *The Pentagon Papers* for the text of documents.

Most of the information in *The Pentagon Papers* was already in the public domain by 1971. Indeed, *The Pentagon Papers* prove that classified documents are often too narrowly focused and much less valuable for a study of foreign policy than such standard open sources as the *State Department Bulletin*, the *Foreign Affairs* series, the *Papers of the U.S. Presidents* series, *The New York Times*, etc. A book that demonstrates this point is George McT. Kahin and John W. Lewis, *The United States in Vietnam* (New York, 1967). Kahin and Lewis did a capable job of exploiting the standard public sources and ordering their material into a reasoned analysis of U.S. policy. (However, they do not indicate that they interviewed public officials about their policy-making roles or that they observed U.S. government activities in Indochina.)

A great deal of worthwhile information can be gleaned from memoirs and firsthand accounts of particular episodes by former officials. The ones which I have found most interesting and useful are (in rough chronological order) those of Cordell Hull, Dean Acheson, George F. Kennan, Anthony Eden, Edward G. Lansdale, Maxwell D. Taylor, John Mecklin, Roger Hilsman, Townsend Hoopes, and Lyndon Johnson. The memoirs of Presidents Truman and Eisenhower serve mainly to indicate the minor importance they attached to events in Indochina during most of their years in the White House.

The Roosevelt and Truman Eras

Besides giving his own (and the State Department's) views on Indochina and Franco-American relations, Cordell Hull's *Memoirs* (New York, 1948) tell us a great deal about the perspective in which Franklin Roosevelt viewed these subjects during World War II. Other valuable works on U.S. Far Eastern policy in the late 1930s and 1940s include: Barbara W. Tuchman's *Stilwell and the American Experience in China, 1911-45* (New York, 1971) U.S. Department of State, *United States Relations with China* ("The China White Paper"), reissued by Stanford University Press, 1967; and three classics by Herbert Feis, *The Road to Pearl Harbor* (Princeton, 1950), *Churchill, Roosevelt, Stalin* (Princeton, 1957), and *The China Tangle* (Princeton, 1953). Also useful are Tang Tsou's *America's Failure in China, 1941-1950* (Chicago, 1963); and particularly Ellen J. Hammer's *The Struggle for Indochina, 1940-1955* (Stanford, 1966).

Dean Acheson's *Present at the Creation* (New York, 1969) describes the context in which the Truman administration began to interest itself in Indochina in 1949. One chapter summarizes most of the key Truman administration decisions on Indochina from 1949 to 1952. The first volume of Ambassador George F. Kennan's *Memoirs* (Boston, 1967) provides extremely interesting insights into the policy-making process during the start of the Korean War in 1950 (including the role played by John Foster Dulles). Joseph Buttinger, *Vietnam: A Political History* (New York: 1968), traces events in Vietnam, including the growing U.S. involvement.

The Eisenhower Era

The most valuable full-length study of Eisenhower's Secretary of State to appear so far is Louis Gerson's *John Foster Dulles* (New York, 1967). Foreign Secretary Anthony Eden's memoir *Full Circle* (Boston, 1960) also contains an extremely interesting description of Secretary Dulles' activities before, during, and after the 1954 Geneva conference on Indochina.

Bernard B. Fall wrote extensively and well on United States involvement in Indochina from the 1940s to the late 1960s. Among his most useful works are *The Two Viet-Nams*, second revised edition (New York, 1967): *Viet-Nam Witness* (New York, 1966): and *Last Reflections on a War* (Garden City, N.Y., 1967). These last two books make available in more permanent form some of the best of Fall's hundreds of articles on Vietnam. His major work, *Hell in a Very Small Place* (Philadelphia, 1967), describes the seige of Dien Bien Phu, including the question of U.S. intervention which was debated at the time. Major General Edward G. Lansdale's *In the Midst of Wars* (New York, 1972) describes the early days of U.S. relations with Diem.

The Kennedy Era

As Assistant Secretary of State for Far Eastern Affairs, Roger Hilsman was closely involved in major Indochina policy decisions of the Kennedy period; his book *To Move a Nation* (New York, 1964) contains many valuable insights into the policy-making process in Washington. A most interesting view of the workings of the U.S. Mission in Saigon during the same period is afforded by John Mecklin's *Mission in*

Torment (Garden City, N.Y., 1965). Of interest also are David Halber-stam's *The Making of a Quagmire* (New York, 1965), Arthur J. Dom-men's *Conflict in Laos* (New York, 1964), and Roger M. Smith's *Cambodia's Foreign Policy* (Ithaca, N.Y., 1965).

The Johnson Era

Lyndon Johnson was the dominant figure in the most critical years of U.S. intervention in Indochina. His memoir, *The Vantage Point* (New York, 1971) has shortcomings; it is obviously ghostwritten and there-fore somewhat bloodless. But it also reflects Johnson's passion for sur-prising his audience. There are many intriguing bits of new information and new documents in the long and detailed chapters in which he defends his major decisions concerning Indochina.

Another major source of information on the Johnson administration (as well as those of Eisenhower and Kennedy) is General Maxwell D. Taylor's memoir, *Swords and Plowshares* (New York, 1972). Also of interest on this period are Hans Morgenthau's *Vietnam and the United States* (Washington, D.C., 1965); Townsend Hoopes' *The Limits of In-tervention* (New York, 1969); Senator J. William Fulbright's *The Arrogance of Power* (New York, 1967); Eugene G. Wyndchy's *Tonkin Gulf* (Garden City, N.Y., 1971); *The President's War* (Philadelphia, 1971) by Anthony Austin; Don Oberdorfer's *Tet!* (Garden City, N.Y., 1971); *The Secret Search for Peace in Vietnam* (New York, 1968) by David Kraslow and Stuart H. Loory; and *Mission to Hanoi* (New York, 1968) by Harry S. Ashmore and William C. Baggs.

The Nixon Era

On the early years of the Nixon administration, Rowland Evans and Robert Novak have contributed *Nixon in the White House* (New York, 1971). My own monograph, *The Expansion of the Vietnam War into Cambodia* (Ohio University Center for International Studies, 1970), was based on press reports and interviews. Eugene P. Dvorkin's (editor) *The Senate's War Powers* (Chicago, 1971) is a useful record of the Senate debate on the invasion of Cambodia in 1970, with some com-mentary by the editor.

Air War in Indochina by the Air War Study Group of Cornell University (edited by Norman Uphoff and Raphael Littauer), Boston: Beacon Press, 1972, provides a useful dispassionate analysis of this subject from 1962 to the end of 1971.

The improvement in U.S. relations with China has made it much easier for journalists and scholars from the United States to visit the mainland. The first new books on China following the thaw naturally attempt to assess the Peking regime's intentions toward Indochina. The group includes: Ross Terrill's *800,000,000, The Real China* (Boston, 1972); *China! Inside the People's Republic* by the Committee of Concerned Asian Scholars (New York, 1972); and *The New York Times Report from Red China*, (New York, 1972) by Tillman Durdin, James Reston, and Seymour Topping.

Congressional Hearings

Congressional committee hearings and reports are an invaluable source of information, particularly on the efforts of the legislative branch to influence policy toward Indochina. Examples include: Reports by Senator Mike Mansfield and a group of senators to the Committee on Foreign Relations in February 1963 and January 1966, following their trips to South Vietnam, Laos, Cambodia, and Thailand; U.S. Senate, Committee on Foreign Relations, *The Gulf of Tonkin, the 1964 Incidents*, Hearings with Secretary Robert S. McNamara, February 20, 1968 (Washington, D.C.: Government Printing Office, 1968); U.S. Senate, Committee on Foreign Relations, *Foreign Assistance Act of 1968, Part 1-Vietnam*, Hearings with Secretary Dean Rusk, March 11 and 12, 1968 (Washington, D.C.: Government Printing Office, 1968); U.S. Senate, Committee on Foreign Relations, *Background Information Relating to Southeast Asia and Vietnam*, Fifth Revised Edition (Washington, D.C.: Government Printing Office, 1969); U.S. Senate, Committee on Foreign Relations, *United States Security Agreements and Commitments Abroad, Kingdom of Laos* (Washington, D.C.: Government Printing Office, 1970); and U.S. House of Representatives, Committee on Foreign Affairs, *Hearings on Supplemental Authorization for Assistance to Cambodia and Other Countries* (Washington, D.C.: Government Printing Office, 1970).

Notes

1. The three versions published in 1971 are: 1) U.S. Department of Defense, *United States-Vietnam Relations, 1945-1967* (Washington, D.C.: Government Printing Office, 1971), 12 vol., referred to here as the "GPO version;" 2) Senator Mike Gravel (editor), *The Pentagon Papers, The Defense Department History of United States Decisionmaking in Vietnam* (Boston: Beacon Press, 1971), 4 vol., referred to here as the "Gravel version;" and 3) Neil Sheehan and others, *The Pentagon Papers as Published by the New York Times* (New York: Bantam, 1971, 1 vol., referred to here as the "NYT version."

2. For Leslie Gelb's comments on the study's strong and weak points, see his Letter of Transmittal of the Study, January 15, 1969 (in both the GPO and Gravel versions) and his article "The Pentagon Papers and *The Vantage Point*," *Foreign Policy* (No. 6, Spring 1972), pp. 25-41.

See also Richard H. Ullman, "The Pentagon History as 'History,' " *Foreign Policy* (No. 4, Fall, 1971), pp. 150-56. Professor Ullman, a Princeton University historian, was a member of the team which wrote the study.

3. Daniel Ellsberg, a member of the study team claims to have leaked the text of the study to *The New York Times* in early 1971, when it was still highly classified. Ellsberg, at time of writing, faces criminal proceedings by the U.S. Justice Department for his alleged actions.

Index